COMMUNITY TREATMENT OF EATING DISORDERS

Paul H. Robinson

John Wiley & Sons, Ltd

Other Wiley Editorial Offices

John Wiley & Sons Inc., 111 River Street, Hoboken, NJ 07030, USA

Jossey-Bass, 989 Market Street, San Francisco, CA 94103-1741, USA

Wiley-VCH Verlag GmbH, Boschstr. 12, D-69469 Weinheim, Germany

John Wiley & Sons Australia Ltd, 42 McDougall Street, Milton, Queensland 4064, Australia

John Wiley & Sons (Asia) Pte Ltd, 2 Clementi Loop #02-01, Jin Xing Distripark, Singapore 129809

John Wiley & Sons Canada Ltd, 22 Worcester Road, Etobicoke, Ontario, Canada M9W 1L1

Wiley also publishes its books in a variety of electronic formats. Some content that appears
in print may not be available in electronic books.

Library of Congress Cataloging-in-Publication Data

Robinson, Paul H., Dr.
  Community treatment of eating disorders / Paul H. Robinson.
    p.   cm.
  Includes bibliographical references and index.
  ISBN-13: 978-0-470-01675-6 (cloth)
  ISBN-10: 0-470-01675-2 (cloth)
  ISBN-13: 978-0-470-01676-3 (pbk.)
  ISBN-10: 0-470-01676-0 (pbk.)
  1. Eating disorders–Treatment.   2. Eating disorders–Patients–Rehabilitation.   3. Community
mental health services.   I. Title.
  RC552.E18R62 2006
  362.196'8526–dc22   2006000887

British Library Cataloguing in Publication Data

A catalogue record for this book is available from the British Library

ISBN-13 978-0-470-01675-6 (ppc)   978-0-470-01676-3 (pbk)
ISBN-10 0-470-01675-2 (ppc)   0-470-01676-0 (pbk)

Typeset in 10/12pt Times by TechBooks, New Delhi, India
Printed and bound in Great Britain by TJ International Ltd, Padstow, Cornwall
This book is printed on acid-free paper responsibly manufactured from sustainable forestry
in which at least two trees are planted for each one used for paper production.

CONTENTS

ABOUT THE AUTHOR

Dr Paul Robinson is a consultant psychiatrist in eating disorders psychiatry at the Russell Unit, Royal Free Hospital, Camden and Islington Mental Health and Social Care Trust. After postgraduate training in general medicine he trained in psychiatry at the Maudsley Hospital, was a family therapist and conducted research into control of eating behaviour at the Institute of Psychiatry and Johns Hopkins Hospital, Baltimore. In the last eight years at the Royal Free he has built up a multidisciplinary team dedicated to the community approach to eating disorders, minimising use of inpatient care and developing safe and effective ways to provide treatment for these distressing, debilitating and at times life-threatening conditions. The team has twice been in the final of the Hospital Doctor Team of the Year Award. His present interests are the treatment of severe and enduring eating disorder (SEED), and the delivery of therapy via email, for which he reached the final of the Medical Innovations Award. He lives in North London.

ACKNOWLEDGEMENTS

For their remarkable enthusiasm, industry and sensitivity I would like to thank all the members of my team at the Royal Free Hospital, past and present. All the current team members contributed actively to the book by allowing me insights into their work in both team meetings and individual encounters. They are (alphabetically):

Anna Carey, art therapist; Mireille Colahan, family therapist and service manager; Sheilagh Davies, consultant psychiatrist in psychotherapy; Yeva Feldman, dance/movement therapist; Nadia Freyther, nurse; Jenny Gray, secretary; Morven Gray, nurse; Yoram Inspector, psychiatrist; Pavlo Kanellakis, counselling psychologist; Pramjit Kaur, nurse; Marie Lewis, secretary; Jeannie Moir, nurse and massage therapist; Julie Moro, family therapist; Jo Myers, clinical psychologist; Ulrike Nau-Deb-hor, counselling psychologist; Michael O'Malley, cleaner; Marianne Paul, dietician and day service manager; Louise Randell, clinical psychologist; Courtney Raspin, counselling psychologist; Heather Warner, family therapist and service manager.

Among previous team members, special mention is due to Adele Wakeham and Dr Liz Bardsley who helped the transformation of the team into a community eating disorders service and the late Seamus McNelis, a nurse who saw in the new ways with enthusiasm. I also thank Professor Gerald Russell who made me, like him, an eating disorders 'addict' (although I think my chances of rehab are better than his) and Sonja, my wife, for putting up with my addiction and, a writer herself, for her editorial help.

Paul Robinson
London, November 2005

INTRODUCTION

This book is intended for all those who are concerned with and responsible for the provision of care for people with eating disorders in their locality. It is aimed in particular at those professionals in the field who are seeking a treatment approach that minimises the use of hospitalisation. It will also be of interest to sufferers from eating disorders and their families, who may find here some insights into the mind of a healthcare provider and be more aware of what they should expect from an eating disorders service.

With this in mind I have set out to make this book accessible to different types of reader in the hope that it can speak to as many people as possible. I have covered some medical topics but hope that I have made them comprehensible to non-medics. I believe that the majority of care for eating disorders is properly provided by non-medical professionals, and that they need to be informed about the sometimes dread physical complications of the disorders so that they can safely and confidently conduct treatment, and know when medical intervention is required.

Community treatment suggests that most interventions should take place while the person receiving those interventions resides either at home or in a place in which they have autonomy, such as a community hostel. Treatment location varies from the outpatient clinic, the day hospital, the patient's accommodation and the community mental health team base. Inpatient treatment is included in community treatment, perhaps surprisingly, but appropriately, because inpatient treatment represents one end of a continuum of intensity of care that extends from the outpatient clinic to the hospital bed. In the last 50 years psychiatry has seen a profound shift in emphasis from hospital to community care, and the closure of thousands of hospital beds has been accompanied by the establishment of a whole range of new approaches, namely community mental health teams, assertive outreach teams, crisis response teams, day hospitals and many new community workers in the fields of housing and occupation. Development of community approaches in eating disorders has been patchy, largely because expertise is available in only a few locations. This book will provide a model for localities to develop their own community-oriented eating disorders services.

It is my experience in building a community-based service that has led to my writing this book, in response to a demand for a handbook on 'How to do Community Eating Disorders'. It should be helpful for eating disorder services at all stages of development, from the glint in the eye of the mental health purchaser to the GP and the consultant in his or her empire. Surveys have repeatedly shown that specialist care for eating disorders is sparse in many parts of the United Kingdom, especially those parts away from the London–Oxford–Cambridge box in the south east. The rule appears to be that funding for eating disorders care, and perhaps funding for other specialist services, is inversely proportional to distance from the seat of government. People residing in those areas have either very little local service or a small unit that cannot cope with local demands. The most severely ill may be referred to a specialist centre, and then be discharged back to the same inadequate provision. This is not an acceptable state of affairs, and many local healthcare providers and purchasers are attempting to get funding together to establish local services. When committing funds, it is necessary to decide how much should go into inpatient care and how much into community care. It is our view that investment in the latter will reduce spending on the former, and evidence is presented in this book that a well-functioning community team can keep people out of hospital.

It has been suggested that a community team could be established for every million population so that in the UK's population of 60 million, 60 teams are required. It has also been suggested that each team should be funded to the level of around £1 million for staffing. This would provide adequate community care for the population, but not fund the beds required. We have estimated that four beds per million, of which half might be low dependency hostel beds, are required which would require one 20-bed unit per five million population.

Needless to say this book is written in an English context and, inevitably, much of the political landscape will be unfamiliar to those in other countries, with purchasers, providers, GPs, the Mental Health Act, the Care Programme Approach and other peculiarly English phenomena. It should, however, be useful to services outside England as a model of how to provide local services for eating disorders, however funded and managed. Conducting seminars in Northern Ireland, France, Spain and Finland has shown the author that the issues everywhere are similar, and invitations to provide workshops arise from a wish to enhance skills in providing community care while according inpatient care its proper place. In most settings it will be possible to recognise the following groups (English equivalents are in brackets): patients, families and carers; primary care teams (general practitioners); secondary care teams (psychiatric services, community mental health teams); and specialist teams (eating disorders, drug and alcohol, etc.), while on the management side there are the government

(Department of Health), local health commissioners (Primary Care Trusts), and local mental health provider organisations (Mental Health Trusts).

The idea for this book arose after a gratifyingly large number of clinics had called the Russell Unit and said 'Can we come and visit? We're developing eating disorders and heard you have an interesting model of care'. We are delighted to host visitors and welcome them to attend our team meeting. This volume represents the idea, 'You've met the team, now here's the book!'

The book is arranged in three sections, beginning with establishing a service and dealing with staff issues in Chapters 1 and 2. The main body of the book, from Chapters 3 to 9, deals with various aspects of care, from initial assessment and physical monitoring in Chapters 3 and 4, through management in different contexts including outpatients, day hospital, other units and inpatient care in Chapters 5 to 8, ending up with the treatment of the patient with long-term illness (SEED – severe and enduring eating disorder) in Chapter 9. The final section, Chapter 10, covers technical aspects such as database development, research, IT and teaching.

For brevity, patients are generally referred to using feminine pronouns, as females make up over 90 % of the clientele of a specialist eating disorders service.

It goes without saying therefore that this book could not have been written without the support of my team who have my admiration, affection and respect. In preparation for the writing I spent an hour with each team member, as well as some patients who had successfully navigated the system. All contributed in their unique way, and their contributions permeate the book. For all of them, past and present members, this is their book.

Chapter 1

ESTABLISHING A HOME-ORIENTED SERVICE

THE TASK

Providing first-class community care of eating disorders is a challenging task. The service must offer high-quality treatment, including therapies known to be effective, and provide safety so that patients who require admission can be identified and provided with timely and appropriate in-patient care. Systems are required to support staff dealing with difficult and demanding clinical situations, to supervise the provision of high-quality therapy and to make sure that patients are monitored for emergence of risk factors. Systems must be in place to deal with extreme physical and psycho-logical difficulties, while staff continue supporting those in intensive day care and in less intensive outpatient care. When patients are admitted, they, their families and the teams looking after them require continuing support and advice. At the same time the team must be in a position to co-work with other community teams in primary care, general psychiatry, drug and alcohol and child and adolescent psychiatry, so that patients' needs are met and they do not slip through the gaps that can appear between services.

PREDICTING AND MEETING DEMAND

In order to receive health care the prospective patient has to negotiate a number of hurdles. If 100 people in a community suffer from a condition, only a proportion will consult anyone about it. Others will discuss it with family or friends, or consult printed or electronic sources of information. Of those who consult in person, many will go to a general practitioner (GP – family physician), who may or may not diagnose the problem, largely de-pending on how it is presented (e.g. weight loss or stomach pains) and how inclined the GP is to look for psychological problems. Once the condi-tion is recognised, the GP will make a decision about referral to specialist services. This decision is based on many variables, including the expertise

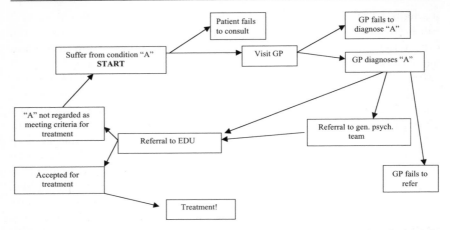

Figure 1.1 Pathways to care: Hurdles that the patient needs to negotiate before obtaining treatment. At every point onward progress may not be made if recognition and appropriate referral fail to occur.

of the GP and resources in primary care, and the availability and quality of specialist services. The sufferer may now have negotiated three of the hurdles (whether to visit the GP, whether the GP will diagnose the problem and refer to a specialist). Between the GP and an eating disorders specialist there may be an additional hurdle, sometimes imposed by the funding agency, in the form of a referral to a general psychiatrist who may or may not refer on to the eating disorders specialist (Figure 1.1). The intrepid patient has now leapt nimbly over three or four fences and arrives at the eating disorders specialist. There is a further hurdle. The specialist has to agree that the patient does have an eating disorder and that it is of sufficient severity to warrant treatment in the specialist unit. These hurdles in referral to specialist care are more substantial and numerous in a government-funded health service as in the UK. They are least in a private service funded by the patient or family and insurance funding tends to make intermediate demands.

Surveys of bulimia nervosa and related disorders in the community in the UK have found that eating disorders are very common, but that consulting a doctor in order to obtain help is relatively rare, generally under 10 % of cases. Reluctance to visit the GP has been attributed to patients' perception of their GPs as sometimes dismissive and uninformed (Newton, Robinson & Hartley, 1993). In a survey sponsored by the Eating Disorders Association and the Royal College of Psychiatrists respondents cited self-help groups, training for GPs and availability of specialist services as key priorities.

In a population of 1 million people, how many are likely to have eating disorders and of that group how many will arrive at the specialist service? Prevalence estimates suggest that 0.4 % and 1 % of young women will have anorexia and bulimia nervosa, respectively. Epidemiology is currently inadequate but a conservative estimate suggests that an additional 3 % will fulfil criteria for clinically significant eating disorders (eating disorder not otherwise specified or binge eating disorder). The proportion of females aged 16–45 in the UK is 32.1 % (9.733 million). This gives an estimate for eating disorders of 450 000 people (adding 5 % males), or 7500 people per million population. Looked at from the other end of the telescope, the clinical eating disorders service at the Royal Free Hospital, the Russell Unit, receives 300–350 referrals per million population per year. This clearly demonstrates the powerful effect of the hurdles: around 4.6 % of the eating disordered population are referred in one year. In a research project described in Chapter 10, students and staff at a large college in the University of London were circulated by email and offered therapy online. Of 97 people accepted for treatment, only 21 had until then received any form of therapy. On the one hand the small proportion of people contacting healthcare services represents a serious failure to address a public health problem. On the other, GP and specialist services would quickly be overwhelmed if all potential patients turned up at once! Given that a unit providing care for 1 million people attracts, on average, five new referrals a week, how many will have bulimia nervosa (BN) and anorexia nervosa (AN)? Epidemiology suggests the proportion should be around 2:1. In practice those proportions are not too far off. At the Royal Free, over a year, the average proportions are 48 % BN and 19 % AN. The figures for binge eating disorder and eating disorder not otherwise specified (EDNOS) are more at variance with statistics, which suggests that they should be in the majority. In the clinic they form only 27 % of referrals, suggesting that 'typical' patients are being preferentially referred. Five new patients a week can be accommodated in an efficiently run new patient clinic. Length and intensity of treatment are needed in order to make an estimate of ongoing staffing requirements. With an average caseload of 10 and a duration of therapy averaging 1 year, and 150 patients eligible for individual psychotherapy, a staffing of 15 therapists would be required. In practice there will be fewer therapists, and therefore a waiting list is inevitable as assessed patients back up while awaiting therapy. If a day hospital is envisaged, staffing needs to take account of groups, meals and key working, while provision for liaison, outreach and emergencies adds further to the demands. The staff numbers in the Russell Unit are detailed in Table 1.1 (see p. 4). The figures are also given in whole-time equivalents per million population, so that they can be used in service configuration.

LOVE OF MONEY: THE ROOT OF ALL EVIL

In the 2001 report (Royal College of Psychiatrists, 2001) from the Eating Disorders Special Interest Group, we came up with a delightfully simple formula: £1 (€ 1.42) for each population member will give you enough to

Table 1.1 Staff members on the team serving an area containing 840 000 people

Staff members	Grade	Whole Time Equivalents	WTE per million
Management	Service Manager	1	1.19
Doctors	Consultant*	1	1.19
	Junior Trainee	0.5	0.6
	Senior Trainee	1	1.19
Nurses	Senior	2	2.38
	Junior	2	2.38
Psychologists	Consultant	0	0.0
	Non-consultant	2.1	2.5
Dietitian	Senior	1	1.19
Massage Therapist	Junior nurse	1	1.19
Art/Movement/Drama Therapists		0.4	0.48
Occupational Therapist	Senior	1	1.19
Family Therapist	Senior	0.8	0.95
Administrative (secretaries)	Senior	1.6	1.9
Total		15.4	18.33

* 0.9 Eating disorders psychiatrist
0.1 Consultant psychiatrist in psychotherapy

provide a good, community-based service for over 18s with eating disorders. In this section we assume that you are developing adult eating disorder services for 1 million people with a mixture of urban and rural populations. Almost all healthcare funding organisations are short of money. When there is a well-developed National Health Service (NHS), as in the UK, private funding agencies are able to limit access to private health care funding, especially for long-term conditions, knowing that the NHS will be there to provide ongoing care. Indeed, private insurers will sometimes demand that, as the time for their funding comes towards an end, the clinician has expressly indicated the NHS alternative treatment package that has been set up. Where access to high-quality free health care is restricted, as in the USA, private care has a real ethical dilemma in how to limit care in someone who very much needs treatment, but is unable to continue to pay for it after insurance or public funding has been withdrawn. In much of Western Europe, specialist care can be obtained and the state will pick up all or most of the bill.

Given that money is in short supply, what can a clinician or manager do to encourage a loosening of purse strings in favour of a specific need such as eating disorders? It is important to be aware that your favourite clinical area is in competition with many others, for example drug misuse, forensic services, early intervention and assertive outreach. In general, the money directed towards a particular area is dependent on a finite number of pressures. Broadly they comprise: (1) costs: both of funding new services and of not funding them; (2) profile: the level of interest in an area both locally and nationally; (3) danger: how dangerous to the public and (less influentially) to themselves are your client group?

I will expand on these three essential areas, and provide information on how to maximise their effectiveness in obtaining funding for a new or developing service.

1. Costs

   As far as can be discerned, funding bodies appear to be motivated by cost, safety, consumer opinion and effectiveness, probably in that order. While the cost of something may be high, funders may well provide the money if the cost of not providing it is higher, in other words, could the service save money? In order to argue this you need to find out what is happening to this patient group at present. It may be that other services, such as general medical or general psychiatric, are attempting to do the work. Find out from clinicians who have tried to treat severe eating disorders how it went. If the patient was in a psychiatric ward for weeks, ran rings round the staff and ended up not gaining weight, while the unit was so short of beds that an acutely ill manic patient needed to be admitted to a private unit, you have a case. The new service, you can argue, would work constructively with the patient and family, probably prevent the admission, and obtain a better outcome. The most telling argument is that the acutely ill general patient would have been accommodated without an expensive and inappropriate private admission elsewhere. If patients with severe eating disorders are being admitted to inpatient units, funded by the local health purchasers, find out how much has been spent in the past few years on these placements. It would not be unusual to find that £200 000, (€ 330 000) had been spent per year. Offer to develop a community service with that starting budget which would give you two nurses, a part-time consultant, manager and therapist. Discuss with great care the question of funding inpatient admissions. If the funding body ask you to pay for admissions out of your own budget remember that one admission could easily put your service in the red. The alternatives are: (a) to hold back a proportion of the budget (say £100 000) to cover admissions or (b) to accept a lower budget from the funding body while responsibility for funding admissions remains outside your eating disorders budget. Because admissions for eating disorders can be so expensive, no one wants to hold the hot potato of the financial risk for them.

2. Profile

   Patients with eating disorders are not that popular (see Chapter 6) but that can work both ways in terms of the support you may or may not get from your colleagues. Some might see eating disorders as relatively trivial and definitely second rank to schizophrenia and depression, while very much wanting someone else to deal with the patients because they can be so difficult to manage especially on general psychiatric wards. Have there been any enquiries or surveys of eating disorders in the area, and what were the recommendations? Is there a local branch of the Eating Disorders Association and what do they think of local services? Is it known that a local dignitary had a relative with an eating disorder, and might lend support to a campaign? (Occasionally a very high profile individual has a family connection with eating disorders, as occurred in France, but in that case, the idiosyncratic services that were set up did not meet with the approval of many eating disorder specialists.) On a national level, look at the guidelines available. In the UK NICE (www.nice.org.uk) has been successful in gathering together the evidence for effective treatments in a variety of areas. It is likely that, in the UK, hospitals will be rated and, perhaps, funded according to whether they comply with NICE recommendations. This will be a tremendous boost for service quality, although where the money will come from to fund the necessary improvements no one knows, as yet. For our clinical gold prospector looking for cash to start or improve a service, the promise of extra funding for a Trust which might come from complying with NICE could well encourage a Trust to 'Spend to Save'.

3. Danger

This is one of the most powerful influences on funding bodies. Serious incident enquiries following the death or serious disability of a patient can have profound effects on services. Risk to others is often even more influential. In England the murder, by a patient with schizophrenia, of a member of the public sparked off a wave of enquiries and reports that led to a fundamental change in the way discharged patients who might move to another area were managed. The enormous bureaucracy known as the Care Programme Approach in which care in clinical and social spheres is documented and the responsible person identified for each intervention, as well as for coordination of care, was a result of this wave. Obtain reports of any enquiries that have been held in cases of patients with eating disorders in the area and in all adjacent areas, and collate the recommendations. Many such reports conclude that specialist help was not available when it should have been or that it was not accessed or heeded at the appropriate time. These findings are strong arguments to persuade funding bodies to release more money.

WHICH STAFF?

Staff from differing professions are like travellers who reach a caravanserai having come from widely differing directions. They will each have a different and unique story to tell and be able to teach their co-travellers about their particular experience, while at the same time having much in common with the others. It is important to have certain skills in a team, but, as will be seen in the following chapters, a healthy team develops in such a way that people can overlap considerably in role, so that underlying training becomes less important. What are the essential tasks that the team requires to perform, and how many staff are needed to perform them? The following tasks are among those required in a community eating disorder service (EDS):

- clinical leadership
- managerial leadership
- psychiatric assessment and management
- medical assessment and management
- dietetic assessment and management
- psychological assessment and management
- family intervention
- guided problem solving
- occupational therapy, and occupational advice and training
- liaison skills with other clinical services
- administrative services.

Many of these tasks are not strictly linked to professions. Clinical and managerial leadership can be provided by any profession. Psychiatric assessment requires psychiatric support and supervision, but much of the information required can be collected by others. The list suggests that a psychiatrist, a psychologist, a dietician, a family therapist and an occupational therapist should be available for advice. Mental health nurses can provide many of the requirements in consultation with the other professions and offer a particularly broad approach, which fits them to act as key workers providing frontline contact to the patient, integrating care and acting as an interpreter of the advice of the other professionals. A team secretary facilitates the work of all members of the team and is a key player.

Table 1.1 shows the current staffing in the Russell Unit and can be used as a guide for services intending to provide a comprehensive community service for eating disorders. The staff required for providing inpatient care to those that require it are not, of course, reflected in these numbers.

This number might be reduced if substantial commitments to work can be obtained from other health agencies such as community mental health teams, primary care, or the voluntary sector. For example, if general practice counsellors can be persuaded to provide guided self-help, many patients with bulimia nervosa could be dealt with in primary care, with supervision from the specialist service.

RECRUITMENT

How to attract people into a service is a major problem in health care. When asked what attracted them to come and work in our team, the most common reasons are: interest in eating disorders, the reputation of the team, limited unsocial hours, the opportunity to engage in therapeutic work, personal connection with a team member; and a number of negatives, including exhaustion on a general ward and fear of personal injury. It is advisable to recruit the most senior people to key posts. As well as bringing their experience to the work, they may engage in academic work including research and teaching, and may attract trainees whose work can substantially increase the amount of staff time available on the unit. Once a unit has achieved a reputation for good work it attracts other professionals, apart from trainees, who can contribute to the number of hands available. Therapists, sometimes experienced in general work, who wish to enhance their experience of treating eating disorders, may offer their services free as long as they can access clients and medical backup. They will often use external sources of supervision. There are many doctors coming from both the European Union and beyond, who wish to gain expertise in the health service and, sometimes, in eating disorders and who are willing to work until they have the expertise, confidence or qualifications to obtain a paid job in the UK. Doctors who are training in general adult psychiatry may wish to join the team for one or two sessions per week as a 'special interest' for which the eating disorders service bears no cost.

While trainees and unpaid visitors cannot be depended upon to appear and are only variably present, they can increase the effective size of a team substantially. Naturally they have to receive appropriate support and supervision.

WHO DOES WHAT?

This is a very sensitive area. Different professions and training programmes bestow differing skills on their participants. These differences have a number of implications, namely a different range of interventions and professional structures, as well as different status, income and power. Teams are, to some extent, organised by these differences, although certain types of work accentuate them more than others. A cardiac transplant team with surgeons, anaesthetists and nurses would find sharing of many roles quite inappropriate, whereas, in a primary care team, the roles of history taking, monitoring, triage and follow up can be shared between, say, medical and nursing members of the team. In psychiatry, medical and nursing roles are quite defined when inpatient care and particularly compulsory admission are prominent parts of the service. In general, the more community focused a team the more can professional roles be shared. The favoured caricature of a psychiatrist is someone who 'studied medicine but doesn't practice it and practices psychology but never studied it'. The medical side is well represented in eating disorders and hardly a day goes past in which I or a medical colleague do not interpret an ECG or a blood test. It is recommended that psychiatrists in eating disorders obtain substantial training in one of the therapies with utility in our patients, be it cognitive, family, analytic or one of the others, in order to avoid the criticism implicit in the latter part of the mostly undeserved dictum.

As can be seen in Table 1.2, there are some differences in the way each profession handles each role, although, in general, most things can be done by most of the team. As the team becomes more mature and confident in each other, the range of roles taken on by each team member expands, and within a role, the balance of work taken on between different professions shifts. This is most clearly seen in medical monitoring (Chapter 4). Patients who present risk of physical deterioration and death are, naturally, of extreme concern to professionals, including psychiatrists. One member of the team, usually the consultant psychiatrist, has to take the lead on standards of medical monitoring in the team. As time goes on, non-medical members of the team develop confidence in assessment of medical risk, including body mass index (BMI), muscle testing and ordering investigations such as electrolytes and electrocardiography. Each professional will decide how far he or she is willing to go in taking responsibility for medical data, for example, whether to call a doctor when a slightly increased urea level is reported, and the level of sharing of the medical monitoring role depends on experience, contact with physicians and availability of a doctor's opinion in cases of doubt.

A similar process pertains in the case of individual therapy. This is in some teams seen as the domain of qualified therapists. This has the advantage that each patient sees an expert in therapy, but in the Russell Unit apart from the psychologist team members we have largely avoided appointing psychotherapists and from the outset encouraged nurses to take on individual patients with appropriate support and supervision (Chapter 2). This allows nurses with basic psychiatric training to gain experience in therapy, has inspired some to take advanced courses in a range of psychotherapies, and is very much appreciated by patients. This sophisticated role for nurses and, more recently, other professions, can only be pursued safely (for both staff and patient) with appropriate supervision from experts in different forms of psychotherapy. The way we have achieved this is described in Chapter 2.

STAFF MANAGEMENT STRUCTURE

Here we must consider two forms of management, professional and line. Professional management is almost always by a more senior member of the individual's own profession, be it nurse, doctor, psychologist etc. The function of such management is to help the individual function as a member of their professional group and to progress professionally and academically.

Table 1.2 Some roles (left hand column) and the way different professions approach them (top row)

	Doctor	Nurse	Psychologist	Family Therapist
Individual therapy	Yes, but rarely available	Yes, routine	Yes, more complex cases	Yes, if available
Meal support	Yes, but rarely available	Yes, routine	Yes	Yes
Medical monitoring	Yes, more severely ill cases	Yes, routine	Yes, routine	Yes, if Key Working
Advice to other teams	Yes, routine	Yes	Yes	Yes
Family therapy	Yes, as trainee	As trainee or Key Worker	Occasionally	Yes, routine
Key working	Rarely	Yes, routine	Yes, routine	Yes, if available

For someone who has recently undergone transition, for example from trainee to qualified worker, or by moving posts, there will be many issues to be dealt with in professional supervision with someone who has traversed the same territory. The professional manager can also be involved in any difficult meeting the person might be required to attend, such as disciplinary hearings.

The line manager has quite a different role. This is to represent the next level of management, right up to the board of management, with the aim of enhancing the individual's contribution to the team with a view to increasing its effectiveness and efficiency. The line manager should support and praise what is going well, but not be afraid to tackle what is not.

The two roles are not uncommonly combined in one person, with the effect that many people are line managed by someone from the same profession. We have found, in the Russell Unit, that in time, as clinical skills become shared and confidence within and between professions increases, line management can cross professional boundaries. Our current staff diagram and the equivalent diagram five years ago are given in Figure 1.2, and it can be seen that, in the later team structure, more line management is done across professions. Cross-disciplinary management can only work when individuals within a team trust each other so that they do not feel the need to retreat behind professional groupings in their management arrangements. In one team known to the author, anxiety in the nursing team was so great that nurses were prevented from consulting other staff groups, with a resulting split in the team that was irremediable.

COPING WITH DISTANCE IN A COMMUNITY ORIENTED EATING DISORDERS SERVICE

Just as in a crisis resolution team in general psychiatry, the aim of the community oriented eating disorders service is to treat people with eating disorders in their homes, or, at least, out of hospital. The different ways in which this can be achieved are described in this book under the headings of outpatient, domiciliary, hostel and day hospital care. Different areas, however, demand differing solutions, and a largely rural area will utilise more peripatetic treatment delivery than a compact urban area. There are several factors that impact on, for example, people's ability to take advantage of a day service. The first is accessibility, and this in practice means the time and effort it takes to get from home to the clinic by private or public transport. Patients seem to manage up to an hour each way and this is a reasonable upper limit, although it could be stretched to 1$\frac{1}{2}$ hours. Ask the patient to make the journey, perhaps with a friend or relative, and report back. Some areas are covered by journey planners on

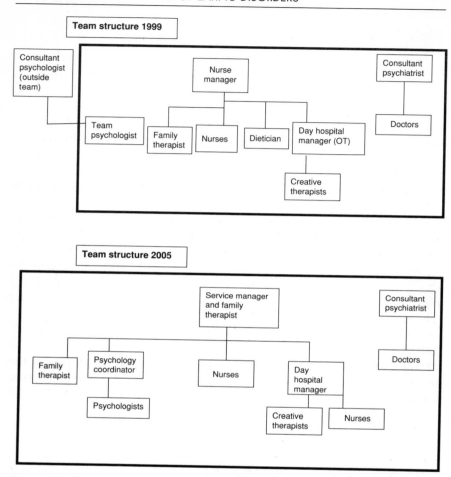

Figure 1.2 Showing changes in management structure of the team between 1999 and 2005. There is increased cross-disciplinary management.

the internet (e.g. www.transportforlondon.co.uk) and these will provide information on recommended routes and journey duration. The second factor is the state of the patient. It is clearly not feasible for a patient with a BMI of 13 and weakness of her legs to make a substantial journey on public transport, including walks, even though she herself may relish the idea of using up all those calories. Related to this is the perception of relatives. Carers, especially parents, who have lived with a child with an anorexic illness for many years may be extremely cautious about them attending a day hospital and some careful family work may be required in order to persuade the family of the safety and benefits of such a course of treatment.

Clinical description 1.1

A young man of 18 was referred to the service. He had developed anorexia nervosa at the age of 13, had a current BMI of 13.5 and had symptoms of bulimia and over-exercising, in which he engaged on an exercise cycle in the home. He was judged as fit for the day programme, but his mother regarded him as too unwell and frail. Two family meetings at the home led to the arrangement, by the clinic, of taxis to collect him from home and bring him back in the evening. This continued until his BMI was 15 when he began to attend using public transport until his full recovery and discharge.

The third factor is motivation of the patient and family. When a patient is safely housed in an inpatient unit, turning up to a therapy group is relatively easy. However, in order to attend a day or outpatient service, particularly on a daily basis, motivation has to be higher, and influences such as ambivalence about treatment and alternative activities, including eating disorder behaviours when the clinic is an hour's journey away may all conspire to keep the patient away. Close attention to motivational enhancement, involvement of the family in a supportive and informative way and adherence to firm rules in the clinic can all help to keep this to a minimum.

The service can respond to the dilemma by enhancing the ability of the patient to get to the clinic, for example by providing taxis, by offering accommodation near to the clinic, in the form of a hostel or using a local hotel, or by bringing treatment to the household, thereby helping and supporting the family in providing care. In planning a service for a mixed urban and rural population, a combination of weekly outpatient treatment, part-time day hospital, full-time day hospital, outreach and satellite clinics, and hostel or hotel accommodation can be provided, giving a wide range of interventions for management of different types of patient at varying distances from the EDS base.

BRICKS AND MORTAR

Clinical description 1.2

A local businessman has a daughter with anorexia nervosa who is admitted with hypokalaemia to a medical ward. She is seen by members of your service and makes a miraculous recovery. He is so impressed he gives the hospital £1 million to spend on providing a good facility for eating disorders.

Given this admittedly unlikely scenario, how should you spend the money?

Location, location, location

The two main issues are the unit's accessibility to staff, patients and other users, and the question of medical support. It makes sense for the service to be located near to bus and rail transport so that it can be reached in a reasonable time. If it is in an area with very expensive housing (that is, in most inner city locations) it should also be accessible to staff living in less costly areas. If there are two or more population centres, consider establishing two centres, perhaps within the geographical area of two funding bodies. In very thinly populated areas consider a mobile outreach service (see Chapter 7) and a day hospital with a hostel (Chapter 8).

Whatever model of care, include as much flexibility as possible. An outpatient unit should be usable as a day hospital or liaison and outreach base so that the service can adjust to changing clinical demands. The proportions of the different elements of community care can be varied depending on the waiting lists for each form of intervention, with staff spending, for example, more time on outreach and liaison when demand for that approach increases and that for day care diminishes.

Staff areas

Adequate accommodation for staff is essential to the welfare and functioning of the team. Individual offices have the advantages of privacy and their potential for interviews with patients or other staff, and the disadvantages of isolation. Individual offices are notoriously difficult to maintain in a state that is suitable for interviews with patients or relatives with abundant opportunities for breaching rules of confidentiality and safety. Open plan arrangements foster team cohesion but some find close proximity with colleagues difficult to sustain. A combination of an open area together with a few rooms for either individual occupation or 'hot desking' for confidential meetings would seem sensible.

Team meetings

A room capable of accommodating the whole team is essential. It should be comfortable so that a meeting of three hours is not unbearable and this means attention to seating, lighting, heating and ventilation as well as the dimensions of the room.

Interview rooms

A few bookable interview rooms will be needed. Patients with eating disorders are not known for their risk of violence to staff. However, alcohol and drug abuse are quite common and precautions such as alarms and escape routes for staff are advisable, especially when new patients are assessed.

In the treatment of eating disorders, from time to time allegations are made that a therapist has acted in a sexually inappropriate manner. No accurate figures are available but there is a perception that misconduct occurs more frequently when the patient has an eating disorder compared to other psychiatric or non-psychiatric consultations. Whether the apparent excess in eating disorders is, in fact, significantly greater than, say, psychotherapy for personality disorder or gynaecology is uncertain. However, a definitive study, in such a sensitive area, is unlikely to be done and all therapists, particularly but not exclusively males, should take precautions to avoid even the suspicion of wrongdoing. Interview rooms should be unlocked and should have a window or peephole fitted in the door. Other staff should be aware that the interview is taking place. Patients should not be interviewed in rooms that are not clearly interview rooms without a chaperone. Such rooms include sitting rooms and bedrooms (during home or hospital visits). If the therapist is aware of a risk of misconduct, because of the patient's behaviour and/or his own feelings, it should be discussed as a matter of urgency with a mentor or supervisor. Allowing a third party to know about the potential for trouble acts as both prevention and a potential source of help should a complaint be made. Lastly, a team should have a clear mechanism for discussing concerns in a manner that does not leave either the concerned staff member or the subject of the concern open to unwarranted adverse consequences. This matter should be addressed as a clinical governance issue before any problem has arisen, just as dealing with potential violence is a routine item for discussion in a forensic team.

Family therapy

A room for seeing families will need comfortable accommodation for up to eight people. The requirement does not end there, however, as will be described in Chapter 5, and the room may need to accommodate a further two to four people for other members of staff joining the session, while a supervising team requires an adjacent room, with a large one-way screen separating it from the therapy room, as well as a sound system allowing the supervising team to hear what is going on in the therapy room, and a microphone allowing the supervisor to speak to the therapist via an

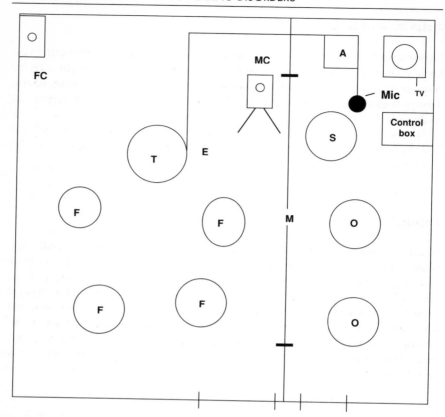

Figure 1.3   Suggested diagram for a family therapy suite.
Notes: T = Therapist; E = Earpiece; A = Amplifier; Mic = Microphone; TV = TV monitor/video recorder; MC = Mobile camera (pan and tilt); FC = Fixed camera (wide angle); F = Family member; S = Supervisor; O = Observer/team member; M = One-way mirror.

earphone. If videotaping is required, a recorder linked to fixed and mobile cameras will be required. If adjacent rooms cannot be provided, the video monitor can act as a tolerable second best for supervision in a distant room. A rough design for such a family therapy suite is shown in Figure 1.3.

Groups

Therapy groups in outpatients (cognitive behaviour therapy, family support, outpatient support groups) and day care require a room with capacity for up to 12 people for up to two hours. Depending on the anticipated room usage, group, team meeting and family therapy rooms can be used for all these purposes.

Activity and large groups

Groups such as dance and movement therapy and art therapy requiring a large group of patients to use equipment or to engage in physical activity require a large room, perhaps two or three times the area of a group room. This sort of room can also be useful for multi-family groups, in which up to 25 people may be using the room at one time, for several hours. Such activities may occur once or twice a week, and this sort of room would not generally need to be exclusively for the use of the eating disorders service, but booked as needed.

Eating

If a day hospital is planned, provision of meals (see Chapter 6) will very likely form a part of the programme. Depending on how meals are provided, a kitchen for serving meals and a dining room for consuming them are the least that will be required. It is useful to have room for a 'beginners' table and a less supervised table, and some patients may require one-to-one help with eating when they are finding the act of eating very hard to perform. Sometimes it is useful for family members to come in to the unit and have a meal with the patient and staff, and this could take place in a number of different areas, or be part of a family therapy session.

SO, WHAT SHOULD WE ASK FOR?

Adding up the above facilities, we get:

- Team office: with enough desk space for all team members required to use it, plus a few for medical, nursing, psychology and other students and trainees.
- Team meeting room: with enough room for the whole team, plus a few more (family, students, visitors).
- Individual offices: for those that require them.
- Interview rooms: depending on number of outpatients seen, and the possibility of borrowing other, generic rooms.
- Group rooms: perhaps doubling with team meeting room.
- Family therapy suite: one room for 3–4 staff and one for a family with one therapist, with occasional visitors.
- Large group rooms: booked as required.
- Kitchen: for preparing or serving.
- Dining room: for day patients, individual and family supported meals.

HOSPITAL OR COMMUNITY?

The location of the eating disorders unit requires some thought. On the one hand, a community location has clear advantages. There is no geographical sharing with an inpatient psychiatric service and there is, therefore, congruence between the 'community' label on the unit and its location. Some patients and families object to the identification of eating disorders as a psychiatric illness, although this is, perhaps, a bit of denial that we should discourage. While a community location is desirable, it is also important that hospital facilities, particularly medical, should be quickly accessible. Given unlimited choice the ideal would be a comfortable house in the vicinity of a general hospital. Given unlimited finance, the house next door would make a fine rehabilitation hostel! (See Chapter 8.)

Chapter 2

STAFF

YOU CAN'T GET THE STAFF!

The single most important factor in the success of a team is the quality of its staff. This sweeping statement is based on my own experience of a number of teams, ranging from the astoundingly successful, to the profoundly dysfunctional. Just as a building will fall down if bricks are substandard, a team will malfunction if work is not of the highest quality. This applies to staff in all parts of the organisation, from the manager ensuring that funding for the service is maintained, to the junior nurse making sure that a serum potassium is checked, as well as the domestic maintaining a clean environment. How to attract staff to work in a particular team and encourage them to stay in the team is an unsolved mystery. Our team has a low vacancy rate, a low sickness rate, low staff turnover and a high pregnancy rate. The team has a preponderance of females, with one male psychologist, a male consultant psychiatrist and junior doctors who may be male or female. The female:male ratio (about 10 to 1) is about the same sex ratio as the referred patients. However, the two men do have more senior positions, so the team to that extent reflects societal tendencies and inequalities. There are currently three black workers in the team: one manager, one nurse and a junior doctor.

Recruitment is helped by a good reputation for clinical standards. Secondly, the range of work needs to be interesting and challenging, stretching the capacity of staff without regularly overloading them. Thirdly, effective line management and clinical supervision help to back up clinical work and control case loads. Fourthly, problems are approached as quickly and effectively as possible, a friendly atmosphere is fostered and lastly the professional development of each staff member is addressed. Each of these areas will be expanded in this chapter.

COME HITHER!

Vacancies arise in a team for diverse reasons. The manager should be worrying if several staff move on because they are stressed or for other reasons are unhappy with work. Pregnancy is probably a sign of a healthy team, and is welcome. Moving abroad or to a distant post occurs when staff experience family changes, including marriage, and is probably little to do with work on the team. Leaving the team to go to another local team at a similar level of seniority may be a cause for concern, and the staff member should have an exit interview to see what reasons may be behind the move.

How to fill vacancies? The first rule is only to appoint a suitable candidate, rather than filling the gap at all costs. It is better to find ways to cover the absent person for a while, rather than appoint someone with no experience and poor qualities just because the person applies for the post. There is often difficulty in recruiting to a particular post at the same level, so discuss with your manager how you can be flexible. A senior nurse, for example, might be replaced by a more junior nurse and the money saved used to buy some psychology time to supervise the new nurse. See if the jobs done by the departing team member could be shared by other team members and some of their roles that require less experience given to the new nurse. See if part-time team members would like to increase their hours.

When the vacancy is caused by a pregnancy or a secondment, in both of which cases the person could well return after 6–12 months, temporary solutions, using existing team members to do more complex tasks and employing a short-term person to restore the numbers of staff, can be more helpful than trying to replace an experienced team member for a few months. While advertising pays, it also costs, and it may not be worth spending a fortune on a national advertisement for a short-term post. It is worth it for a permanent position, and, in addition, personal contacts between team members and other members of their professions can be an important source of information about who might be interested in joining the team. You should also use local websites that are accessible to people outside the institution. At interviews, make sure that senior team members are on the panel, including the consultant and service manager, for key positions. It is also useful to have a member of the human resources department at hand, and a senior manager in the organisation can complete the interview panel.

INDUCTION AND MENTORING

When a new person starts work, she should be allocated a mentor, generally of the same professional group, who shows her round, introduces her to the team, and tells her how the team functions and what her expected role is. A handout describing the work of the team is useful at this stage and, unless she is very experienced, she is not expected to take on patients for assessment or therapy for several months. During that time, the new team member shadows her mentor and observes other team members

performing new assessments and meeting with patients in a variety of contexts. She is gradually introduced to the various tasks she is required to
perform and works increasingly independently. The rate at which this process occurs naturally varies between individuals, depending on training,
experience and personality. If the new person is the only representative of
a particular profession on the team, say occupational therapy or a dietician, induction should still take place, but a delay in dealing with referrals
cannot usually be introduced.

FORMAL STRUCTURES: LINE AND PROFESSIONAL MANAGEMENT

Line management is traditionally provided by the same profession as the
person being managed. However, this does not need to be the case, and is
largely a product of professions being unwilling to entrust management
to another profession. Our experience is that line management can follow
functional divisions in a service, so that one person manages the day hospital and all staff associated with it, another manages the outpatient service
and another the outreach and liaison service. This means that a dietician
may be managing a nurse, or an occupational therapist. Some professions,
such as medicine and psychology, are rather more resistant to this form
of flexible management than others, but there is no reason why a nurse in
charge of, say an outreach service, should not manage a doctor working
wholly within the service. The line manager is responsible for agreeing the
weekly timetable, ensuring adequate support, supervision and caseload
management, as well as monitoring attendance, sickness and any disciplinary issues. This form of management is separate from professional
management, in which the individual meets with a member of her own
professional group and discusses career progression, training and continuing professional development. If there is a problem in the individual's per-
formance, which could lead to disciplinary action, it is often useful for the
professional and line manager to meet with the person to discuss the issues
relatively informally, and the professional manager can act as a support.

SUPERVISION

In a team in which individuals with basic professional training such as
mental health nursing take on for therapy people with eating disorders,
provision of adequate supervision is essential so that clinical standards
are maintained, safety is addressed, the therapist is not given an excessive clinical burden and the patient feels confident in the therapy she is
receiving. Clearly the need for supervision in general varies depending on
training, experience and confidence. Supervision is a broad term and can
be divided into a number of types.

1. Medical supervision

This sort of supervision consists mainly of consultation with other professionals and trouble-shooting. It is done informally 'in the corridor' and more formally in a weekly meeting. This latter is termed the 'Current Concerns meeting' and occurs on a Wednesday morning between 9 and 10. A list is generated from a computer database containing the names of patients that people wish to consider. The meeting is chaired by a team member on a rotating basis. The patients are discussed and the situation resolved in a number of ways. Some examples follow:

Clinical description 2.1

A nurse working with a patient with anorexia nervosa is concerned because the patient reports feeling like harming herself and she describes depression of mood and hopelessness. The patient is discussed in the Current Concerns meeting and the outcome is that one of the doctors agrees to see her within a week, assess her mental state and recommend appropriate management.

Clinical description 2.2

The consultant receives an urgent faxed referral of a patient who has been admitted to a medical ward in a hospital some five miles away. He brings the case to Current Concerns and a visit within a few days is arranged by the liaison and outreach nurse and one of the team doctors. The case is brought back to Current Concerns the following week and arrangements are made for the patient to attend the day hospital after she is discharged from the medical ward.

Clinical description 2.3

A trainee psychologist brings a patient to Current Concerns. The patient, aged 27, has been offered two appointments for individual therapy but has failed to attend, after confirming both appointments. She has a five-year history, is slightly underweight (BMI 18.4) and vomits regularly. The trainee is asked to write to the GP, discharging the patient back to the GP, but asking that the GP actively monitor weight and potassium and refer back if the patient wishes to engage in treatment.

More informal versions of this level of supervision occur any time that staff are together. After a particularly gruelling session support and encouragement given by other staff members can be very helpful. One of the most difficult tasks is to monitor a high-risk patient, for example one who maintains a low weight and whose potassium level frequently threatens to dip to dangerous levels. The first task is for the therapist, whether nurse, psychologist or occupational therapist, to meet, decide on a management plan and complete a risk assessment. The plan might be to measure potassium three times a week, and to perform an ECG at baseline, and then if the potassium falls below 3.0 mmol/l. The nurse will continue to require support in the form of informal discussions with the doctor about the patient's current potassium, and a joint look at her latest ECG. The doctor may be reassured or wish to have the views of a cardiologist about the patient's current ECG.

2. General psychotherapy supervision

In this form of supervision, the therapist meets, often in a group, with an experienced clinician, who may be a consultant psychiatrist in psychotherapy, a psychologist or a psychotherapist. One or two patients are generally discussed in a weekly meeting lasting 1–2 hours, depending on the number of attendees. The supervisor comments on the session and may discuss feelings of the therapist elicited by contact with the patient. The discussion is quickly opened up to other members of the group who will comment based on their own experiences of similar problems. While supervision is clearly influenced by the therapeutic training of the supervisor, whether psychoanalytic, cognitive behaviour therapy or other modalities, the emphasis of this approach is to help the therapist solve the problem that she has brought, without imposing a therapeutic model. In this model of supervision, the supervisor facilitates discussion in the group and it is the entire experience of the group, rather than the specific training of the supervisor, that guides the conduct of supervision. In a variant of this form of supervision, practised at the Russell Unit, the supervisor interviews the therapist presenting her work in front of the other group members. They are then encouraged to discuss what they have heard while the therapist and supervisor listen. This approach is reminiscent of the 'reflecting team' often used in family therapy.

3. Specific psychotherapy supervision

Staff providing specific therapies such as cognitive behaviour therapy (CBT), interpersonal therapy, psychodynamic or psychoanalytic therapy and dialectical behaviour therapy demand specific supervision by a professional suitably trained in the modality. Equally, staff engaged in family therapy, dance movement therapy and art therapy will require supervision.

Whether these types of supervision are provided within the team or not is a management decision and partly depends on the number of people requiring it. In our team Cognitive Behaviour Therapy, Interpersonal Therapy (Klerman, Weissman, Rounsaville & Chevron, 1984), family therapy and psychodynamic therapy supervision are provided within the team by a psychologist, a family therapist and a consultant psychiatrist in psychotherapy. Liaison and outreach work (see Chapter 9) is supervised monthly by the consultant psychiatrist, and weekly during the Current Concerns meeting. The art and dance movement therapists each have their own supervision outside the team. All outside supervision is funded from the team budget. In addition, the team members who provide supervision are themselves supervised by outside supervisors. This complex system of supervision is illustrated in Table 2.1.

4. Case and caseload management

A different but important form of supervision is case management (see Table 2.1). Here, the progress of the patient is assessed, intercurrent psychiatric and physical problems noted, and the shape of therapy planned. If a patient fails to attend a certain number of times she would be discussed in case management and brought to the Current Concerns meeting for discussion and possible discharge back to the GP. Alternatively, if a patient has been attending for longer than average (as a rule, over one year) the reasons for this need to be discussed in case management and if it is thought that there are difficulties ending therapy appropriately, because, for example, a patient becomes extremely dependent on the therapist, the case would be taken to general or specific psychotherapy supervision to work out the issue.

In caseload management, the number of patients held by a particular therapist is considered and discussed. The appropriate number depends on many factors including the experience and skills of the therapist, the time taken by other duties (such as day hospital care and new outpatient assessments) and the difficulties presented by current patients. Sometimes, however, taking all this into account, a therapist is taking on either too few or too many cases, and if this is the case she will need help in order to restore balance. Generally, discussion in caseload management is enough to resolve any problem. Occasionally the therapist's line manager may need to be involved if, for example, competing responsibilities are difficult to alter, and it may require action at a higher level to rearrange duties so that a therapist can achieve the caseload agreed with the supervisor.

The case and caseload supervisor can be any senior member of the team, and in the absence of a suitable person, the role can be assumed by the line manager (see above).

Table 2.1 Structure of supervision for different therapeutic approaches in the team

Type of supervision (see text)	Type of therapy	Therapist	Supervisor	Details of supervision	Functions of supervision
Medical	Any	Any team member	Psychiatrist	Informal and weekly group	Identification and management of psychiatric or medical problems
General Psychotherapy	Supportive individual	Any team member	Consultant psychotherapist	Weekly, group	Identify, solve problems
General Psychotherapy	Supportive individual	Any team member	More senior team member	Weekly, individual	Areas not addressed in the group
Specific Psychotherapy	Psychodynamic group	Psychologist, trainee psychiatrist	Consultant psychotherapist	Weekly, group	Manage group, address transference and counter-transference
Specific Psychotherapy	CBT individual	Any team member	Psychologist	Weekly, group	CBT approach
Specific Psychotherapy	CBT group	Psychologist, nurse	Psychologist	Weekly, group	Manage group, CBT approach
Specific Psychotherapy	Family therapy	Family therapist, family therapist trainee, other team member	Family therapist	Weekly, live supervision	Support family interventions
Case and Caseload Management	Any therapy	Any team member	More senior team member	Weekly, individual	General management, caseload management
Medical and Case/Caseload Management	Liaison and outreach work	Nurse, doctor	Psychiatrist	Monthly, group	Discuss, advise on case management
Informal and peer support	Any	Any team member	Peer	Any time, one to one or group	Informal discussion of difficulties

5. Informal and peer support

This form of supervision is hard to define but extremely important. It takes place in the team office, over lunch, in the corridor and sometimes in the pub or coffee shop after work, and involves sharing difficulties in clinical management with colleagues outside the supervision system. If supervision has not helped resolve a problem, then peer support can help by refocusing priorities and assisting the therapist to use the supervisory structures more effectively, 'Why not talk to x about it?' or 'Have you thought of opening it out in Current Concerns?'

Informal and peer support can be semi-formalised into a peer supervision meeting in which all the participants are therapists and no supervisor is present.

STAFF DEVELOPMENT

Professional development in staff is the remit of the professional manager (see above). However, various activities within the team can help individuals make choices about their future professional lives. Senior members of the team regularly receive information about courses, some of which may be relevant to the team. It is useful to have a file of such information and to maintain a notice board to display forthcoming events. A library of relevant books including texts on the main eating disorders, obesity, the main therapeutic approaches and several self-help books for guided self-help is very useful and a team member should be given the responsibility of looking after such a collection and devising a way to keep it reasonably intact, as well as maintaining the information file on upcoming courses and the notice board. As consultant I find it helpful to meet with each team member twice yearly for an informal discussion on where they see themselves in the team, and where they would like to be in the future. Feedback suggests that the team appreciates this session in the knowledge that their contribution is acknowledged. The informal meeting is also an opportunity for the staff member to indicate whether any particular course would be helpful in their work with the team, whether it be CBT, family therapy, management skills or nutrition. If a training budget can be established realisation of these proposals can be achieved, and the team member as well as the whole team, and, of course, the patients, all benefit. As part of preparation for writing this book, I spent an hour with each team member which gave me a much clearer idea about how the team as a whole functions. Some team members also related that spending this time helped them view their work in a more positive light. It is difficult to know the effects on morale and on the quality of team functioning that ensue when senior team members spend time with individual team members, but my suspicion is that it can be considerable. The team needs to have sufficient confidence to approach informal meetings such as this without the fear that they might give themselves away and so be liable to be criticised. Individual staff members use the informal meeting with the consultant in different ways. For some it is an opportunity to request support for funding a particular course, perhaps with a view to becoming a qualified therapist. Others feel content in performing their role and do not wish to train to do anything else, and this must be respected and supported. Knowing how the staff see their careers is very helpful when a staff member leaves and the team needs to find ways of covering that individual's work. Even so, some people who seem to have decided to keep their work unchanging may agree to increased responsibility if the opportunity presents itself.

SOCIALISING

Some teams, and subgroups within a team, may socialise together in diverse ways that can include having lunch together, engaging in sport and going out for an evening meal. This aspect of the team's functioning cannot be forced but when it occurs it can be a very cohesive influence. While there is no reason why more elderly members of the team should not accept an invitation to visit a night-club, for example, they should withdraw home well before they have had the opportunity to embarrass themselves and everyone else by their attempts to emulate their younger colleagues on the dance floor!

Food appears to be an important subject in the team. On Wednesday mornings, after the Current Concerns meeting, we enjoy a banquet (lasting a maximum of 15 minutes) of French cheeses, chocolate and pastries, washed down with fresh coffee and tea. I sometimes wonder whether we are eating for the patients, and a recent series of pregnancies in the team raised the question of whether we were also reproducing for them! Unconscious and, perhaps, conscious motivations for our behaviour (including our choosing eating disorders as a field) undoubtedly abound. Perhaps if we had continued our staff support group (see next section) we would be more aware of them. However, we did not, and such insights as we have emerge from our private thoughts and conversations, within and outside the team.

STAFF SUPPORT GROUPS AND AWAY-DAYS

There is general agreement that looking after patients with eating disorders is stressful and difficult and that some sort of support is a good idea. Clearly the best support is accurate information and timely intervention, provided by a plethora of supervision sessions and clinical meetings. Further support is given informally in meetings with individual colleagues, group discussions and social events. Many teams do have a support group, although our experience of such a group is that although it was useful its effectiveness was limited. The group tended to be split into talkers and non-talkers, and the latter group comprised mostly the most junior staff. The result was that the senior members of the team, which included doctors, the manager, psychologists and some senior nurses, did talk and resolved some issues. The junior members of the team, mostly junior nurses, hardly ever talked and there was a feeling that although there were important issues to discuss they were too inhibited to talk freely in front of their managers and seniors. The process gave rise to a belief that there were, indeed, substantial problems in the team that should be discussed, but they could not be because of the constraints of the group. Individual members of the 'silent' group would admit that they were just too shy to talk in front of such a group, and that the other professions, especially doctors and psychologists, were so good at talking, it made them feel even worse. Eventually, we unanimously decided to terminate the group, which had persisted for some two years.

Away-days are different. They are a way for NHS staff, often working in rather grimy buildings, to get out for a day to a pleasant location and to discuss the future workings of the team. They are useful when substantial change is forecast, for example due to changes in senior staff or in catchment area. The idea of the staff support group can be applied here, but in a less unrelenting way. Invite a reliable outside facilitator to help the team discuss a particular issue, for example, 'Who should sit with patients at meal times?', or when a number of key people have left within a short time, to discuss team structure and work allocation. The facilitator will charge, probably quite highly if he or she is good, but the improvement in team functioning within a difficult period can be palpable. When the facilitator is absent part of the day can be devoted to small group work in which other issues are discussed, perhaps less contentious ones, and one person from each group asked to feed back while the proceedings are recorded on a flip chart (which documents, in my experience, always become completely incomprehensible as soon as the next day has dawned 'What did that extra thick arrow and those asterisks mean?'). The day can also contain brief presentations from team members on their particular hobby horses like 'Why we should introduce acupuncture into the therapeutic programme' or a presentation of some research one of the team is set to do.

The location of the away-day should, as the name implies, be away, but not so far as to place undue burdens on the team members' time and money. It should be as pleasant as possible, within the means of the budget, and refreshments and perhaps meals should be provided.

The patients are, of course, given a day off from therapy and the away-day is in that respect similar to a weekend or national holiday. Just as occurs prior to a weekend, the ability of patients to cope without support should be considered, and arrangements made to cover clinical needs such as taking blood for a potassium level and looking at and acting on the result.

INVOLVING THE STAFF IN MANAGEMENT

The away-day is one way in which the staff can both hear about developments in the management sphere and contribute to them. Throughout the year, we have established two forms of management meeting: the business meeting, to which all staff are invited; and the management meeting, open to a small group of senior staff. Both occur monthly, for one hour, and the management meeting is scheduled to take place a week before the business meeting, so that issues for the larger meeting can first be discussed in the smaller. In the management meeting there are representatives from the day hospital, the outpatient service, and the therapy service and these individuals meet with the service manager and the consultant. The agenda follows a predictable form:

Management meeting

Date, place

1. Present and apologies
2. Previous minutes
3. Matter arising from previous minutes
4. Reports from different professional areas
   a. Nursing
   b. Medical
   c. Therapies
   d. Administration
5. Reports from different service areas
   a. Outpatients
   b. Day hospital
   c. Outreach and liaison
   d. Inpatients
6. Manager's report
7. Any other business
8. Date and time of next meeting

The meeting is chaired by the service manager and minuted by one of the secretaries.

Business meeting

The monthly business meeting follows a similar format, with information being provided to the team by members of the management team. This meeting is chaired by the consultant psychiatrist and is also minuted. All minutes are sent out by email.

PROBLEMS

The combination of good staff, sensitive management, relevant supervision and friendly relationships means that significant interpersonal difficulties occur rather rarely. When they do they can be related to the job itself, to a personality clash in the team, to personal problems or even to mental disorder in a staff member or a variety of other issues.

Job-related unhappiness commonly occurs after someone is promoted to a more senior position in the team. There may be overt or covert competitiveness among staff who have applied for the post. Be aware of staff who have been trainees together – they may exhibit a particularly intense form of sibling rivalry. When the appointment has been made the disappointed losers can make life impossible for the person selected. If such a situation develops it must be challenged as soon as possible by the service manager.

Sometimes individuals clash within the team. One person may feel deserving of more recognition and act autonomously without the authority of the service manager. The activities (e.g. starting a therapy group without discussion with management) may not strictly be against the rules but a number of such digressions can undermine the established systems of responsibility and accountability in the team and the team member will need counselling, perhaps with the individual's professional supervisor, so that work in the team can be harmonised.

The third type of staff problem occurs when an individual, who may be experiencing difficulties in their private life, develops some form of psychiatric disorder. As long as it is recognised and treated and time is taken off work as appropriate, the main issue is covering that person's work which, in a well-functioning team, occurs by 'rallying round'. If the staff member does not recognise or admit to a problem the impact can be substantial. Someone with an eating disorder, for example, may struggle to keep up with the work, dogged by perfectionism and the demands of a bulimic disorder and end up working all hours and breaking down at work. By then it is usually obvious that the individual needs help and the advice of the occupational health service can be sought. Staff members who require treatment for an eating disorder must clearly be treated elsewhere, and if they live in the eating disorder's area of cover the funding organisation will need to approve an external referral. This also applies to members of staff about whom rules need to be established locally. There are a number of levels of such 'special caseness':

1. Team members.
2. Staff and students working within the same organisation (e.g. mental health service provider). In this group the staff and students can be offered care within the team but will usually opt for treatment in another unit. If they are treated within the team, their files should be kept in a separate, locked cabinet, they should not appear on lists for distribution within the team and in meetings students should be asked to withdraw while fellow students and professionals are discussed.
3. Members of staff in related health and social care organisations. This includes general hospital services, often managed separately these days, local GPs and their trainees, and staff in hostels and social services. They can often be managed in the service but should be given the choice of being treated elsewhere.

The two important principles here are confidentiality and the right to effective treatment. Too often health staff seem to be denied the latter because of fears about the former and we must develop strategies to avoid this unhappy outcome.

Chapter 3

INITIAL OUTPATIENT ASSESSMENT

SOURCES OF REFERRAL (Figure 3.1)

The various hurdles that need to be negotiated by a person with an eating disorder if she decides to access treatment have been described in Chapter 1. The specialist service managers have to decide whether and how to restrict referral rights to their service. There are a number of reasons to restrict access, although in health systems in which the public is accustomed to decide for themselves which specialists they consult, such as in France or the United States, such restriction may not be popular. In general, more restrictive filters demand more of non-specialist services and the demands on the eating disorders service may be less. The levels of specialisation at which referrals could be made are as follows.

Level 1: self-referral

Patients or relatives can refer to a service (the general public)

This is, understandably, popular with patients and relatives, and could lead to a very high referral rate and a high false positive rate, i.e. a large number of people without eating disorders applying for treatment. Evidence against the latter proposition came from our email treatment trial (see Chapter 10). Of 110 people who wrote in requesting treatment, over 97 % had eating disorders according to the questionnaire for eating disorders diagnosis, which generated DSM IV (the Diagnostic and Statistical Manual of Mental Disorders, 4th Edition) diagnoses. This suggests (predictably) that people with eating disorders know what is wrong without seeing a doctor, and that a service that is open to self-referral should not expect to see a large number of inappropriate referrals, although they may well receive a very large number of appropriate referrals which could swamp the service. This is not the only reason that a service might decide against self-referral. Responsibility for care and monitoring when the person has self-referred is entirely a matter for the patient and the specialist service, unless a GP is willing to endorse a referral after the patient has

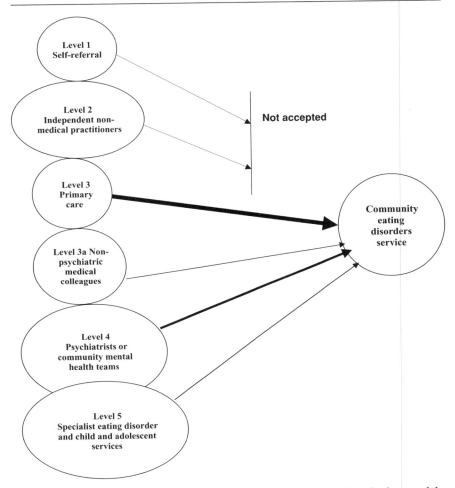

Figure 3.1   Sources of referral to the Eating Disorders Service. The thickness of the arrows reflects the proportion of referrals from each source.

self-referred and been assessed. If not, the weight of responsibility on the specialist service is heavy, and this may limit the number of patients that can be taken on.

Level 2: referrals from independently practising non-medical practitioners

Referrals are accepted from therapists, dieticians, psychologists and any other non-medical practitioner who is not part of a multidisciplinary team (independent non-medical health workers)

Patients referred from these sources will be in therapy, which may be dynamic or cognitive behavioural psychotherapy, dietetic counselling and many others, and will have an assessment written by the practitioner. As in self-referral, however, responsibility for monitoring of physical state is uncertain, and the GP would need to be approached to endorse the referral. In some cases, the practitioner has already informed the GP who has agreed to the referral and the GP can therefore reasonably be approached to share medical assessment and monitoring.

Level 3: referrals from primary care

Referrals are accepted from GPs and members of the primary care team (GP and team)

In many specialist services, this is the most common mode of referral. The patient visits the GP who makes an appropriate referral to the specialist team. The GP continues to hold responsibility for monitoring, prescription of medication and emergency attendance, but this responsibility is shared with the specialist team who are required to advise and support the GP and to take over elements of responsibility as agreed with the GP, e.g. for prescribing. Primary care referrals usually come from the GP, but may also come from a practice counsellor or nurse, with the approval of the GP.

Level 3a: referrals from non-psychiatric medical teams in secondary care

Referrals are accepted from medical or non-medical members of teams providing non-psychiatric medical care (general medical and surgical doctors and teams)

These services include gastroenterology, bariatric (weight-reduction) surgery, rheumatology, gynaecology and endocrinology, all of which may be consulted by people with eating disorders whose symptoms bring them to physicians for diverse reasons including irritable bowel syndrome, weight reduction, osteoporosis, infertility and amenorrhoea. Responsibility for these services is generally restricted to treatment within their speciality, and the GP usually needs to be informed and brought in to share care with the eating disorder service. Referrals via accident and emergency departments should be regarded as coming from this level of referrer, even if a psychiatrist has written the referral letter, often after seeing the patient in the accident and emergency department following an act of deliberate self-harm.

Level 4: referrals from psychiatrists or non-medical practitioners in multidisciplinary psychiatric teams

Referral can be made by psychiatrists or medical or non-medical practitioners acting as representatives of a team that includes a medical practitioner, usually a psychiatrist (psychiatric, non eating disorder specialist teams)

Psychiatrists in any field of psychiatry including general psychiatry, drug and alcohol misuse, forensic psychiatry and psychotherapy make referrals to the eating disorder service, usually informing the GP. In such a case, responsibility for risk monitoring is shared by the eating disorders service, the psychiatric service and the GP, although what precisely is required of which element of this highly complex system has to be worked out in a meeting including the referring psychiatrist, the GP and the eating disorders psychiatrist. If this is not done, professionals may not know what they and others are required to contribute, and patient care, as well as professional nerves, can suffer. Non-medical referrers at this level include community psychiatric nurses (CPNs) and social workers in community mental health teams (CMHTs). These referrals can be regarded as coming from the team as a whole, and if there are medical assessment and monitoring issues, these can be addressed with the medical and nursing members of the team. The referrer is sometimes a worker with coordinating responsibility for the patient's care, and is hence a very valuable member of the patient's support and treatment network.

Level 5: referrals from other specialist eating disorder services and child and adolescent services

Referrals are accepted from specialist eating disorder and child and adolescent services

Child and adolescent teams are classified at this level because adolescents with eating disorders usually form a substantial proportion of their caseload. These referrals are usually *transitional*, that is, they occur when a patient transcends either a geographical boundary, moving from the catchment area of one eating disorder service to another, or a developmental boundary, moving from the age range of one service to that of another. Referrers may be the consultant or another team member in specialist eating disorders or in child and adolescent teams. When the referring team is a specialist eating disorders team, the patient or the GP now fall in the area of another team, and when referrals come from child and adolescent services, the patient is frequently around the age at which transfer to adult services is anticipated (usually 18 years). In both cases the referring team is unlikely to offer any further involvement after transfer

Table 3.1   Issues encountered in referral from different sources, including risk sharing and handover meetings when relevant. Note that levels 1, 2, 3 and 3a are not specialist psychiatric resources, level 4 is such a specialist resource and at level 5 a fair degree of eating disorders expertise can be assumed

Referrer level	Referral Source	Likely referrers	Responsibility shared by:	Handover meeting attended by:
1	Self	Self, relative	EDS	N/A
2	Lone therapist	Therapist, dietitian etc.	Therapist, EDS	N/A
3	Primary care	GP, GP counsellor, Practice nurse	GP, EDS	N/A
3a	Non-psych. Secondary Care	Physician, surgeon	GP, EDS. ?referrer	N/A
4	Psych. secondary care	Con. psychiatrist, Psychologist, Nurse	GP, Mental Health Team, EDS	Referrer, GP, EDS
5	Other EDS, Child and Family Service	ED psychiatrist, therapist, nurse	GP, EDS	Referrer, GP, EDS

Notes:
Level 1: Self-referral
Level 2: Lone therapist
Level 3: Primary care
Level 3a: Non-psychiatric secondary care
Level 4: Psychiatric team
Level 5: Eating Disorders or Child and Adolescent team

of care has been completed. Accordingly, primary care and perhaps general psychiatric services may need to be involved in the handover meeting, as well as the referring team and the receiving eating disorders service.

The different levels with their characteristics and interrelationships are depicted in Table 3.1. Setting up a new service provides the opportunity to decide at which levels to accept referrals. The decision will have a profound impact on workload, the nature of the work performed by the team and the capacity of the team. Except for level 5, any patient referred brings the potential for the referring agency to remain involved in treatment. When the referrer is the patient or relative this is self-evident. A lone therapist referring may well agree to continue working with the patient, at least until therapy can be provided by the eating disorders service (EDS). Rapid transfer of care may be required if, for example, treatment is being paid for by the patient who is no longer able to fund it. Often, however, a therapeutic relationship, once built up, is better continued, as long as adequate liaison can be established with the EDS. At level 3, the most common referral source, continued involvement of the patient's GP allows sharing of risk management so that out-of-hours medical cover is provided by primary care (increasingly commonly through an agency) and interventions such as medication, monitoring of weight and electrolytes can all be performed in primary care. Whether this sharing is practicable depends on the quality of service provided in primary care, and if the EDS consultant wishes the GP to be actively involved, a phone call or a meeting are usually better than a letter on its own to establish the expectations of each party. At level 3a, the referring physician or surgeon may continue to provide care, for example continued management of osteoporosis or polycystic ovarian syndrome, or surgery for obesity, but risk management will usually have to be arranged between the EDS, the GP and the general psychiatric service if they are engaged. At level 4, the community mental health service makes the referral and could potentially stay involved. They should be encouraged to do so if there are any complicating factors such as self-harm, comorbid serious psychiatric morbidity, or a long-standing illness with major social, accommodation and occupational problems. They will also be helpful in smoothing the way if the patient requires a general psychiatric bed, and if compulsory treatment is needed. Moreover, it may be possible to train and supervise an interested member of the community mental health team to provide treatment for some eating disorders. Confining referrals to those coming from level 4 has the advantage that patients will receive a psychiatric evaluation prior to coming to the EDS and the mixed blessing that the number of referrals is likely to be controlled. This is probably because patients are less likely to agree to referral knowing they will require a general psychiatric evaluation prior to being seen in the eating disorders service. Raising the barriers to care in this way does more than simply reduce the referral rate. It can also increase the average severity of illness in patients who do reach the EDS so that complex care such as including individual and family therapy, day care and admission, is more likely to be required by these patients. This is a good illustration of how simply counting referrals may not be an accurate way to indicate workload. 100 patients referred with bulimia nervosa, treated in 10 therapy groups of 10 patients each lasting 20 weeks, do not require the same staff time as 100 patients with anorexia nervosa, self-harm and alcohol misuse requiring intensive case management, as well as day and inpatient care.

At level 5, the referrer is not usually involved in further care, and risk management, as in level 3a, will need to be arranged with the GP and, perhaps, the local psychiatric team.

In 203 consecutive referrals in 2004–5, the proportions of each type of referral were as follows:

- Levels 1, 2: none
- Level 3: 67 %
- Level 3a: 4 %
- Level 4: 28 %
- Level 5: 1 %

INFORMATION REQUIRED

It is useful to decide in advance what information you would ideally like to receive from the referrer. In order to determine this, consider what decisions need to be made when you receive the referral letter.

1. Is the patient correctly assigned to my service? To answer this you will need the patient's age, address and the address of the GP, depending on whether and how your service is restricted by age or geography. Most adult eating disorders services are required to assess and treat patients in the adult age range, i.e. 18 to 65, and need to decide whether they will accept referral of a 70-year-old patient with bulimia nervosa.
2. Does the patient appear to have an eating disorder? You will require a few details of the presenting problem, be it weight loss, amenorrhoea, bingeing, vomiting, body image disturbance, etc.
3. Is this an urgent referral? The letter may say 'urgent', but this is sometimes a reflection of the pressure that has been put on the referrer rather than of the severity of problem. In a sense, all referrals are urgent because a patient, perhaps with several years of illness, may have finally agreed to specialist treatment and this moment should be seized as quickly as possible. In practice, however, because of the large number of referrals, it is not always possible to respond immediately, and some sort of triage is required. If triage is done according to risk factors (see Chapter 4, Figure 4.5) the main information needed is BMI or height and weight, purging behaviours, serum electrolytes and suicidal behaviour. We have found that referrers often do not provide this information when relevant, even after a sustained educational campaign. In the 203 consecutive referral letters to the Russell Unit, alluded to above two-thirds from primary care and one-third from secondary care, information on height and weight adequate to calculate BMI was provided in 35%. The proportion of referrers providing information on BMI according to source of referral is given in Table 3.2. There was no significant difference based on source of referral.
4. Is the information on address and phone number up to date? This is particularly important for students and foreign patients, both of whom tend to move regularly.

Table 3.2 Proportion of patients referred to the Russell Unit eating disorders service in which details of height and weight were included in the referral letter. There was no significant difference found (using chi-squared, $p > 0.9$) when letters mentioning 'weight loss' were compared with those in which weight loss was not mentioned.

	n	Weight %	Height %	BMI or Wt + Height
Primary care	136	45	25	45
Secondary care	67	59	51	52
Total	203	39	27	35

5. What is the previous treatment history and the current treatment provided and planned? Previous treatment allows notes to be obtained prior to the interview. Moreover, it is very helpful to know if the patient has been started on antidepressant treatment and referred to a counsellor and especially if referred simultaneously to psychiatry, eating disorders, psychotherapy and dietetics in the hope that one will yield fruit. The resulting confusion does little to help an already chaotic individual.

The following referral form (Figure 3.2) elicits the above information and can be a useful aid to communication. It is likely that referrals will in the near future be made electronically, in which case such a form could be available online. Many people regard referral forms as of limited usefulness as they are usually difficult to find when actually needed!

URGENCY

People who are insistent and assertive often get more rapid attention than the shy and retiring. As already noted, however, a referrer's indicator 'urgent' does not necessarily mean that the case must be prioritised. We fast-track the following referrals, based on information received in the initial referral letter:

1. BMI <19 whose weight is falling
2. BMI <15
3. Electrolyte disturbance
4. Recently or due to be discharged from an inpatient eating disorders service
5. Anorexia nervosa, <25 years old with a short history (<1 year)
6. Child of the referred patient known to be at risk.

Each service must develop its own criteria for urgent assessment. The three principles embodied in the above are to prioritise those at high physical risk and those in whom research has shown an improved outcome following earlier intervention.

Specialist Eating Disorders Service

Referral Form
Date of referral
Urgency (circle): Routine Urgent
Reason for urgency (circle): Low weight Electrolyte disturbance Self-harm Child at risk
Other (specify) ……………..
Name of patient:……………………………….Date of Birth………. Sex: M F
Address

Home phone:
Mobile Phone:
GP:
Address

Phone:
Email:
Referrer (if not GP):
Professional role:
Address

Phone:
Email:

Suspected diagnosis (circle):

Diagnosis	Subtype	
Anorexia nervosa	restricting	Bulimic
Bulimia nervosa	purging	non-purging
Binge eating disorder		
Eating Disorder Not Otherwise Specified	Specify weight loss, weight gain, bingeing, purging as prominent symptoms	

Height (m):
Weight (kg):
BMI:
Symptoms (circle): Weight loss, Amenorrhoea, Body image disturbance, Bingeing
Vomiting, Laxative abuse
Electrolytes measured? Yes No. Normal Abnormal

History including reason for referral
_____
_____
_____
_____

Signed

Figure 3.2 A referral form for use by GPs and other referrers to the Specialist
Eating Disorders Service

INFORMATION GATHERED BEFORE
FIRST ASSESSMENT

Many services require a prospective patient to complete a questionnaire
prior to assessment. This is useful for a number of reasons. It ensures
a certain degree of motivation to attend the appointment, it alerts the

interviewer to important factors to explore, it gets the referred patient thinking about the process of assessment and it provides a first-aid kit for an interviewer who finishes the session without asking a key question. The content of a preassessment questionnaire depends on its purpose. A list of potential areas follows:

- Demographic information including current name and address, mobile phone number and email address, GP details, ethnicity.
- Details of the current problem, eating disorder symptoms, height and weight, any additional problem, physical problems.
- Family history, childhood trauma, abuse.
- Previous treatment.
- Expectations of current referral.

DNA AND THE OUTPATIENT CLINIC

It has been noted that a proportion of patients invited to attend hospital for assessment for any problem, whether it be back pain, a skin rash or an eating disorder, fail to attend (DNA – Did Not Attend) and it has been calculated that if all the staff time wasted on people who do not turn up is added together and saved, the NHS would never have any financial problems. It is, of course, a waste of resources when people do not turn up for an appointment, but it is also a fact of life that there will be a proportion of people failing appointments that is probably irreducible. This is because the reasons that people miss their appointment will always be there. The patient might have got better, or more likely, her motivation for treatment, so apparently strong in the GP surgery, may have waned. She may have moved away, gone for private care or been on holiday. It is probably significant that DNA rates are much higher in a free service such as the NHS when compared to a private service. There are some things that can be done to reduce the DNA rate, but they must be used cautiously. It has been shown (Killaspy, Banerjee, King, & Lloyd, 2000) that patients in general psychiatry clinics who fail to attend outpatient services are, in general, more ill than those who do make it. We must be careful not to exclude the most ill patients from treatment because they do not get to our clinics. Confining appointments to patients who confirm them is one reasonable way to improve attendance. The appointment is sent out several weeks in advance and a date by which time a confirmation needs to be received is included with the appointment. If the confirmation is not received by that date, the appointment is given to another patient, generally someone prioritised as urgent and waiting for an appointment as soon as possible. If this is done, the referral letter should be scrutinised and advice given to the referrer based on information received, for example, self-help (see the reading list supplied in Table 3.3), monitoring of weight or potassium level, re-referral at a future date. In the case of inpatients referred with possible anorexia

Table 3.3   A useful reading list for outpatients and referrers to foster self-help in eating disorders

Condition	Recommended text
Anorexia nervosa	Janet Treasure (1997) *Breaking Free from Anorexia Nervosa: A Survival Guide for Families, Friends and Sufferers*. Psychology Press. R.L. Palmer (1989) *Anorexia Nervosa, a Guide for Sufferers and their Families*. Penguin. A.H. Crisp (1980) Anorexia Nervosa: Let me be. Plenum.
Bulimia nervosa and binge eating disorder	Ulrike Schmidt & Janet Treasure (1993) *Getting Better Bit(e) by Bit(e): Survival Kit for Sufferers of Bulimia Nervosa and Binge Eating Disorders*. Psychology Press. Chris Fairburn (1995) *Overcoming Binge Eating*. Guilford Press. Peter Cooper (2006) *Overcoming Bulimia Nervosa and Binge-eating Self-help Manual*. Constable and Robinson.

nervosa, and deemed at risk (see Figure 4.5, risk factors or high risk, on p. 73) the referrer should be contacted for a discussion about how to proceed, including the possibility of seeing the patient in the GP's surgery or at home.

THE ASSESSMENT CLINIC

When referrals rates are high, it is important to have a system that efficiently combines a number of important functions, namely:

- A comprehensive assessment of eating disorder, general psychiatric, and physical history.
- An assessment of current physical state.
- A discussion of treatment options and a decision on further management.
- The writing of a full report for use by the referrer, the patient and the EDS.

The system in use at the Russell Unit over a number of years appears to fulfil these objectives and it will be described here in detail.

PHASE ONE: THE ASSESSMENT INTERVIEW

Prior to the patient's arrival at 10 am she is allocated to one of the team members assigned to the clinic. The professional background of the assessor is

Table 3.4   Areas to cover in the initial assessment of a patient with anorexia nervosa

Area	Specific areas to cover
History of eating disorder	Weight/BMI history
	Menstrual history
	Intake on the day before the assessment
	Compensatory behaviours
	Body image
	Physical complications of over/underweight
General psychiatric history	OCD, depression, anxiety, self harm
General medical history	Other diseases
Early personal and family history	FH of eating, affective disorder; weight in family; history of abuse, bullying or neglect
Treatment history	Specialist treatment, therapy
Mental state	Depression, body image
Physical state	BMI, SUSS (see Figure 4.1, p. 63), hypotension
Expectations and motivation	

of secondary importance to their ability to complete the assessment in an hour. In our team, nurses, doctors, psychologists, family therapists, occupational therapists and students in most of these areas have acted as assessors. They meet with the patient and conduct an interview in which information is collected on all relevant aspects of the referral. Usually the patient's preassessment questionnaire as well as the referral letter will be available, and should have been read before the interview. To guide questioning, the interviewer uses a checklist, which indicates the areas to be covered in the session. This covers the areas indicated in Table 3.4 and the full checklist is provided in Appendix 3.1 (see p. 49). It may seem daunting for the first few times and neophytes should observe a few assessments until they are confident enough to do them alone. When faced with the alarming array of questions to ask, it is also worth bearing in mind a few key issues that need to be addressed in the clinic:

- Does the patient have an eating disorder? If not how can we help her access appropriate care?
- Does she have risk factors or high risk (see Figure 4.5, p. 73). If so what investigations, monitoring and treatment does she require over the next few days/weeks?
- What treatment service offered by the EDS is most appropriate for her needs?
- Does she have any serious symptoms related to other medical or psychiatric problems and, if so, what treatment do they demand?
- What are her own ideas about what she wants from the service?

Naturally, in a full assessment other issues, including those of possible causality, are also addressed and are of great interest. However, if the above questions can be answered fully, the interviewer has gone a long way towards a helpful assessment.

PHASE TWO: THE TEAM DISCUSSION

After an hour during which 3–5 patients have been assessed, the assessors meet together with the consultant psychiatrist and the outpatients nurse manager to discuss the new patients and come to a decision on what further information is required or requires clarification and what investigations and therapy would be most appropriate. Patients who have not turned up are discussed and further actions planned. This usually means referral back to the referrer with a self-help reading list, unless there are risk factors, in which case the referrer may be asked to monitor weight or potassium, to try and refer the patient again, or to arrange for an outreach worker at the EDS to see the patient at a community location, such as the GP's surgery.

Presentation of a complex history in 12–15 minutes takes a certain amount of skill, but is achievable for any competent team member, including students of nursing, medicine, psychology and occupational therapy. Occasionally a patient has such difficulty in providing a history that by the end of an hour the increasingly anxious interviewer does not have the requisite information. It is very important that team members understand that this can happen for a number of reasons outside their own control. Some patients have so much to say that they spend the hour going over some very complicated problems that preclude discussion of other parts of the history. Some present very difficult assessment problems.

Clinical description 3.1

A young male patient was referred because of a weight loss of about 25 kg over six months. After spending an hour with him the nurse joined the team discussion somewhat distressed by announcing that she was no wiser about his eating problems than she had been at the beginning. The consultant interview later in the morning provided little more explanation, although it was clear at that interview that the patient, who subsequently proved to have schizophrenia, was displaying profound thought disorder.

In our experience, such extreme difficulty, which can also occur with a very obsessional patient, occurs rarely and interviews by team members' have been found to provide a useful basis for deciding on therapeutic intervention the vast majority of the time.

During the presentation, areas which have been left out or which were unclear are identified so they can be covered during the subsequent consultant interview. The consultant also fills out a data sheet in which basic demographic and clinical information is recorded. This has a number of functions:

1. It acts as an *aide-mémoire* during the subsequent interview of up to five new patients in an hour.
2. Information on the data sheet is transferred to the database (see Chapter 10) and is used for clinical audit.
3. It is used during the following team meeting to provide basic information about new patients seen that week, in case the person assessing the patient is not around that day. The data sheet in use at the Russell Unit is reproduced as Appendix 3.2 (see p. 52). Each team will need to decide on what information they require in their work, and the form is linked to particular interests in the Russell Unit.

One advantage of the team approach is that several team members get to hear about other patients with eating disorders and their problems, even if they have not come to the clinic, and to observe senior members of the team deciding on appropriate management and this can be a very powerful and rapidly effective learning experience for students and new team members.

While the team deliberates the patients have an hour during which they are asked to do the following:

- Read a description of and sign consent to the clinic procedure (being interviewed by the consultant in the presence of team members and students, being examined and weighed and having blood tests).
- Read and sign consent to a report being written to her GP or other referrer and to herself receiving a copy of the report.
- Complete a number of eating disorder related questionnaires. In our clinic we ask all patients to complete an eating disorders inventory, a Beck Depression Inventory and the Bulimia Investigatory Test Edinburgh. These are repeated at the end of treatment to obtain an idea of gains during therapy.

PHASE THREE: CONSULTANT INTERVIEW AND TREATMENT PLANNING

At 12 pm, each patient is asked to join the team for a discussion, mainly with the consultant or deputy. After a user survey, in which it was widely reported that facing a large group of professionals at this stage was very difficult, we discuss with patients their feelings about seeing a group and, if the patient wishes, we ask students to leave along with any staff member not considered essential. The essential staff members are the consultant and junior doctors, the outpatients nurse manager, and the interviewer (who may be a student). If the patient is a local student, we would exclude from all discussion about the patient any student in the same area of study.

During the consultant interview, the aim is to clarify the diagnosis, and establish that the provisional diagnosis reached in the assessment and in the team discussion accords with the consultant's own views. Sometimes, if the patient has a psychosis, personality disorder or obsessive compulsive disorder in addition to the eating disorder, a secondary diagnosis needs to be reached and the consultant may have an important role here.

The value of specific diagnosis in eating disorders needs to be examined. So many patients fall into the 'atypical' or 'eating disorder not otherwise specified' (EDNOS) group, at least in community settings, that one wonders whether the system really serves a valuable function. The antipsychiatry movement of the 1960s saw diagnosis as a way of controlling dissidence and, in the former Soviet Union, it was used in just that way, with political non-conformists being given the label 'sluggish schizophrenia' and incarcerated. There are people who believe that the anorexic lifestyle is a valuable one that should not be challenged. Their views can be found on 'Pro-Ana' websites. It is possible that many people with eating disorders who do not seek treatment hold these views. Even so, the celebration of the anorexic lifestyle would not preclude diagnosis. The main value of diagnosis is in its brevity. If we were to diagnose every patient we see as having an 'eating disorder' we would then have to add a problem list including low weight, purging behaviours, amenorrhoea, sexual difficulties in men, growth retardation in children, body image problems, bingeing, anorectic drug abuse as a minimum. This would be possible, although rather cumbersome.

Diagnosis does seem to be with us for at least a while, and in the team discussion there is usually not much doubt about which diagnosis to write, even if it often is EDNOS, and the main function of this brief (10–15 minute) interview is to assess motivation and to agree on a management plan. It is useful to have team members present, such as group, individual and family therapists, to engage with the patient in a discussion of the details of the different therapies, although that discussion can be conducted by the consultant. In general, the care pathways for different conditions are fairly well established, and the majority of treatment plans fall into the following categories:

- Bulimia nervosa or binge eating disorder without major comorbidity, other than depression and anxiety: referred for assessment for group CBT. Offered family therapy if interested.

- Anorexia nervosa: individual with or without family therapy. If the patient does not show risk factors or high risk (see Chapter 4) she can be monitored in primary care, otherwise she is considered for urgent treatment in the EDS.
- Bulimia nervosa or binge eating disorder with major comorbidity, e.g. frequent deliberate self-harm, alcohol or other drug abuse, psychosis: consider individual therapy and joint working with another specialist team, e.g. general psychiatry, psychotherapy, drugs or alcohol team.

Any patient engaging in purging behaviours such as vomiting or laxative or diuretic abuse has a blood test for urea and electrolytes. Any patient with a history of over six months weight-related amenorrhoea receives a bone mineral density scan (even if currently of normal weight). A patient who is at risk because of low weight may be referred for a blood test for electrolytes, blood count, liver function and creatine kinase, and an electrocardiogram.

PHASE FOUR: WRITING THE REPORT

This can also be daunting for the uninitiated. Those happy to use word processors type their own, otherwise administrative time for typing is required. The report should go to the referrer and the GP as well as the patient, if a copy is requested. It is useful to provide interviwers with an outline of what is required in the report. If possible the report should not exceed three A4 pages. It contains the following sections:

- Name and address of referrer
- Date and date of clinic
- Name, address, phone number and date of birth of patient
- A brief outline of the assessment with diagnoses made
- Physical measures: weight, height, BMI
- Suggested treatment
- History of present illness
- Relevant personal and family history
- Drug, alcohol, forensic, psychiatric and medical histories, as relevant
- Discussion of motivation and treatment, alluding to consultant interview
- Name and signature of assessor and consultant

A fictitious example is provided in Appendix 3.3 (see p. 54).

After the assessment session, it is important to have a system whereby the production of the report is logged. This is because, with so many people writing reports, including students who may only spend a few weeks in the service, the occasional report risks getting lost or not done, with potentially disastrous consequences. One member of the team, for example the person responsible for coordinating outpatient assessment and treatment, keeps a list of assessments made and referrals received. The list of referrals awaited including the date of assessment, is made available at the team meeting, for example during the Current Concerns meeting (see chapter 2) and if a letter has not been logged as received by, say, four weeks after assessment, the assessor, or the person responsible for the assessor's work (e.g. the consultant psychiatrist in the case of medical students) makes sure that the person is contacted and the assessment received. It is also useful to list management decisions made about each new patient (e.g. check electrolytes, order bone density scan, refer for individual and family therapy), and make sure that the decisions have been carried through.

COPYING LETTERS TO PATIENTS: ACCESS TO MEDICAL RECORDS

In the UK patients now have virtually unlimited access to their medical records. Only if seeing a document is deemed by the consultant psychiatrist to carry a substantial risk of harm to the patient, can access to a particular document be blocked. Equally, if a document contains information that has been provided by a third party, such as a relative, without the patient's knowledge, then the document can be withheld for the same reason. An extension of this access is that correspondence can now be copied to the patient if she wishes. This has a number of advantages, not least that errors of fact in the assessment can be corrected. Opinions with which the patient disagrees (such as a diagnosis of personality disorder or assessment of risk to others) are less likely to be altered by the author of the report. Consent to copying letters to the patient and, crucially, the address to which the letter should be sent, is collected from the patient during the new assessment clinic.

OTHER WAYS OF ACCESSING THE EATING DISORDERS SERVICE

In general, it is helpful to channel referrals through the assessment process described above. Patients coming to the attention of the team through the outreach and liaison service (see Chapter 7) usually gain access to the service via an outreach and liaison worker. In such a case the consultant should make efforts to see the patient, with the outreach and liaison worker, as soon as practicable, so that the latter is not left vulnerable if things go wrong. Sometimes, other teams may have the view that as soon as the patient with an eating disorder is referred to the EDS the latter should take them over as soon as possible. This may not be appropriate, for example, in the case of a patient with frequent self-harm who has been treated in a community mental health team for a number of years. The intervention of a senior member of the EDS may be required to restore expectations to a realistic level. It is also worth remembering that however egalitarian your team is other teams may dismiss a nurse's opinion and accept that of a doctor, because of the power differential. This is highly regrettable, and seems most prevalent on medical units, but for the present at least is a fact of life.

APPENDIX 3.1 RUSSELL UNIT EATING DISORDERS SERVICE STRUCTURED HISTORY CHECKLIST

Interview Details
Date:
Place:
Interviewer: Interviewer's profession:
Interviewer's email address:

Demographic Details
Name:
Address:
Post code: Phone no.:
Email address:

Sex:
Ethnicity: Nationality:
High risk occupation Y/N   Specify ....

Presenting Complaint
Nature:
Duration:
Frequency:

Eating Disorder Symptoms
Diet: food eaten on day before appointment
Food restriction
Overeating episodes
Self-induced vomiting
Chewing and spitting
Laxative abuse
Diuretic abuse
Exercise abuse
Thyroxine abuse
Anorectic drug abuse

Weight History
Height (m)
Premorbid weight
Weight fluctuations before onset
Weight at onset of symptoms
Lowest adult weight
Highest adult weight
Desired weight
Current weight

Associated Symptoms
Obsessive compulsive symptoms
Depressive symptoms
Anxiety symptoms
Psychotic symptoms (delusions, hallucinations)
Deliberate self-harm
Drug misuse
Shoplifting

Physical Symptoms
Gastro-intestinal
Gastric fullness
G-I bleeding (vomiting blood, passing blood or melaena)
Dysphagia (difficulty swallowing)
Constipation
Diarrhoea
Abdominal pain

Neurological
Muscle weakness
Sensory loss
Paraesthesiae ('pins and needles')
Memory loss
Disturbance of consciousness (fits, faints)

Endocrinological/Gynaecological
Age of first period:
Last menstrual period:
Duration of amenorrhoea (total, mths):
Weight (Kg) at last period:

Skeletal
Bone pain
Fractures
Skeletal changes (loss of height, deformity)

Cardiovascular
Postural hypotension (dizziness on standing)
Chilblains

Personal and Family History
Family history of:
Eating disorder
Depression
Alcohol misuse
Other psychiatric or physical disturbance
Divorce, deaths, separations

Family Relationships
With and between parents and sibs
Extended family
Members of family living at home with patient

Personal History
Childhood neglect or abuse (verbal, physical or sexual)
Childhood psychiatric symptoms
Obesity
Problems in family
Pressure to lose weight
Difficulties at school (e.g. teasing, bullying)
Occupational difficulties
Relationship history and problems
Sexual problems
Alcohol or drug misuse

Past Medical/Psychiatric Illness
Previous episode of eating disorder/other psychiatric disorder
Physical illness (e.g. osteoporosis, infertility, gastric problems)
Medication, past and present
Other treatment received (psychotherapy, family therapy, admission)

Mental State
Depression (suicidal ideation)
Anxiety
Body image distortion (feeling fat when not), disparagement (hating body parts)
Low self-esteem
Dichotomous reasoning (black and white thinking)
Psychotic symptoms (delusions, hallucinations)
Cognitive deficits (poor concentration, poor immediate and 5 min recall)
Insight

Diagnoses
Eating disorder
Anorexia nervosa (restricting or bulimic)
Bulimia nervosa (purging or non-purging)
Eating Disorder Not Otherwise Specified (EDNOS)
Obesity (Grade 1: BMI 30–34.9, Grade 2 35–39.9, Grade 3 >40)

Other Psychiatric Disorder
Personality disorder
Depression
Other . . . .

Physical disorder

Further information required

Investigations

Treatment offered

Expectations

Motivation (precontemplation, contemplation, determination, action, relapse prevention, relapse management)

APPENDIX 3.2 RUSSELL UNIT – EATING DISORDERS SERVICE DATA SHEET FOR NEW PATIENTS

Name
Age/Sex/Origin/Ethnicity
Address
Tel: home/mobile
Hospital no.

OUTCOME OF ASSESSMENT
i. Individual/other waiting list
ii. BN Group assessment
iii. BED Group assessment
iv. Day Care
v. Inpatient
vi. Medical Review
vii. Other
PCT for GP

DIAGNOSIS
Anorexia nervosa (restricting)
Anorexia nervosa (bulimic)

Bulimia nervosa:
  Purging
  Non-purging
Binge eating disorder
EDNOS
Morbid obesity
Personality disorder
Other psychiatric disorder
Physical disorder
Interventions
Date first appointment
Interviewer at first appointment
Children M/F ages
Occupation
Lowest weight (kg) (BMI)
Highest weight (kg) (BMI)
Desired weight (kg) (BMI)
Stable premorbid weight (kg) (BMI)
Current weight (kg) (BMI)
Height (m)
Age at onset of eating disorder
Months amenorrhoea

OTHER HISTORY
Personal:
Child sexual abuse (<16)
Child physical abuse
High risk school
Sexual or physical abuse (>16)
High risk occupation

Medical:
Hx of anorexia nervosa
On oral contraceptive

Family:
Maternal eating disorder
Other first degree relative
  Eating disorder
First degree rel c psych disorder
Has a child at risk

PROBLEMS (ED)
Weight loss
Current amenorrhoea
Self-induced vomiting
Laxative abuse

GENERAL PSYCHIATRIC
Overdoses
Depression
Psychosis
Deliberate self-harm

SUBSTANCE MISUSE
Alcohol misuse
Amphetamines
Cannabis misuse
Cocaine misuse
Heroin misuse

PROBLEMS PHYSICAL
General:
Current pregnancy
PCOS

Related to AN:
Osteoporosis
Fractures

Related to BN:
Hypokalaemia
Dental erosion

Diuretic abuse
Chewing and spitting
Thyroxine abuse
Anorectic drug abuse
Bingeing
Excessive exercise
Chronic ED >10yr

Related to obesity:
Arthritis
Hypertension
Nocturnal apnoea
Raised cholesterol
Diabetes mellitus
For bariatric surgery?

APPENDIX 3.3 FICTITIOUS SAMPLE LETTER TO REFERRER

Russell Unit
Royal Free Hospital
London NW3 2QG
Tel: 0207830 2295
Fax: 0207830 2876

Monday, 11th July 2005
Dr Mary Brown
The Health Centre
First Street
London NW3 8EG

Dear Dr Brown,

Re: Cynthia Jones, d.o.b. 1.2.65, address 4 Surrey Road, London NW3 8QU
Phone 020 7712 0500, 07891234567

Diagnosis: Anorexia nervosa

Weight/Height/BMI: 35kg 1.62m BMI 13.3. Maximum weight 58kg BMI 22.2 Recommended treatment: Blood for U and E, LFTs, CK. ECG. Close monitoring of BMI, muscle power and investigations. Individual and family therapy. Day Care advised.

Thank you for referring this 40-year-old lady, whom I saw together with her husband George as an emergency at the Royal Free on Friday 8th July. She has been losing weight for the past 10 months from a previous weight of 58kg to her present 35kg.

There have been a number of behaviours and symptoms that are consistent with anorexia nervosa. George has noticed that the fridge is filling up with low calorie foods such as lettuce, Cynthia is drinking 8 or more cups of coffee a day, she has developed a liking for salt, mustard, pickles, pepper and cinnamon, and gets through a medium pot of Marmite a week. She has also had disturbed sleep, with only a couple of hours a night. She has less energy, has difficulty climbing stairs, has been as active as possible walking during the day and ironing at night, although she does not feel that her activity has been excessive. Menstruation stopped in January of this year, and she has noticed reduced libido. She has not experienced any bingeing, vomiting or laxative abuse and she agrees she is thin, although regards her ideal weight as 50kg (BMI 19.2).

There are no symptoms suggestive of any other cause for weight loss, namely no cough or haemoptysis, night sweats, bowel disturbance, apart from occasional constipation and no urinary or gynaecological symptoms, apart from amenorrhoea. She has had aching in her leg for a number of years, of obscure origin. There is no history of any other illness and she does not drink, smoke or take illicit drugs. She had three miscarriages in her twenties at 7, 12 and 18 weeks, and was, understandably, especially distressed at the latter. She looks tanned but assured me that she had been in the sun. The electrolytes being normal argue against but do not exclude Addison's Disease. She is on Vitamins, Iron and Calcium tablets.

Currently her physical state is poor for someone at a BMI of 15.9 and this is because of the rapidity of her weight loss. She lost 2kg in the week before I saw her.

I asked her why she thought she was losing weight, and she replied that she had not been eating as much. She had been depressed and lost her appetite since being criticised at work as a teacher by her Head Teacher. Her diet the previous day was:

BK: 2 bowls of porridge made with water with some sugar

LN: Green salad, $1/2$ slice bread, piece of smoked salmon

DN: Steak (small portion), salad, Ryvita, apple with Marmite.

Through the day: 8 cups coffee, plus herbal teas.

Family and personal history

The couple have two sons. Charles is 15, and was diagnosed as having Growth Hormone Deficiency as an infant and has been on GH treatment. Cynthia had no problems with eating at the time that Charles was an infant, or during pregnancy. He is now 5ft 2in, developed otherwise normally through puberty and has a girlfriend. Richard is 17 and well. George alluded to a very stressful time for a number of years. His father died 4 years ago, his mother is now ill and Cynthia tends to take on the carer role.

In her family of origin, her father died of a heart attack when she was 10. Her mother is 66, and has been depressed. A male maternal cousin suffered from anorexia nervosa at the age of 15 when Cynthia was 16 and was treated at St Georges Hospital. The death of her father had a tremendous impact on the family. She became very close to her mother although she describes no other problems in childhood. She and George met in 1989 when she was 24. She had had few boyfriends before. Their relationship has been strong. Recently Cynthia has objected to George encouraging her to eat, and he has now backed off, which has made her feel less depressed but has not changed the rate of weight loss.

Her ECG and electrolytes were normal and she had problems sitting up without help. This gave her scores on the SUSS (Sit Up Squat Stand) Test of 3/3 on the Squat test (able to stand up without difficulty) and 1/3 on the Situp test (able to sit up from lying flat only with help of hands).

In summary, I thought she was a lady who had become very upset following criticism at work, who has lost weight as a result of self-imposed dietary restriction and now fulfils criteria for anorexia nervosa. Other conditions should be excluded but there is no clinical indication of any other diagnosis. Additional factors in the aetiology are likely to be the early death of her father, and the three miscarriages.

Management requires first monitoring for risk assessment. Currently she is at moderately high risk because of her muscle weakness and rapid weight loss. If any of her blood tests become abnormal she would qualify for high risk. I enclose a risk algorithm for your interest.

I asked her to join the day hospital right away. She will be reviewed in a few days and if her weight has gone down or any parameter has deteriorated (BMI, SUSS, Blood tests, ECG), I think she should be considered for admission, probably to a medical bed.

Yours sincerely

Matt Smith   Dr P Robinson
Medical Student   Consultant Psychiatrist
cc: Cynthia Jones

Chapter 4

PHYSICAL ASSESSMENT AND MONITORING

DEATH AND THE MAIDEN

The statistics on eating disorders and mortality are stark. They hold the highest standardised mortality ratio for any psychiatric condition, along with heroin abuse, much higher than affective disorders and schizophrenia (Harris & Barraclough, 1998). Of course, more people die who suffer from the latter two disorders. The reason the eating disorder figure is higher is that the patients die younger, and the standardised mortality (which takes account of years lost) is greater. Anyone who wants a glimpse of the distress behind these cold statistics should look at the In Memoriam page on the Something Fishy website (www.somethingfishy.org). There, a candle represents a person who has died of an eating disorder, sometimes two in a family, and the number of candles is enough to evoke a First World War grave image. The enormous power of anorexia nervosa is clear when a clinician, or a relative, is faced with someone whose BMI hovers around the limits of survival, and who continues to defend her anorexia literally to the death, by restricting, exercising, falsifying her weight and attempting, often successfully, to persuade carers and staff that she is 'all right'. This experience ensures that you will never entertain the thought that the patient should 'just eat' or 'stop being so silly', pieces of advice that have been handed to many patients with anorexia nervosa by well-meaning clinicians.

READING THE REFERRAL

Referral letters vary enormously in the detail provided to a specialist eating disorders service. They often lack the most important information, the patient's height and weight. In an audit of referrals to our service, this information was provided in only 35% of referrals (see Table 3.2, p. 39), and sometimes weight was not provided even when the provisional diagnosis was anorexia nervosa, and the referrer was concerned about recent weight loss. Pressures on time, particularly in primary care, make it difficult to make these measurements, although it is unlikely that a referral to a hypertension clinic would not mention the blood pressure. It is hard to make a proper assessment of urgency without this information, however, and services are urged to liaise with both primary and secondary care to encourage height, weight, symptoms, reason for referral and treatment history in their referral letters. Having a member of staff, usually a secretary or other administrative staff, call the referrer and obtain missing information can improve things considerably. Refusing to see the patient until the information is provided is, I believe, going too far, because of the potential for referred patients being in a poor physical state, but some would disagree.

With the letter in front of you, what can you discern? The first task is to divide letters into probable diagnosis: anorexia nervosa, bulimia nervosa and binge eating disorder. Separate out complex cases, with additional symptoms such as severe depression, self-harm, psychosis, diabetes mellitus and inflammatory bowel disease. These patients will probably already be seeing other specialists and might be seen jointly with them. A liaison member of the ED team can see a new patient in a diabetic or gastroenterology clinic or a community mental health base. These cases are dealt with fully in Chapter 7. Back to the three piles of eating disorders. You have a new patient clinic (Chapter 3) which has a three-month waiting list. Not ideal, but not unbearable if the patient referred has a five-year history of bulimia nervosa or binge eating disorder. These patients, at normal or high BMI, with bulimic disorders, are placed on a 'routine' waiting list, and sent an appointment for a new assessment. The letter may indicate that the patient is vomiting or abusing laxatives. These patients are at risk for hypokalaemia, and the referrer can be advised to check the serum electrolytes while the patient is waiting for an appointment. (A suggested letter to the referrer is provided in Appendix 4.1.) If the letter in a case such as this includes a request for an urgent appointment, and the reason for urgency is not apparent from the letter, the referrer should be contacted to clarify, so that a decision to place the patient ahead of others referred earlier can be made. There are various reasons for accelerating such an assessment, including psychological distress, severity of bulimia and weight loss. If the reason is risk of self-harm, it is reasonable to ask the referrer to apply to general psychiatric services for support until the appointment in the ED clinic comes up.

The pile of referrals of underweight patients should be, in general, treated as more urgent, because of the higher risk of dangerous physical problems in this group. If, however, a patient has been stable at a BMI of, say, 15 for a number of years, it would be reasonable to see her non-urgently. Be alert, however, to a number of key indicators. They are documented in Chapter 3. However, they are not the only indicators.

Mental state, including severe depression, suicidal ideation or deliberate self-harm, makes a referral urgent, but usually can be dealt with by liaising, or asking the referrer to liaise with the psychiatric crisis service. It will be noted that at the preassessment stage, risk assessment concerns similar factors to those taken into account post-assessment (Figure 4.5, p. 73). Lastly, if a referral is faxed or phoned, the chances are that the referrer is worried. It may be that he or she is under particular pressure from the patient, the family or even the local member of parliament, but more usually such a referral means that the patient's health is at substantial risk.

If you class a referral as urgent, after perusal, you or a member of the team (with a designated liaison role), should call the referrer, discuss the clinical situation, clarify the urgency and the usual outcome would be an assessment within the next 72 hours. Ideally, see the patient with the referrer in the surgery or clinic or in the patient's home, when family can be included. Otherwise, she could be slipped into the weekly assessment clinic as an 'extra'.

FIRST CONTACT WITH THE PATIENT

Whether you see the patient in your clinic or elsewhere, there are certain pieces of information which inform your risk assessment. The standard medical approach to illness is to collect information from the referrer, the patient's history, information from the family and others, from physical examination of the patient, and from blood tests and other special investigations.

We have looked at the referral letter, although as the assessor might not be the same person, look at it again. It may contain a piece of information that alters your whole assessment, such as a history that she suffered a cardiac arrest at a potassium level of 2.3 mmol/l.

RISK INFORMATION FROM THE HISTORY

The areas of importance from the history are the weight history, the nutritional history and symptoms of nutritional deficiency. In Chapter 3 you will find a checklist for the initial evaluation which contains many important questions, although clinical enquiry using open and closed questions will still be required.

In the weight history the lowest weight the patient has been is a rough guide to what level of malnutrition she has survived in the past, the weight at last menstruation is an indicator, but not the only one, of healthy weight, and recent changes in weight may provide very important information on risk. A patient who has maintained a low BMI of, say 14, for two years is at less risk than a patient whose BMI has reduced from 19 to 16 in two months. Sometimes, at low BMI, weight loss accelerates, so look for an increase in the rate of weight loss. Plot the weights and BMIs on a chart, to identify such changes. Be wary of accepting the patient's report of her current height and weight: she may be inaccurate in both.

Nutritional history is very important because it gives an indication of a number of potential problems. Extreme restriction can lead to vitamin and other micronutrient deficiencies, including anaemia, scurvy, beri-beri and haemorrhage caused by vitamin K deficiency. Restriction in the volume of food eaten, and confining meals to one part of the day, can lead to reduced gastric emptying rate. This has a number of effects. It causes bloating and excessive fullness after meals, which exacerbate undereating and can increase the rate of weight loss. Secondly it can lead, during refeeding or bingeing, to acute gastric dilatation, a rare but very dangerous condition in which the stomach, weakened as a result of weight loss and functioning slowly because of delayed gastric emptying, is unable to cope with a large meal. This meal can be in the form of a binge, in a patient with bulimic anorexia nervosa, or as the initial phase in nutritional treatment. Food will remain in the stomach, which then dilates as the stomach wall stretches and thins, so that it ends up as a large, thin-walled balloon. The result is severe and involuntary vomiting which, in this situation, is sometimes mistaken for bulimic vomiting. If not treated appropriately, the stomach may perforate in which case peritonitis may set in and the outlook for the patient is often very poor. Gastric perforation has developed in patients with bulimia nervosa, not very underweight, who have found vomiting physically impossible after a large binge, which has ruptured the stomach (Robinson, 2000).

Symptoms of nutritional deficiency vary according to the organ or system affected, and a whole textbook would be required to document them. Some of the most important are physical weakness caused by muscle wasting, 'pins and needles' in the extremities which can be due to alkalosis associated with potassium deficiency[1] (usually related to vomiting or laxative abuse) and feeling faint, especially on standing, which is a symptom of low blood volume, due to dehydration, and poor cardiac output, related to both

---

[1] Paraesthesiae, or 'pins and needles' are caused by increased excitability of the peripheral nerves due to reduction in available calcium. Vomiting stomach acid leads to alkalosis and this changes the ionisation of calcium in the blood so less is ionised and therefore, available.

Table 4.1   Weight (Kg) ranges for BMI from underweight to obese

Clinical classes	BMI	1.54 (5′0″)	1.59 (5′2″)	1.64 (5′4″)	1.69 (5′6″)	1.74 (5′8″)	1.79 (5′10″)
Severe AN	14.0	33.1	35.4	37.7	40.0	42.6	45.1
AN	17.5	41.4	44.2	47.1	50.1	53.2	56.4
Normal	19.0	45.0	48.0	51.2	54.4	57.8	61.2
Normal	25.0	59.2	63.2	67.3	71.6	76.0	80.5
Obesity Grade 1	30.0	71.0	75.8	80.8	85.9	91.2	96.6
Obesity Grade 2	35.0	83.0	88.5	94.1	100.0	106.0	112.1
Obesity Grade 3	40.0	94.7	101.1	107.7	114.6	121.6	128.9

dehydration and wasting of the heart which is not spared in someone who has lost muscle due to starvation.

EXAMINATION AND RISK

The most important measurements on examination are height and weight, from which body mass index can be calculated (BMI = weight (kg)/(height (metres) squared)). The BMI is reliable above the age of 16. Below it, BMI can still be used, but as the normal range varies with age, a percentile chart needs to be used in conjunction with the BMI. In adults (18+) the important levels of BMI are:

- The normal range: 19–25.
- The level below which the weight criterion for anorexia nervosa is satisfied (17.5).
- The level below which mortality increases sharply (14).
- The lower level for overweight (25)
- The lower level for obesity, Grades 1, 2 and 3 (30, 35 and 40).

These levels, for different heights are provided in Table 4.1 for those who have a hostile relationship with calculators!

BMI is important, and any patient with a BMI below 14 is at risk for serious medical complications and should be considered for inpatient treatment. However, it is not the only factor in deciding on the level of risk. Chronicity plays an important part. As noted above, a patient at a BMI of 14 who has maintained that level for a number of years may not be at very high immediate risk. Secondly, some patients falsify their weight and their measured BMI is not a true reflection of their actual status. Thirdly, other factors, such as low potassium level, may provide a threat, completely independent of weight, which may demand inpatient care.

FALSIFICATION OF WEIGHT AND OTHER MEASURES: DETECTION AND MANAGEMENT

This takes a number of forms. The patient is usually in a treatment programme, outpatient, day patient or inpatient, and is seeking to avoid intensification of her treatment (by an increase in her diet, hospital admission, or close observations) by artificially increasing her apparent weight on weighing. Often this involves adding weight of some sort to the body just prior to weighing, or making the weighing machine indicate a higher weight. The various techniques encountered (discussed at greater length later in this chapter) include water loading, carrying weights and interfering with the weighing machine.

This sort of falsification can be very dangerous when the observer is falsely reassured that weight is not falling, when it is. There are a number of approaches to overcoming this problem. The simplest is to weigh the patient at an unscheduled time and to compare the result with the weight taken at the usual time. The other approach, which should be occurring in any case, is not to rely on weight as the only measure of progress. Here, physical examination will be covered, while investigations including blood tests are considered in the next section.

MEASURING AND MONITORING MUSCLE POWER: THE SUSS TEST

Muscle is abundant in the body, and it is not surprising that under conditions of poor nutritional intake, it is used as fuel. Measuring muscle power at the first evaluation, and monitoring it thereafter in selected cases is therefore a key element in assessing risk. The method favoured by neurologists (the MRC scale; Medical Research Council, 1975) is found to be too insensitive for use in anorexia nervosa. It depends on whether a limb can be moved against gravity or resistance, and patients with anorexia nervosa can do this even though they are very severely emaciated. Most patients are between 4 (joint moves against gravity and some resistance) and 5 (normal power) on the MRC scale. The technique developed at the Russell Unit is known as the SUSS test, meaning sit up and squat stand (see Figure 4.1).

Sit up: the patient lies flat on the floor and sits up without, if possible, using her hands or arms to help. Scoring is as follows:

0. Unable to sit up even using hands to help.
1. Able to sit up, but only by using hands to help. Any use of hands or arms counts, such as placing the hand on the knee or leaning with the elbow.

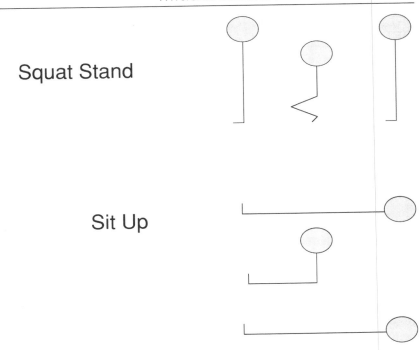

Squat Stand

Sit Up

3: No difficulty observed
2: Some difficulty observed
1: Subject only able to perform the test with (any) help of
hands
0: Subject unable to perform test

Figure 4.1   The SUSS test, a guide to scoring.

2. Able to sit up, without using hands, but with noticeable difficulty.
3. Able to sit up, not using hands, with no difficulty.

Squat stand: the patient squats so that her thighs and calves are in contact. She then stands up without, if possible, using her hands. Scoring is similar to the sit up:

0. Unable to stand up even using hands to help
1. Able to stand up, but only by using hands to help
2. Able to stand up, without using hands, but with noticeable difficulty
3. Able to stand up, not using hands, with no difficulty

Most patients (but not all clinicians!) can manage to score 3 on the SU and 3 on the SS, when they are reasonably well. Recording of the results on a monitoring sheet, along with weight, BMI and relevant blood tests, can greatly help maintain safety for patients at low or declining weight.

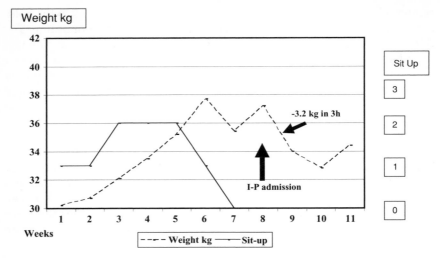

Figure 4.2 Use of the SUSS test in a patient falsifying her weight. The patient's weight increased steadily up to week 6 then oscillated. Her Sit Up test improved from week 1 to 3 then fell to zero at week 7. At admission a week later she admitted to water drinking to falsify her weight, and the latter fell by 3.2 kg on the day of (compulsory) admission.

Clinical description 4.1 (See Figure 4.2)

An 18-year-old patient was being followed up as an outpatient. Her BMI was very low, and she was being monitored regularly with a view to admission which she rejected. For five weeks her weight steadily increased, by a total of 5 kg and her SUSS test remained satisfactory. After that time, although her weight increased, her sit up scores fell to zero, and, in spite of further weight gain, she was admitted against her will to an eating disorders unit. On the day of admission she lost 3.2 kg and admitted to having water-loaded over the previous two weeks.

OTHER USEFUL PHYSICAL TESTS

Naturally, if a patient's symptoms demand a particular physical examination, it should be done. A patient who complains of dizziness on standing up is probably dehydrated and a standing and lying blood pressure measurement is useful. Body temperature should be done using a low reading thermometer (sometimes surprisingly hard to locate – try the elderly services ward or accident and emergency, but after the crisis buy your own) as hypothermia is not uncommon in low weight patients, especially in the winter. Indeed, some patients deliberately expose themselves to the cold, inadequately clad, in order to aid weight loss by shivering. For bulimic patients check for an irregular heart rhythm and have a look in the patient's mouth for dental problems (the teeth look thin and translucent due to wear on the front and back) and under her chin for parotid swelling. You may wish to check her arms for self-harm she may not have wished to mention.

Blood investigations

Syphilis used to be called the 'great imitator' because of the multiplicity of systems in the body that could be affected. Eating disorders have a substantial claim to that title in that virtually every organ of the body can be affected. Many abnormalities found in special investigations can be of very serious import and can lead to rapid admission to hospital, even from the first outpatients clinic visit.

Electrolytes

Changes in serum potassium, sodium and chloride are common. Low potassium levels are found in potassium losing states such as vomiting in bulimia nervosa and laxative abuse. The danger of low potassium is that it causes cardiac irritability and, potentially, sudden death. The aetiology is not straightforward. It is thought that in vomiting, loss of gastric acid causes a deficit of acid (metabolic alkalosis). This can only be corrected by exchanging hydrogen (acid) for potassium in the kidney, leading to a loss of potassium but retention of hydrogen (acid), and improvement of alkalosis. There is a lot of potassium in the body, most of it within cells. During chronic metabolic alkalosis potassium is progressively lost from cells to replace that lost in the urine. When intracellular stores fall to low levels, the serum potassium falls. Hypokalaemia is therefore a sign of severe total body potassium depletion, the correction of which will not occur with a few Slow-K or a few hours of a potassium chloride infusion.

Liver function tests

These include transaminase enzymes (ALT, AST, GGT) and blood pigments (bilirubin). It is not clear why transaminase levels increase with weight loss. I used to tell patients, risking upset to the vegetarians, that the body was so short of nutrition it was having a meal of paté from its own liver. There is another possible, though unproven, explanation, which is that there may be intestinal leakiness, which allows bacteria to reach the liver, causing a mild hepatitis. Whatever the explanation, rising transaminase levels are a worrying sign in a patient losing weight, and indicate severe starvation, in the absence of another cause such as alcoholic or other liver disease.

Glucose

It is not surprising that many patients with anorexia nervosa have low blood glucose. It arises from a combination of poor food intake, very low reserves and physical exercise. Carbohydrate is stored in the body as *glycogen* in the liver and muscles, which is converted to glucose when needed. It is depleted rapidly by poor diet and exercise (as marathon runners know). When it disappears energy is drawn by metabolism of fat and protein. In anorexia nervosa, fat stores are also depleted and low blood sugar often occurs. In extreme cases it can be very dangerous (see Chapter 7, p. 130). It is common for patients with anorexia nervosa to engage in *micro-exercise*. In this, the patient constantly makes small movements, such as flexing and extending the ankle or making small kicks with a leg crossed over the other knee. When an emaciated patient is *micro-exercising* it can tip the blood glucose into hypoglycaemia, especially when it is prolonged and accompanied by constant standing and sleep avoidance, other means of increasing calorie consumption.

In less extreme circumstances, the finding of a low blood sugar in an emaciated outpatient should prompt an enquiry into episodes of blackout, or fainting. If it is suspected that hypoglycaemia may be contributing to such episodes the patient should be advised against driving.

Creatine kinase (CK)

This is an enzyme found mainly in muscle, both skeletal and cardiac. It rises when there is muscle damage, for example after an injury, and when the heart suffers loss of blood supply, as in a heart attack. In anorexia nervosa the CK levels rise when muscle is being used as a source of nutrition, and a raised CK therefore indicates severe malnutrition. There are two types of CK, one coming mostly from skeletal muscle and one mostly from cardiac muscle. The latter, known as CK-MB, should not constitute more than 5 % of the total. In patients with anorexia nervosa who have raised CK, the CK-MB often exceeds 5 %, suggesting that cardiac damage, not usually apparent on an electrocardiogram, may occur at low weight in anorexia nervosa. However, athletes may normally have up to 15 % CK-MB in skeletal muscle and this may explain some of the rise in CK-MB seen in anorexia nervosa patients who overexercise.

There is, moreover, an interesting interaction between CK and exercise. It is well known that vigorous exercise alone can raise CK levels. If weight is low, however, CK can rise to very high levels, and if the patient then exercises, the levels rise even further. This is well illustrated in the following case:

Clinical description 4.2

A patient was admitted to a medical ward because of low weight (BMI 11.6) and high CK levels. On admission her CK was 1037 iu/l (NR 32–267). She was placed on close nursing observations and within five days her CK was 358. Nursing observations were removed and the level increased to 914, they were reinstated again and the level fell to 134. She was known to be a compulsive exerciser who admitted to vigorous exercise on the ward when not being observed closely.

Electrocardiogram (ECG)

The ECG is often a difficult area for psychiatrists whose last contact with the PQRST complex may have been as a house officer. For the purposes of assessing a patient with anorexia nervosa, the level of expertise is not excessive. Concentrate on the following:

1. Rate and rhythm. A low rate, say 40 beats per minute, is not unusual in low-weight patients and is a normal adjustment to reduced body demands. The blood pressure will also be low, and this is not, in itself, a cause for concern as long as the patient does not have postural dizziness. The principle is: if the pressure is enough to maintain brain function when standing, we don't need to be too worried about the numbers. Abnormal beats (extrasystoles) should be noted and if more than occasional, regarded as possibly abnormal.
2. QT interval: this is important, because the more prolonged the interval between the QRS complex and the T wave the more likely it is that abnormal rhythms will occur, with potentially fatal results. QT interval varies with heart rate, and the corrected QT (QT_c) should be used. This is almost always calculated helpfully by the machine. If not: the QT interval is the time from the beginning of the QRS complex to the end of the T wave. $QT_c = QT / \sqrt{(RR \text{ interval})}$. (The RR interval is the reciprocal of the heart rate.) The normal range varies but any level over 460 ms should be regarded as abnormal. Conditions that alter the QT_c include neuroleptic medication and hypokalaemia as well as low body weight. The effect on QT_c needs to be taken into account when using a neuroleptic to sedate a patient with anorexia nervosa.

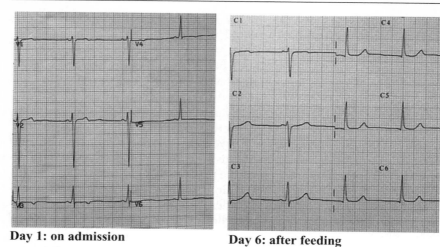

Day 1: on admission   **Day 6: after feeding**

Figure 4.3   ECG chest leads 6 days apart in patient with BMI 15 and recent rapid weight loss from BMI 19. On admission there are inverted and flattened T waves in V3-V6 which have normalised by Day 6. Electrolytes were normal.

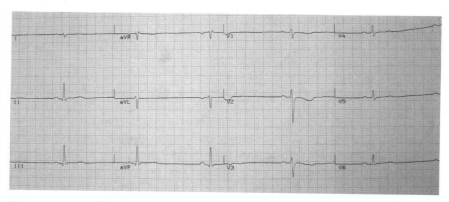

Figure 4.4   An ECG taken from a patient with a BMI of 12 and a body temperature of 34.5°C. There is sinus bradycardia (34/min), and T wave inversion in V2 and V3.

3. Changes suggesting ischaemia (Figure 4.3): rarely, changes that look like an impending heart attack are observed (raised or lowered ST segment, inverted T waves). These are alarming, and need to be taken very seriously. They are sometimes related to hypothermia (Figure 4.4) with, presumably, reduced oxygenation of cardiac muscle. The creatine kinase (noted above) is often raised in patients with severe anorexia nervosa and the cardiac fraction of CK (CK-MB) may also be raised. It is not clear whether or not this indicates that cardiac muscle is being damaged but is would seem prudent to assume that it does.

TRICKS OF THE TRADE: HOW ANOREXIA JOINED THE MAGIC CIRCLE

Patients with anorexia nervosa often behave as if they are obeying a secret commander. Anorexia tells them what is allowed and not allowed, and passes comments on the advice of well-wishers such as family, friends and mental health workers. Indeed, many patients report an inner voice saying things such as 'you are fat', 'don't eat that, it'll make you fat' etc. The voice usually fails to meet criteria for a psychotic experience, but sometimes it is hard for a psychiatrist to distinguish such a voice from those encountered in schizophrenic and depressive psychoses. In eating disorders such experiences are generally classified along with obsessive ruminations and thoughts associated with anxiety, rather than psychoses. Nevertheless they can be very powerful, and patients who are forced into situations, either in the family home or in hospital, in which they have to eat and gain weight, will often obey the 'voices' and do their best to avoid weight gain. This includes resorting to, sometimes ingenious, ways of opposing staff. Some of these practices have already been mentioned in this chapter. Because the patient's main aim is to avoid weight gain, the behaviours are all directed to that end. They are much more common when the patient has been admitted to hospital, although they also occur in day care. They can be classified as follows:

1. Avoiding food provided at meal times
   Patients have a number of ways of concealing food and getting rid of it. They hide it in clothing, especially baggy jackets with wide sleeves. They slip it into furniture and out of windows and patients have been known to paint the tablecloth with butter or margarine. Cats in households with an anorexic daughter sometimes become uncharacteristically obese. Locations for hiding food can reflect a good deal of ingenuity.

Clinical description 4.3

A patient spent several weeks in a general psychiatric ward during which time she was given a considerable amount of food but failed to gain weight. Some time after her discharge the stench coming from the bathroom led to the discovery, when bath panels were unscrewed, of a large cache of rotting food.

2. Secretly vomiting, spitting or taking laxatives
   Some patients are able to vomit extremely efficiently. For example, with a turn of the head and a cough, in front of a nurse or parent, a patient may have vomited into a sleeve. Some patients freely vomit after meals when sitting with a patient group or family, others fill plastic bags with

vomitus and leave them around the house or clinic, where their smell usually leads to discovery. Other patients chew their food and spit it out, either as an obsessional symptom or as a way of reducing calorie intake. Pieces of tissue containing food are subsequently found tucked into furniture. Laxatives are frequently unearthed in room searches in hospital, as are diuretics, some purchased over the counter, some provided by a doctor for 'bloating'.

3. Falsifying weight

There are many ways in which patients manage to make the team or family believe that weight gain has occurred when it has not. Three of these are waterloading, wearing weights and interfering with the weighing machine. Drinking up to 3.5 litres of water before weighing is a common ruse. Its danger lies not only in deceiving carers and clinicians, but also in causing fits due to low sodium levels that occur following ingestion of large quantities of water, and which can be used as a marker of this practice. Some patients, especially those with bulimia, vomit after waterloading, when they have been weighed, which reduces the risk of hyponatraemia but probably increases that of hypokalaemia. Some patients conceal weights in their clothing including batteries in underwear, a radio suspended from a belt under a dress and exercise weights taped to the belly. One patient of the author's acquaintance used her very long toes to grip the base of a weighing machine and pull up, thereby increasing her apparent weight.

4. Recruiting another illness that makes weight gain more difficult

The most frequent offenders here are allergies, irritable bowel syndrome and diabetes mellitus. It is not unusual to be faced with a patient who states that she has been diagnosed as suffering from a combination of allergy to wheat and candida infection and told to avoid wheat products. She has then cut down her diet and an eating disorder, anorexia or bulimia nervosa, has developed or worsened, sometimes requiring hospital treatment. Reputable specialists in clinical allergy generally find no strong evidence of allergy, and no indication to restrict nutrition. Irritable bowel syndrome is a disorder of exclusion and one that is very common among gastroenterology clinic attenders. The symptoms can be very severe, and treatment often unsatisfactory. Patients may find or claim that certain foods, usually carbohydrates, make their symptoms worse, and this can make the dietary treatment of anorexia nervosa very difficult. Close collaboration with a gastroenterologist, with the patient seen jointly with an eating disorders worker, can be helpful. Diabetes mellitus is one of the most dangerous conditions to have in combination with an eating disorder because it provides an additional method of weight control, namely failure to take insulin leading to glucose 'leaking' into the urine, and raised blood glucose which can result in fatal hyperglycaemic coma. Poor blood glucose control damages eyes, kidneys, heart and nervous system with resulting major disability and reduced life expectancy. Such patients may require intensive case management and individual and family therapy, day care, joint working with a diabetic team, and admission to medical and eating disorder inpatient services when required.

5. Making an unholy alliance with a team member (team splitting)

Splitting is most clearly observed when the patient has an advisor external to the team, such as a nutritionist, who provides incompatible advice to the patient. It is then difficult to pursue a consistent therapeutic line and the patient usually deteriorates. Something similar, but less apparent, can happen within a team, when the patient has a special relationship with a team member (who may or may not be the patient's therapist) who argues that, for example, insistence on weight gain is not appropriate at the time, and that if the team would only wait, results would follow. Such waiting can go on for months and cause considerable friction within the team.

MEDICAL MONITORING: WHEN, HOW, BY WHOM

Following an initial evaluation, the decision may be that little monitoring is required while the patient remains on the waiting list for treatment. However, most patients present some physical problem that should be monitored. A patient with bulimic symptoms, for example, requires monitoring of serum potassium, and, if the first measurement is normal, this can be in primary care, perhaps monthly. Weight, also, if low but above BMI 15 and not falling, could be monitored monthly by the GP, as long as arrangements are made to feed the results back to the eating disorders service. Low mood and self-harm may also need to be monitored either by the GP or a member of the eating disorders or general psychiatry team.

Patients who require frequent medical monitoring should be identified as a specific group, and a clear policy developed for them. At the Russell Unit, factors taken into particular consideration in assessment and monitoring include weight and weight loss, purging behaviour, electrolyte and ECG changes, mental state, including risk of self-harm and recent discharge from inpatient care.

The rate of monitoring can be monthly, weekly or several times a week, up to daily. The decision on frequency is important and often requires senior medical input. Monitoring itself can be done by a wide variety of individuals, including members of the eating disorders, general psychiatry or primary care teams, members of the family or, sometimes, the patient herself. It is important, however, that it is made clear who collects the information and to whom the information is transmitted. The system at the Russell Unit is for monitoring data to be discussed at a weekly meeting of the whole team under 'Current Concerns'. A computer database is used to generate a list of patients giving rise to current concern. This includes:

1. Current patients at risk for medical or psychiatric reasons.
2. Patients referred who appear to be at risk.
3. New patients seen that week.
4. Recently assessed patients in whom a report has not yet been sent to the GP.
5. Patients in inpatient services.

Frequent medical monitoring applies to the first two categories.

The methods used to monitor patients will vary according to their specific needs. However, the list is usually drawn from the following:

1. Weight and BMI.
2. SUSS test (see above).
3. Blood tests: urea, electrolytes, liver function, creatine kinase, platelet and white blood cell count, phosphate, magnesium, glucose.[2]
4. ECG.

The algorithm (Figure 4.5) gives a series of pathways. In the algorithm, we allocate the patient to one of three risk categories: low risk, risk factors present or high risk. In a patient deemed high risk, monitoring of physical and mental state is arranged, depending on the problems. It is possible for a patient to have two or more high-risk areas, say low weight, hypokalaemia and depression, and therefore require several types of monitoring simultaneously. Moreover, the list of factors in Figure 4.5 is not exhaustive, and other less common risk factors such as solvent or analgesic abuse could lead to significant concern and the need for frequent monitoring. Use of monitoring data in deciding whether to admit to hospital will be dealt with in Chapter 8.

PATIENTS WITH AN EATING DISORDER COMBINED WITH ANOTHER MEDICAL CONDITION

Diabetes mellitus

This has already been mentioned as an illness which causes weight loss and is therefore an aid to dieting. The juvenile onset form, which is the

---

[2]Refeeding syndrome (Chapter 10) can be detected by daily measurement of phosphate, potassium, magnesium and glucose, and treated with oral or intravenous correction should any of these fall.

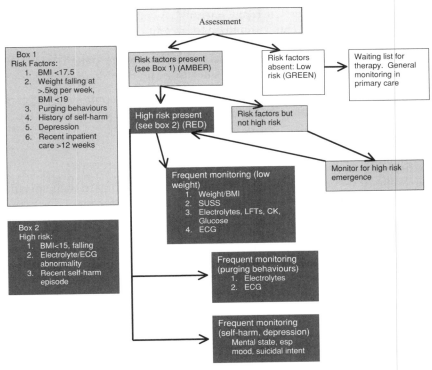

Figure 4.5 The Russell Unit Eating Disorders Risk Algorithm.
Notes:

- At assessment, determine whether RISK FACTORS or HIGH RISK are present. If not, assign to waiting list and monitor in primary or secondary care.
- If any of the RISK FACTORS are present, monitor regularly in case HIGH RISK appears. (Treating physician and team to determine frequency and nature of monitoring.)
- If HIGH RISK is present, assign to frequent medical monitoring, which can be for weight loss, electrolyte disturbance or mental state. (Treating physician and team to determine frequency and nature of monitoring.)
- Risk factors are the most common ones seen, and not the only ones encountered.

one usually associated with anorexia nervosa and bulimia nervosa, is due to failure of the pancreas gland to make insulin. The result is that glucose cannot get into cells to be used and the body wastes away, while the unused glucose is passed in the urine (hence mellitus – like honey). The drawback, however, of this form of weight control is that uncontrolled diabetes mellitus leads to acute complications such as coma, and chronic complications including blindness, kidney failure and neuropathy. Therefore, although patients with diabetes mellitus who reduce their insulin dose may lose weight, their health and life expectancy suffer. There is a readily available test to check a diabetic's control, the HbA1C (a form of haemoglobin, the blood pigment). The level of HbA1C is related to the average blood sugar level over the previous three months (the life of an average red blood cell). So, the higher the HbA1C (the normal level is under 7 %) the worse the control, and the more likely it is that the eating disordered patient has been underdosing with insulin, bingeing, vomiting and combinations of same.

This is a condition in which a combination of medical monitoring, psychological therapy, including family therapy, and liaison with both diabetic services and primary care are all helpful.

Crohn's disease

This is one of the inflammatory bowel diseases, the other main one being ulcerative colitis. Some patients who take steroid treatment to control the diarrhoea, which is a main symptom of both conditions, leave out their medication after bingeing in order to encourage diarrhoea and reduce weight. As in diabetes, the danger of this practice is that complications (such as holes between gut and other organs or the skin in Crohn's and cancer in colitis) may develop if the disease is not properly treated. In these conditions, and in irritable bowel syndrome, mentioned above, a link with the gastroenterology team, seeing the patient together if possible, can be very helpful.

Pregnancy

Pregnancy is arguably a medical condition, but it is definitely a cause for concern in a patient with an eating disorder. The areas of concern are for the mother, for the developing foetus, for the care of the newborn and for the parental relationship. As in all pregnancies, the mother's reaction will vary according to how welcome a new member of the family feels at the time. In addition, the physical changes that accompany pregnancy may not be that welcome and a major adjustment is required by all women, some more than others. For the woman with anorexia nervosa, who has kept her weight and shape under strict control, the growing baby represents a serious challenge to that control. The feelings accompanying increasing body size and loss of control over body shape may lead to increased eating disorder symptoms, including food restriction, exercise and purging behaviours such as vomiting or laxative abuse. On the other hand, concern for the growing baby in the knowledge that foetal malnutrition is a danger, may lead to a suspension of symptoms during pregnancy. What actually happens is determined by a balance between the two sets of influence. In bulimia nervosa it is not uncommon to find symptoms improving markedly during pregnancy, only to reappear after the baby is born. In anorexia nervosa there is limited evidence that weight gain may occur fairly normally in the first six months, only to decline in the last trimester, when increasing body size triggers more intense body dissatisfaction, increasing dietary restriction and, perhaps, purging behaviours (Treasure & Russell, 1988). Our practice during pregnancy is to allocate a key worker from the eating disorders service, and for that person to consult with the eating disorders psychiatrist and liaise with the obstetric team, accompanying the patient to at least some antenatal appointments. Therapy for the eating disorder may need to be intensified to weekly or even day hospital care and if foetal malnutrition appears to be occurring, with maternal weight gain falling below expectations and declining foetal growth rate (usually measured on the ultrasound as bi-parietal diameter and femoral length) consideration should be given to admitting the patient to hospital for inpatient feeding perhaps up to delivery. A discussion about care of the child and addressing the parental relationship is given in Chapter 5.

PATIENTS UNDER THE CARE OF OTHER TEAMS

The eating disorders team will occasionally be asked to consult about a patient whose main care is within another service. This rarely occurs when the main problem is an eating disorder, as most general teams are happy to hand over care of such a patient to the eating disorders service. However, if there is something else which leads to a medical referral, the eating disorder symptoms may emerge and demand treatment after the referral condition has been initially addressed. This can occur in any of the situations already mentioned, including diabetes, bowel disorders and pregnancy. Referral to medical services can be for osteoporosis, amenorrhoea, infertility or any of many conditions, and this can give rise to confusion and inappropriate treatment.

Clinical description 4.4

A 32-year-old woman with longstanding anorexia nervosa (BMI 17.3) was referred to an endocrinologist because of osteoporosis. She was placed on a long-acting biphosphonate, Alendronate. Unknown to the endocrinologist she was then referred to an infertility clinic because of inability to conceive. She was treated with IVF but failed to sustain a pregnancy. Shortly after she became pregnant spontaneously. She was taken off the Alendronate because of its theoretical potential for teratogenicity

In this case, a drug with a known half life of 10 years was given to a woman not only of child-bearing age, but having active treatment for infertility.

The ethics of treating a woman whose infertility is due to anorexia nervosa need examination. Most would agree that in weight-related amenorrhoea, return of menstruation and fertility through weight gain is the most appropriate course. Should infertility treatment be offered to a woman who is unable to gain weight? The arguments against are the known increase in foetal morbidity in anorexia nervosa and the difficulty women with eating disorders have in feeding their children (Stein et al., 2001). There should not be a blanket embargo but it would seem prudent to make a psychiatric examination by a specialist in eating disorders a part of the assessment for fertility treatment in such patients, and to hold a multidisciplinary conference prior to treatment being agreed.

Some patients are mainly looked after by general psychiatric teams or community mental health teams. Eating disorder services cannot look after everyone with an eating disorder. They can offer quite prolonged treatment, as well as urgent interventions when life is threatened, but in a disorder which can last 40 years or more, some of the long-term care is appropriately provided by the community mental health team. They are more likely to have access to social work, funding for rehabilitation, occupational therapy and housing support that patients with long-term disorders, whether anorexia nervosa, depression or schizophrenia, require. Nevertheless, there must be clear guidelines for such teams in dealing with nutritional decline. A patient who is losing weight, or who fulfils criteria for High Risk in Figure 4.5 must be referred back to the eating disorders team, because they may require urgent admission. A liaison worker in the eating disorders team who is in regular contact with a worker in the psychiatric team can keep an eye on this and make sure the general services does not bite off more than it can chew. The same applies to patients with anorexia nervosa being looked after in primary care. For those at the lower end of the BMI range (<15) contact with the eating disorders team is highly desirable, even if the patient is not seen regularly by the eating disorders team. Some patients with borderline personality disorder fulfil criteria for bulimia nervosa. However, if they are also taking frequent, near fatal overdoses or regularly cutting their arms and legs, they may be better managed in the general team with support from an eating disorders liaison worker. Multidisciplinary meetings with members of each team present can be useful in parcelling out responsibility and avoiding splitting which is so likely to occur in these clinical situations.

Clinical description 4.5

A 30-year-old woman was admitted to a psychiatric ward and referred by a general consultant psychiatrist. She had been bingeing and vomiting but also blood-letting so that she became profoundly anaemic (haemoglobin 4.5 g/dl). She declared that she preferred to be anaemic as it blocked out reality and that it helped her lose calories. She was a patient for whom the descriptor anaemia nervosa seemed appropriate as well as borderline personality disorder. She agreed to meet with her local team and to see the eating disorders psychiatrist as an outpatient. She was discharged but failed to keep any appointment. She was readmitted because of repeated self-harm and anaemia.

In this case, while the patient did not comply with treatment, there was a useful alliance between the general and eating disorder services that the patient could access if she developed the motivation. Helping to reduce anxiety in staff about patients' management should not be underestimated.

WHAT IS HEALTHY WEIGHT – HOW LOW CAN YOU GO?

In the mind of someone with anorexia nervosa, body weight is probably the single most influential piece of information. The lower the weight, the more successful she is. It is, naturally, a delicate subject during treatment. The therapist has in view aims which he or she labels 'healthy'. They include regular menstruation, weight within a statistically normal range, avoidance of osteoporosis and some psychological and social aims such as freedom from weight and food concerns and better social and occupational adjustment. There is usually little argument with the patient about the latter aims. However, the aim of a healthy weight as well as the physical improvements in menstruation and osteoporosis may well not be shared by the patient. There are several ways to approach the determination of healthy weight, and each of them has some value.

1. Normal weight range: the most common measure to use in adults is the body mass index (see this chapter, page 61). The normal range is from 19 to 25. A BMI of 19 is a useful level at which to aim in refeeding but it has a number of drawbacks. It bears no relation to the individual's frame and weight history and it is not related to physiology.
2. Previous menstrual weight: this is the stable weight at which the patient previously menstruated regularly and normally. It has the advantage of being linked to a physiological process and being related to the patient herself. However, it is often difficult to apply in practice because the patient may have a fluctuating weight history and may have been obese or overweight in the past, making it difficult to be sure of a stable premorbid weight. Moreover, if weight was obese in the past, it may not be in the patient's best interests to return to that level, even if she was willing

to do so, which is very unlikely. Lastly, it obviously does not apply in males in whom the previous stable weight with normal sexual function could be used as an approximate equivalent.

3. Menstrual weight predicted by pelvic ultrasonography: This is a useful approach which has the advantage that it is tailored to the patient's own physiology. It requires fairly elaborate equipment and skills, so may not be available everywhere. The way it is used in the Russell Unit is as follows:

   – When the patient's BMI reaches 19, she has a pelvic ultrasound scan. This can give one of three appearances: Stage 1: immature stage. No discernible internal ovarian structure. Stage 2: multifollicular stage. The ovaries are full of small, roughly equally sized follicles. Stage 3: one ovary contains a dominant follicle (>18 mm in diameter). Other follicles are suppressed and smaller than in stage 2.

   – If the scan shows stage 3, she is encouraged to hold the weight and expect a period. If it is stage 1 or 2, she is asked to put on 2 kg, and have a further scan. This process is repeated until stage 3 is observed or a period occurs.

Clinically this approach has the advantage that the 'decision' on weight is made by the patient's body rather than the doctor, and the patient can then take more control of her own health rather than depend on the doctor to decide for her what her weight should be. This very much fits with the self-reliance that is encouraged in the Russell Unit, exemplified by the emphasis on day care and domiciliary treatment. Again, this approach is not applicable in male patients. For them, the combination of a BMI above 19 and a return of sexual functioning, manifested by increased libido, morning erections and masturbation can be used as an equivalent system.

Menstruation returning at low BMI

This sometimes occurs in patients with a long history of anorexia nervosa, and in non-white Caucasian patients, especially from the Indian subcontinent. The possible explanations are: (i) The hypothalamus (the part of the brain responsible for managing the menstrual cycle) has been reset at a lower weight by years of illness. (ii) The patient has a genetically low level of BMI at which menstruation begins (check with female relatives). (iii) She is having anovulatory periods due to monthly fluctuations in oestrogen levels, but not accompanied by ovulation. (iv) She is falsely declaring that menstruation has occurred. There may be other reasons, such as changes in body composition, with a relative increase in percentage body fat. None of these explanations has been fully explored in research, however. It is not known whether menstruation at a BMI <19 has implications for long-term health including osteoporosis and infertility. We have decided to introduce a little flexibility and to agree to a minimum BMI of 18.5 in patients who menstruate at low levels of weight. Measurement of progesterone on day 21 of the cycle will confirm ovulation if the level is over 38 nanomol/litre (Prelevic, personal communication). We also monitor bone density in patients who have regained periods at low weight and recommend weight gain to normal if bone density is declining.

APPENDIX 4.1 LETTER TO A REFERRER OF A PATIENT WITH PURGING BEHAVIOURS

Dear Dr Smith,

Re: Jane Brown

Thank you for referring the above named patient. She will be sent a new patient appointment within three months. In the meantime, as she suffers from bulimic symptoms that place her at risk for electrolyte disturbance, especially *hypokalaemia*, I would be grateful if you would arrange to check her electrolytes and let me know the result.

Yours sincerely

Chapter 5

PSYCHOLOGICAL INTERVENTIONS

INTRODUCTION

Eating disorders are among the most 'medical' of psychiatric disorders. Diagnosis is often made on the basis of physical symptoms such as weight loss and amenorrhoea and the most worrying aspects of treating eating disorders are frequently medical problems such as low potassium or emaciation. Oddly, apart from food (taken at least three times a day) very few medical interventions have been found to be helpful in treatment. Antidepressants have all been shown to suppress bulimia to some extent, but they do not teach healthy eating patterns and patients often relapse after treatment is withdrawn. The recommended treatments for eating disorders (e.g. National Collaborating Centre for Mental Health, 2004) are mostly psychological, including individual, group and family approaches. In this chapter, the various treatments that can be provided will be described, and some information given on how to implement them in a way that maximises individual autonomy while ensuring safety as far as possible in a dangerous set of conditions. Supervision and support for staff seeing patients individually is covered in Chapter 2.

WAITING LISTS AND PRIORITIES

In a service in which 200–300 new patients are referred per year, some will fail to engage, some will be treated with urgent day or inpatient care, but the majority will be recommended for some form of individual therapy. As I have already described (Chapter 2) staff with basic nursing training can successfully treat patients with severe eating disorders as long as they are properly supported, trained and supervised. In our team at present there are seven whole-time equivalent (WTE) staff mostly in the professions of mental health nursing and psychology who take on individual patients for therapy. Assuming all caseloads are full, and each WTE takes on 10 patients (a reasonable caseload) and assuming an average duration of therapy of one year, a patient referred may have to wait a year to be seen. In practice the waiting list is variable, and dependent on many factors, mainly length of therapy of existing patients and availability of suitable therapists, taking into account absence due to training, maternity leave and sick leave, as well as delays in filling empty posts. Waiting for therapy is a serious problem, which seems to be endemic in public sector provision. The team's efforts have to be directed to several areas at the same time. Patients presenting in crisis have to be treated, day patients require daily intervention and responsibilities to outpatient group and individual clients have to be met. In a service aiming to reduce reliance on inpatient admission, the resulting pressure on staff to deal with emergency and routine work can be very heavy. Some services have solved this dilemma by specialising in one level of urgency, either high (e.g. accident and emergency departments) or low (e.g. outpatient therapy units). The eating disorders team, like the community mental health team, has to decide how to respond to problems of different urgency without neglecting one group.

There are a number of ways in which the waiting list for individual therapy can be kept under control (see Table 5.1). At the level of referral, it is possible to set criteria for assessment so that patients with less severe eating disorders or none at all are not assessed. Consider the following example:

Table 5.1 Some ways to control the waiting list for individual therapy

Level of referral pathway	Intervention	Likely effect
Referral	Restrict to patients meeting diagnostic criteria	Decrease referrals. Increased treatment required in primary or secondary care
Assessment	Accept for therapy over a threshold (e.g. meets ICD-10 criteria, World Health Organisation (2003))	Decrease therapy provision. Increased treatment required in primary or secondary care
Therapy	Use only groups for some patients (e.g. BN)	Increased drop-out for patients rejecting group therapy
	Recommend self-help manual	Small decrease in need for therapy
	Use guided self-help	Reduce need for full therapy
	Use supervision to actively manage caseload	Quicker turnover of patients in therapy
	Discharge patients after agreed number of missed sessions	Increased drop-out from therapy
	Provide agreed limited number of sessions	Some patients inadequately treated

Dear Doctor,

Re: Samantha Jones

Please see this patient who has a history of bulimia nervosa and now presents with depression and difficulty accepting her body image. Her current BMI is 23.4.

Yours sincerely

Dr Rush

In this case, you may write back:

Dear Dr Rush

Re: Samantha Jones

Thank you for referring this patient. It does not appear from your letter that she suffers currently from an eating disorder. If you believe that she does, I would be grateful if you would complete the enclosed referral form and send it back. Otherwise I suggest that you may wish to consider referring her to a general psychology, counselling or psychotherapy service.

Yours sincerely

Dr Treet

Enc: Referral Form (see Figure 3.2 on p. 40)

Secondly, when the patient is seen for assessment, she might not meet criteria for treatment in your service. This can present difficulties, particularly if she has waited a long time for assessment. However, if her eating disorder, which appeared severe at referral, has now abated, it would be reasonable to give her an appointment with a senior team member (e.g. the consultant) in three months to decide whether treatment needs to be undertaken. In this case she should be placed provisionally on the waiting list at initial assessment so that she does not have to wait longer than necessary for treatment if therapy is required. In a more straightforward case, a patient with morbid obesity is referred because of possible binge eating. At assessment she is found to be snacking continuously throughout the day, with no evidence of binge eating disorder. Such a patient should be seen for dietary counselling and medical assessment and treatment of obesity, and this is outside the remit of most eating disorder services, although this might change in the future.

After the patient has been assessed and accepted for treatment the process of therapy can be accelerated in a number of ways. Self-help has received some research attention (Treasure et al., 1996) and it has been shown that providing a self-help manual for patients with bulimia nervosa results in recovery for a proportion. Adding professional support in a treatment called guided self-help (GSH) increases the proportion so that recovery rates approach those achieved using cognitive behaviour therapy (CBT) in the traditional way. We have found that GSH can be administered by a psychology assistant and can reduce the need for later therapy. Another 'minimal' treatment is therapy delivered via email, described later in this chapter. This has not been fully evaluated from the time/cost-effectiveness perspective but in our controlled trial therapists found that it compared favourably with face-to-face therapy in time commitment.

Group therapy is, in general, more efficient than individual and can be offered routinely for certain groups of patients. This includes separate CBT groups for patients with bulimia nervosa and for those with binge eating disorder. Patients who are averse to groups will require to be seen individually.

At the other end of the therapeutic process is the question 'How long is therapy?' Woody Allen, in the film *Sleeper*, on awaking after a 200-year sleep declares: 'I missed over 200 years of analysis. My therapist was a strict Freudian, I would almost be cured by now'. Different therapeutic approaches demand differing frequency of sessions lasting various durations. In bulimia nervosa and binge eating disorder, 16–20 sessions over 4–5 months is favoured (National Collaborating Centre for Mental Health, 2004). Family therapists usually provide a session every 2–4 weeks for 6–12 months. In supportive or analytic therapy often used in patients with anorexia nervosa, or in those with personality problems, weekly sessions can go on for 1–2 or more years. It is in the latter forms of therapy that active supervision and caseload management (see Chapter 2) can be helpful in supporting a therapist in planning the termination of therapy when some gains have occurred but problems still remain after a substantial duration of therapy. The problem can also be managed by offering a contract for, say, three months' therapy after which time the contract can be renewed.

MOTIVATION: THE LIGHT BULB HAS TO WANT TO CHANGE

Motivation to change is a crucial quality without which we are wasting our time trying to force change upon someone in whom the forces of staying anorexic outweigh those directed towards recovery. Learning from the motivational interviewing approach of DiClemente and Prochaska (1998) applied to the eating disorders field by Treasure et al. (1999) we can first elicit from the patient a statement which encapsulates a significant proportion of the problems associated with their eating disorder. For example: 'My eating disorder leads to significant health problems, including back pain and depression, and has alienated me from my friends, with the result that I spend most evenings alone, socialise only once a fortnight and I do not have anyone I could call in the night in an emergency.' It is also useful to elicit a statement which expresses the positive aspects of the eating disorder for the patient. 'Anorexia is my life. It helps me deal with anything I find difficult, protects me from having to face close relationships and is a wonderful hiding place for when I feel bad. I do not have to do anything really, and if I do succeed in something, people are so impressed because I did it while I was so ill.'

Next, decide, with the patient which motivational level fits her current intentions:

1. I do not recognise I have a problem (although other people do think I have one). DENIAL, 'It's your problem if you don't like thin people.'
2. I recognise I have a problem, but I'm not ready to do anything to change it. It's not that serious, and anyway the cure would be worse than the disease. PRECONTEMPLATION. 'Get fat to prevent osteoporosis in 25 years? No thanks!'
3. I recognise that I have a problem and although I'm not intending to do anything about it right now I am thinking seriously about it. CONTEMPLATION. 'What exactly is CBT?'
4. I have made the decision to take action to solve this serious problem. DETERMINATION. Where do I show up?
5. I recognise the problems and I am in the process of taking action in order to try and solve them. ACTION. 'This is tough!'
6. I've taken action, the problems are under better control and my task now is to prevent relapse. RELAPSE PREVENTION. 'Feels a bit like walking the high wire!'
7. I took action, improved, but now I'm a bit worse again and I have to deal with that. RELAPSE MANAGEMENT. 'Damn, thought I'd beaten it!'

Many patients hover between levels 2 and 3. As they get near to change, their anorexic side wakes up to what is going on and pulls the patient back into symptoms and poor motivation to change again.

In the person with a prolonged illness, identifying their disabilities in the physical, psychological and social domains may well help to increase motivational level. That level can also be different for different symptoms, so that motivation may be higher for improving social network than increasing weight. Decisions on what to offer a patient may depend critically on motivational level. For example, if a patient is at level 2, treatment should be aimed at increasing motivation to change, rather than dealing with symptoms.

SUPPORTIVE THERAPY

Supportive therapy is the name given to therapy that has no theoretical home. It is provided by a wide variety of individuals including secretaries who field questions on the phone, receptionists who welcome the patient, may recognise them and pass a comment, doctors who may only see the patient once in three or six months, and therapists who may be seeing the patients under the rubric of a therapy with a name such as CBT, Interpersonal Therapy (IPT) (Klerman, Weissman, Rounsaville & Chevron (1984)) or Cognitive Analytic Therapy (CAT) (Treasure, J. L. & Ward, A. (1997), but who nevertheless include support as an essential, probably therapeutic aspect of the work. No-one who has not been ill and required the services of a professional can imagine the importance of the visit to or by the doctor, nurse, therapist etc., someone who is willing to give you their attention even if only for a few minutes. This aspect of therapy, the attention of a person interested in your suffering, is rarely acknowledged, but is probably one of the most important. Providing therapy in the same room at the same time, and not being late, form a very important part of treatments such as psychodynamic and cognitive behavioural therapies. They are supportive aspects of treatment because they convey the message that you will be there at the same time and in the same place, in other words you are reliable.

Support, therefore, is intrinsic to all therapies. It forms the central approach in some. Supportive individual therapy is the main form of treatment provided individually at the Russell Unit for people with anorexia nervosa and atypical and more complex eating disorders not suitable for group therapy because the patient has specific needs that would not be addressed in a monothematic group for bulimia nervosa or binge eating disorder. It can be provided by a mental health worker with basic professional training such as mental health nursing as long as regular supervision is provided (see Chapter 2). The essence of the therapy is that the patient is provided with a regular one-hour slot, which is usually weekly but this can reduce with time, in which any subject of concern is discussed. The approach is problem based, with emphasis on the difficulties that the patient brings, whether to do with nutrition, mental state or social, occupational and family functioning. The therapist also has an agenda in that outcome in the service is measured by body weight changes, menstruation in patients who are low weight and improvements in eating disorder and depressive symptoms in all. Accordingly these areas are usually addressed and if patients deny the need to, for example, discuss changes in weight, this is tackled using motivational enhancement, looking at advantages and disadvantages of change (see Chapter 9 for more details). A patient who is physically compromised in any way, such as by low weight, muscle weakness, abnormal blood tests, is monitored physically (medical monitoring) at a rate that is agreed with a physician. The duration of therapy is not predetermined, and it can go on for a year or more. This has adverse effects upon the waiting list, but is felt, in the team, to be the correct approach because different patients take differing amounts of time to get the most out of therapy. The ending is planned well in advance and sessions are sometimes spaced out to several weeks in preparation for the end of therapy. If a patient fails to progress, misses several sessions or deteriorates, the case is brought to the Current Concerns meeting where the patient may receive an appointment to be seen by a senior member of staff, often a doctor or psychologist, for review of motivation, therapy model or physical state or the patient may be discharged back to the referrer or GP. Any patient being discharged at the end of therapy is brought to Current Concerns for a brief discussion accompanied by approving noises when the patient has done well and sympathetic ones if she has not.

MEDICAL MONITORING

This is proposed when a patient is at risk (see Figure 4.5, p. 73) and is not willing or appropriate to engage in regular individual therapy or in day hospital treatment. In these approaches medical monitoring occurs routinely as part of the treatment. Some patients, however, are unwilling to engage in therapy, others are so involved in the eating disorder that the most they can cope with is a fairly brief meeting during which physical measures are taken. For these patients, monitoring of their medical state is essential, so that, should they deteriorate physically, appropriate action can be taken, sometimes including hospital admission, perhaps against the will of the patient. The case will almost always be discussed in the Current Concerns list with medical personnel, so that judgements about safe medical management can be made, the rate and nature of medical monitoring discussed and treatment arranged. The monitoring can take the form of weekly weight, SUSS, ECG and blood tests for electrolytes and liver function, in a moderately compromised patient, but a patient with a low potassium level due to continuing vomiting or laxative abuse can be monitored using electrolyte levels and ECG on a daily basis until risk is less pronounced. This form of observation is very stressful for the key worker, whether a nurse, psychologist or other team member, because patients at risk evoke the spectre of the death of someone who is frequently a young woman, distressing enough in itself, but always followed by a series of enquiries in which the professional competence of the key worker, the consultant and other team members may be questioned. Medical monitoring of a compromised patient should therefore be a matter for the whole team so that the individual at the front line can be adequately supported in this difficult and responsible task.

Intensive medical monitoring is routinely reviewed weekly at the Current Concerns meeting (Chapter 2) and at any time required by the key worker.

Sometimes a patient is unwilling to engage with the team at all, and in these circumstances monitoring will need to take place in primary care, with support given to the GP and other primary care workers as required.

INDIVIDUAL THERAPY

Supportive individual therapy has already been discussed. Depending on the skills of the staff and the needs of the patient any form of individual therapy can be provided. Patients who would normally be offered group CBT, because they suffer from bulimia nervosa or binge eating disorder but are not suitable for group therapy may be offered individual CBT. The possible reasons are diverse. Some patients are averse to discussing their private thoughts with a group of strangers. Some suffer from social phobia and find groups elicit feelings of panic. They could be offered a series of CBT sessions aimed at overcoming the phobia, although in practice the phobic symptoms are intertwined with the eating disorder and separating them is difficult. A third group comprises people such as doctors, well-known faces and local students of medicine, nursing and other health professions. Students in the latter categories might best be treated in another unit, away from their training school, as long as funding can be arranged, although they often wish to be treated 'at home' being either more confident in the home team or fearful about their treatment under a rival establishment! This issue is further discussed below under 'Confidentiality'.

A substantial group of patients have problems for which individual therapy appears to be the most appropriate option. They tend to have complex needs as a result of a coexisting medical condition such as diabetes mellitus or a psychiatric disorder with pronounced symptoms such as frequent deliberate self-harm. These complex patients are often treated by a number of people working together (see Chapter 7, Liaison and Outreach) and individual therapy for the eating disorder may form part of this package. There has been considerable interest in dialectical behaviour therapy (Linehan, 1993) an intriguingly named approach that combines cognitive approaches with affect management skills training, intensive case management and zen mindfulness. The effective ingredients of this mixture are uncertain, but the intensity of involvement with the therapist, including permission to call the therapist out of hours, may well be important. It has been used mostly for patients with a diagnosis of borderline personality disorder, many with frequent deliberate self-harming and it probably should be reserved for this group of patients who are in general very difficult to treat, and often end up in hospital.

FAMILY INTERVENTIONS

Although one of the first writers on the subject of anorexia nervosa, Sir William Gull asserted that 'relatives are the worst attendants', family members almost always have to live with or at least meet the person with an eating disorder and they are understandably confused about how you treat a daughter, sister, wife or mother who appears to be attempting to starve or purge herself to death. This experience usually represents the most difficult challenge that has ever faced the family and it is not surprising that they say the wrong thing, get angry, frustrated, depressed and feel generally helpless. When a child of 14 develops an eating disorder, it is often the family that brings her for treatment, so they are involved from the outset. When the patient is 18 or more, she may come for help because of her own distress, or with the encouragement of others, including family, friends, tutors and employers and, from the age of 18 she has the option of excluding her family from her care, and preventing them from knowing details of her condition and care, such as her weight or potassium level, which would naturally be shared with worried parents. This can put parents in an extremely difficult position. They have a young person living in the house for whom they hold great hopes for the future. They see her restricting her diet, hear her vomiting and can tell under layers of clothes that she is wasting away, and yet they cannot have the information about the current risks to her health, information which they used to receive when she was younger. The result may be that they deny what they observe, and fail to worry when they should, or they react to every piece of evidence of the eating disorder and become overanxious and over-reactive which can be equally unhelpful. In addition, it is not unusual for parents to disagree about how worrying the situation is, and what needs to be done. A father, for example, may see that his daughter is undereating and insist that she finish adequate meals. Her mother may be in finetune with her daughter's emotional state and be aware of the distress eating adequately will cause her. The young woman becomes aware of this and, as all children do, go to the more sympathetic parent and arrange for the other one to be undermined.

Clinical description 5.1

A young woman of 20 is suffering from anorexia nervosa with prominent obsessional symptoms which result in prolonged mealtimes during which she cuts her food into tiny portions. Her father encourages her to speed up her eating, and gets frustrated and angry when she cannot. Her mother spends hours sitting with her during her eating rituals. Supper begins at 7.30 pm, preparations last until 11 pm when she starts to eat. This stage lasts for four hours and she finally finishes the meal at 3 am, by which time her mother, who has a day job, is exhausted. The father is unable to understand his wife's behaviour and spends less and less time discussing the matter. Mother and daughter become an increasingly isolated dyad from which father and siblings become more and more distant.

Clinical description 5.2

An 18-year-old engages in severe dietary restriction and her BMI falls from 19 to 17 in six months. She will not allow her parents to know her weight, and this results in them becoming extremely anxious, her father commenting angrily on every meal she takes, and arguing with her mother who feels that her daughter is dying and becomes very distressed. The patient agrees for her parents to be contacted and told that her condition is serious but not immediately life-threatening which reassures the family that their daughter is being monitored, even if they cannot be informed of the details, and helps them deal with the situation in a more realistic and effective manner.

Carers groups have complained bitterly that they are sometimes excluded from being informed about their adult children's health when they continue to feel responsible for their welfare and safety. This is clearly a difficult area, and a compromise needs to be reached. A patient who clearly states that she does not want her family informed or involved in treatment, or even contacted, must be respected. However, in this case, it may be that effective treatment will be deemed difficult or impossible unless carers are involved, and the patient and referrer must be made fully aware of this. Most patients are not so strict, and will allow some contact with relatives, even if they do not wish them to be fully informed of their condition. This latter demand may be reasonable when a patient is attempting to become more independent. Parents can then be involved to the extent that they can attend a support group and see a staff member for general information about eating disorders, and to ask questions which can be answered without giving information about their daughter that she has indicated she does not want shared.

Clinical description 5.3

A 23-year-old female patient living at home indicates that she does not want her parents informed about her medical state, refuses to have them in care planning meetings but does not object to them being seen. They attend a relatives support group and meet with the general practitioner, consultant and key worker. They describe in detail how their daughter restricts her diet, overexercises and demands that the family comply with her obsessional symptoms, for example storing empty food boxes in the living room. The mother wished to take a tougher line and preserve the family way of life, whereas the father was much more permissive and believed that as their daughter was ill and at risk, she should be allowed to do whatever she wished. These differences were addressed and a helpful compromise was reached between the parents who were seen regularly for parental counselling sessions by a family therapist.

Family therapy suffers from the legacy of theoretical approaches that overtly blamed families for mental illness, beginning with the 'schizophrenogenic mother' and the infamous 'refrigerator mother' who was supposed to cause autism. The anti-psychiatrists of the 1960s were also highly critical of the family (e.g. Laing and Esterson, 1964) and much distress was caused to families, especially mothers, as they were tacitly accused of being the cause of mental illness in their children. Freud blamed hysteria on sexual abuse by fathers until he recanted after realising that if he was correct, his own father would have had to have abused his sister, causing her neurosis. He then changed his theory to suggest that fantasy of sexual union with the father was the cause, shifting the blame back onto the patient.

The 1970s saw some improvement in professional attitudes to the family, although it was widely reported that although parents did not cause mental illness they did precipitate relapse due to being excessively critical or excessively close to the patient. The 'expressed emotion' hypothesis linked the health of the patient with the behaviour of the parents. This time, however, at least there was some empirical evidence to demonstrate that there was something in the idea.

Most recently, the geneticists have had their say, and have asserted that a substantial proportion of the variance in mental disorders including eating disorders, is attributable to inheritance. Sadly, parents feel they are at fault here as well!

Given the assault on parents that there has been in the last century, it is not surprising that many families come to family therapy convinced of two things: (i) I'm the cause of my child's illness; (ii) I'm going to be told just how bad I've been. Approaching family therapy rather like a criminal, convinced of his own guilt, approaches a trial, renders the family, and especially the parents, very sensitive to what is said. Many families, when asked about treatment, rate family therapy as the most unpleasant part of treatment, and report that they were told that they were the problem, and some say that they were told that they had probably sexually abused the young person with the eating disorder. How much of this reflects what is actually said and done, and how much is a reflection of the sort of suspicion I have described is difficult to tell. As a result of this problem, some family therapists have gone to the opposite extreme, and deny that the family has anything to do with the problem. This is equally unhelpful, because even if parents acknowledge the very important influences of life events, peer relationships and of other adults, they still regard themselves as important contributors to their children's development, and find it confusing when professionals deny them this role. A middle ground is required, with family interventions informing and supporting, and providing a context in which to work through family difficulties and negotiate better ways of handling them.

Family interventions can be regarded as analogous to individual ones. With individuals we provide support, information, therapy, groups and so on. There is no reason to restrict our interventions with families to family therapy, even though that can be extremely effective and helpful when it is required. A range of family interventions would include family support, information sessions, family therapy and group family therapy. Each of these approaches has its place in a comprehensive service and these approaches form an integral part of a community approach to eating disorders treatment.

FAMILY/CARER SUPPORT

A family support group allows different families and carers to meet in the absence of the patient and exchange views about life with someone with an eating disorder. It also allows relatives to express their views, sometimes negative, about treatment, and, in some cases, to continue to receive support after a relative with an eating disorder has died. In our service, the Carers Support Group meets once monthly in the evening and lasts $1\frac{1}{2}$ hours. It is facilitated by two team members on a rota, so no team member has a frequent evening commitment. Coffee and biscuits are provided, an informal atmosphere prevails and conversation is encouraged between family members and information is provided when requested.

No particular commitment is demanded, and relatives can drop in as they wish. Naturally no specific information about individual patients is revealed.

FAMILY THERAPY

This is provided by a senior family therapist working with a team of other interested professionals, and the list has included trainees from a family therapy training course, senior psychiatric trainees, both in general psychiatry and in psychotherapy, the consultant psychiatrist (myself, also family therapy trained) and a mental health nurse who subsequently qualified as a family therapist. Once a month a senior family therapist attends our clinic to supervise the work of the senior family therapist and myself.

Families are booked in for 1½ hours and are seen by the therapist, who may be any one of the team, while the rest of the team observe the session via a video link. The rooms are not adjacent, so a one-way mirror is not feasible. The therapist wears an ear 'bug' through which one of the team, usually the same person throughout a session, passes messages. After 45–60 minutes the therapist comes out to join the team, has a discussion and returns to convey any useful thoughts, arrange the next session and round off this one. We leave it to the patient to bring whoever she thinks could usefully attend, and we have seen a variety of different groupings including parents, siblings, partners, spouses, children and friends. Sometimes the patient's key worker comes into the family session as a support to the patient. When this occurs, we have agreed that the key worker should not leave the room to join the rest of the team when the therapist leaves, and to this extent the key worker is regarded as a member of the system receiving therapy.

Techniques vary with therapist and supervisor. Eliciting the history of the family, with the aid of a family tree, is frequently an important part of therapy, as well as discovering who is concerned about what in the family, so that an agenda can be developed which reflects the wishes for change in each member of the family. It is fairly unusual that we would try and increase anxiety about the eating disorder, as often occurs when the patient is 15 or less. We often find that, after years of eating disorder in which parents have been in a state of permanent anxiety, the family may be frozen with the patient unable to develop and the parents unable to leave her for fear of what may happen. They may not have had a holiday for years, and may feel trapped in a relationship which is damaging them, and failing to help their daughter. Family therapy in such a situation may be more about helping parents let go of their daughter and allowing responsibility for her to shift from them to her and the eating disorder (and general psychiatric and medical) services.

Clinical description 5.4

An 18-year-old had developed anorexia nervosa at the age of 16. During family therapy her parents supervised her eating and she gained weight to the normal range, although never accepted the weight gain. After a year of supervision she decided to go abroad for a year, during which time she lost most of the weight she had previously gained. Her parents, who had experienced substantial liberation during her trip, decided that as she was now 19, she should take responsibility for her own weight, and that if she wished to have more help to gain weight this should be provided by the eating disorders service, a decision with which the patient concurred. The patient continued at a low but survivable weight, and her parents continued to live their own lives.

The parents in the above case went through a considerable amount of guilt in coming to their decision to stop providing intensive meal support to their daughter, and so allow her weight to fall. During family therapy they reasoned that they had given her an opportunity to recover under their care, she had become an adult, and now should reasonably seek help from the services available, with their general support and encouragement.

The theme of separation comes up repeatedly in the therapy of patients with eating disorders. A mother becomes depressed following a cot death and the next child is overprotected while the relationship with the husband suffers. This next child finds it very difficult to separate and when she goes to university she develops anorexia nervosa and her mother finds herself spoon feeding her as if she were a baby. In the treatment of adults with eating disorders the role of the family therapist is more often to help parents disengage from their ill child, than to encourage them to become more and more involved in their eating and other behaviours.

This disengagement may lead to the child becoming more dependent on treatment services, and the space created in the family can help her recover, as well as opening up the possibility of improvement in other relationships in the family, particularly that of the parents.

What of siblings? They may seem fine, skating along the outer reaches of the family, staying out a lot, arranging to spend months on a kibbutz or in Argentina and almost always applying for university well away from home. This does not mean that they do not have needs. They have just learnt that it is difficult to have normal needs met when there is a constant crisis in the family. Their dilemma recalls that of some children of Holocaust survivors, used to hearing 'It's not as bad as Auschwitz' when they try and complain about their lot. Siblings can be seen with patient and parents in whole family therapy and they can prove very helpful as a support from the same generation when parents are being hard on the patient. While they are often willing to help prevent the patient acting as an unsupported 'bad guy', their own experience of the illness in the family and how it has been handled must also be elicited. If the sibling is in a relationship or a new family he may decline the opportunity to relive his childhood, having packed it away or dealt with it in the new relationship – sometimes with someone who needs a lot of care.

ACTION TECHNIQUES IN FAMILY THERAPY

The family therapy literature is replete with examples of charismatic therapists doing dramatic things in the presence of bemused families, throwing a ball around the room and observers bursting into the room for example. Families with children with anorexia nervosa have been encouraged to force feed the child and in another case to go through arrangements for the child's funeral. Use of these techniques is largely a matter of personal taste and in my own practice I was more inclined to them in my youth. The family picnic therapy session was pioneered by Salvador Minuchin and can either be very successful or profoundly damaging.

Clinical description 5.5

A patient of 17 with a one-year history of anorexia nervosa was invited with her parents and sister to bring a picnic to the next therapy session. A basket was prepared by her mother with sandwiches, drinks and biscuits. She absolutely refused to eat a mouthful. The therapist encouraged the parents to make sure the patient ate what they thought she needed (she had a BMI of 14) and asked the younger sister to support her sister in what was a very difficult experience for her. The parents, having been granted permission to do what they had long wished to do, became very firm with their daughter, the father backing up his wife, and they succeeded in forcing her to eat a mouthful of a sandwich, after a struggle during which another sandwich had ended up plastered on the therapy room ceiling. After this the patient obediently ate what she was given and gained a normal weight within three months. In the last session the subject had changed from weight and food, which they had solved, to the problem the parents were having in getting their daughters to bed at a reasonable time. The tables were turned in a conversation between the girls: younger sister: It's awful, they want us to go to bed at 10, much earlier than my friends! Patient: Yes, but that's just because they keep wanting to go to bed earlier! There followed an embarrassed exchange of looks between the parents. At a later session with parents alone, it was clear that the experience of overcoming their daughter's eating problem together had resolved a relationship difficulty and the result was that their sex life had improved greatly, leading to them wishing to turn in earlier than their children wished to retire.

Clinical description 5.6

In this case, the patient had been ill for five years. The parents were, again, encouraged to feed their daughter but she did not give in at any point, and after 40 minutes the parents became exhausted and demoralised, feeling that they had failed their daughter, but also angry that the therapist had put them through such an ordeal. The therapist and the observing team also felt that they had asked the family to do more than they were capable of, and also left the session feeling demoralised. The patient developed chronic anorexia nervosa.

Presiding over what can be such a violent family confrontation has always been a source of discomfort for myself and other therapists. It has been demonstrated that a proportion of patients with anorexia nervosa admit to having been sexually abused, even though the proportion affected is no different from other psychiatric disorders. Allowing, and even encouraging, forced feeding in a patient who may have suffered sexual abuse, runs the risk of re-enacting an abusive act and compounding the original abuse. If, in a patient who has indeed been abused, the abuser turns out to have been a parent, forced feeding becomes even more traumatic. The figures suggest that about 30 % of patients have been abused, although a proportion will not divulge the information, so the real figure is likely to be higher. At the present state of knowledge, however, it is a minority that have suffered abuse, and if the family therapist believes that a family meal is likely to improve the outcome then the balance of good to ill might tip in favour of the former and the above concerns need to be kept in mind while the therapist guides the session.

FAMILY SCULPTS

This technique when applied in family sessions can be very powerful. The family is asked to elect a *sculptor* whose role is to place the other family members in the physical positions that reflect their emotional relationships. The *sculptor* is coached by the therapist to use a range of postures, including crouching or lying down or standing on a chair, and to use physical variables to represent relationships. Thus, one family member may be leaning on another, pushing someone away, being pulled in two or more directions, to represent what the *sculptor* feels is happening.

When the postures have been achieved to the *sculptor's* satisfaction, she puts herself into the sculpt so that her position in the system can be observed.

The therapist then asks the group to maintain the position for a few moments, and asks each member of the group to report on *how it feels* (not whether he or she agrees with it). It can be difficult for family members to keep up an uncomfortable position for a long time, but is also helpful in making overt something uncomfortable that has been happening for years.

When everyone has fed back on how they feel in a particular sculpt, another family member is chosen to modify the first sculpt according to his own views of the family, and the same process of reporting is pursued.

A patient with anorexia nervosa was asked to sculpt her family. She placed her mother and stepfather together and her sister to the side of their mother, with her beside the sister, rather an outsider. She said there was something missing from the sculpt and took a chair, holding it above her head and asking her mother and sister to help support it. The chair represented her father, who had died when she was a small child. The sculpt with the chair made the stepfather into the outsider, with the mother and two daughters united by the memory of the dead father.

Clinical description 5.7

A man of 20 with a three-year history of anorexia nervosa placed himself in a family sculpt surrounded by his mother and sisters. He put his father at a distance of 2 metres away from the group. The sculpt evoked an emotional exchange between father and son. Father: why do you put me here, I thought we were close? Son: you're ashamed of me, you won't take me with you to the pub. I'm too thin, you want a strong son you can be proud of. Following the session, the father invited his son to come to the pub with him and this became regular. The son preferred not to stay in the pub until closing and persuaded his father to leave earlier. This reduced the father's heavy alcohol consumption and had a beneficial effect on the parents' marriage. The patient gained weight, pursued individual therapy and made a full recovery over the following year.

Clinical description 5.8

A patient with severe longstanding anorexia nervosa sculpted her family. She placed her mother closely surrounded by her daughters with the father some way off. She placed a pillow in the corner of the room, under an armchair. This represented a sibling who had died a few days after birth. She placed herself outside the family but reaching towards her mother. Asked to repeat the sculpt as she saw it in five years' time she placed the mother and her sisters even closer, and the father more separate, clearly on his own, possibly separated from the mother. She placed herself on the floor, by the armchair, in the grave with her dead brother.

This powerful sculpt suggested that the anorexia may have been linked to the neonatal death. In such a family, death of a new-born, or a late miscarriage, both more common than average in families of adolescents with anorexia nervosa, can lead to a subsequent child being overprotected because of fear that she may die. It has been suggested that this could be linked to difficulty separating from the family in adolescence and that this may trigger anorexia nervosa.

The therapist can feel free to suggest modifications of the initial sculpt, for example 'Sculpt in five years', 'Sculpt without the anorexia present', 'Sculpt when the older child leaves home to go to university', 'Wished for sculpt', 'Most feared sculpt'. More creative families can be asked to enact a 'fantasy sculpt' to embody their dreamed of wishes and fears.

MULTIFAMILY AND MULTICOUPLE GROUPS

This modification of family and couple therapy derives from the work of Dare, Eisler, Scholz and Asen in the UK and Germany. Our approach to multifamily groups has been described in Colahan and Robinson (2002) and will only be summarised here.

In multifamily groups, several families are brought together for the whole day during which activities are arranged by the therapists, which foster improved understanding of the eating disorder and how it impacts on relationships in the family. The time commitment of meetings varies between exponents. We ask families to attend for one whole day, followed by another one week later, then a third after a month, then a follow up in three months, totalling four days. The days are carefully structured (see Figure 5.1) and staffing has included two family therapists, a key worker for each family, and other staff members to take notes and make video recordings if needed. In the first session, a family member describes the family and draws, or has drawn for them, a family tree. This is a good way of introducing the families to each other, and to observe the place of the eating disorder in the family. On subsequent days, this session is used to feedback on homework tasks agreed on the previous multifamily group day. After the coffee break, creative workshops take the form of art therapy, in which a family produces a joint family picture and presents it to other families and movement therapy in which, for example, a tug of war between family members can provide a lot of information on how individuals in the family support each other. The midday meal can be a family picnic, or arranged so that the families swap patients, and afterwards feed back on how it was to have a meal with a person with anorexia nervosa who was from a different family. After lunch we may have a goldfish bowl discussion in which all the patient's generation discuss a topic (such as how food is managed in our family) while the parents look on. Then the

Timetable

0930–11.00	Family tree / homework feedback
11.00–11.30	Break
11.30–13.00	Creative workshops
13.00–13.45	Lunch
13.45–14.00	Feedback on meal
14.00–14.30	Break
14.30–16.00	Goldfish-bowl discussions
16.00–16.15	Break
16.15–17.00	Homework planning

Figure 5.1   Timetable for Day 1 of the Multi-family Group

groups swap, and the parents go into the goldfish bowl to discuss their re-actions to their children's opinions, and express their own about the topic. On other days we have held a family sculpting session (see above) with a multifamily variation. The families had all eaten with an eating disordered child of another family. In the sculpting session the initial *sculptor* was the eating disordered child with whom they had shared lunch, and who often produced a very insightful sculpt.

After another break, the families discuss with a key worker a small positive change they could make in the time until the next session. It might be that the family spend some time each week talking together, that father and son go to the pub (see above, p. 96) or that the patient will have gained a certain amount of weight.

Feedback after the multifamily groups indicated that all family members found them helpful, the patients somewhat less than the other family members. Too few families overall have gone through the system to judge their effectiveness, and demand has changed so that more recent workshops have collected a number of couples in which one member has suffered from an eating disorder. So far the eating disordered member has been the woman, although one male partner quickly admitted to his own eating disorder during the first day.

The preferred form of family involvement in eating disorders has yet to emerge. Some units favour groups of relatives in which the patient is absent and the relatives feel more able to discuss their fears and frustrations. Perhaps a combination of multifamily groups in which patients sometimes attend will prove to be more helpful. This is certainly an area in which outcome research for treatment of anorexia nervosa could develop. The NICE report on eating disorders (National Collaborating Centre for Mental Health, 2004) discovered no adequate studies in which a treatment that was effective for anorexia nervosa had been examined. Perhaps a combination of multifamily group and carer workshops could be added to individual therapy in a controlled trial of therapy in adult anorexia nervosa.

COMPLEXITY THERAPY

No such therapy at present exists. However, chaos and complexity theory does have things to say which are relevant to our work with patients and families. In the systemic view of eating disorders the observer imagines a theoretical point outside the system which contains the person with the eating disorder. This point is imaginary, because any observer is always part of the system. The patient, family and any other person chosen to be within the system are surrounded by a boundary and comments made about the properties of this imaginary system. The properties are quite helpful in thinking about the clinical issues. One such, homeostasis, described the compensatory action that follows any change in the system. For example, an increase in a daughter's starving behaviour may be matched by an intensification of her mother's attention to the daughter, a doubling of her father's alcohol intake and a halving of her sister's attendance at family meals.

Chaos and complexity theory (Gleick, 1996), a relatively new science which can be seen as an extension of the systemic approach, implies that complex processes including the weather and human relationships, are governed by underlying mathematical functions that are chaotic. Such chaotic systems are sometimes said to follow a mathematical expression called a strange attractor. These interesting beasts have the remarkable property that their components never repeat but do not stray outside defined boundaries. These ideas are helpful in understanding human behaviour including mental illness, because they offer the opportunity to model the chaos within boundaries that characterises such behaviour.

If we consider two people with eating disorders: Anna is socially inhibited, underweight, restricts her diet, cuts her food up into tiny fragments and is obsessionally tidy. Maria is also underweight and restricts her diet, but in the evening she binges on large amounts of fattening food and then vomits, her moods fluctuate wildly and she cuts herself to relieve her severe tension states.

These two individuals have very different strange attractors, both chaotic. However, Anna's is within a much more restricted range than Maria's. Could Anna ever turn into a Maria? This does happen in clinical experience when patients with one diagnosis (restricting AN) experience symptoms of another (bulimic AN). *Emergent properties* in a chaotic system refer to new phenomena, hitherto absent, appearing as a result of *bifurcations*. These latter occur when a process (say, food restriction) splits into two options (e.g. restriction and bingeing) opening a novel behaviour in the system. There are, however, strong forces at work in Anna that inhibit her from following any 'Maria' behaviours that threaten to appear as a result of bifurcation, and the appearance of a new behaviour is only likely to occur as a result of a fair amount of energy being introduced into the system, for example as a result of a sexual assault.

The idea of an underlying equation which could describe (mathematically) an individual's characteristic behaviour suggests a sort of stability. I use the idea of the *chaostat* when thinking about individuals and systems. Two drawings in Figure 5.2 illustrate the idea. Figure 5.2(a) represents Anna

(a)

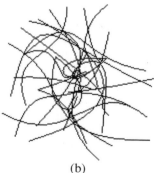

(b)

Figure 5.2 Chaostats. Illustrations suggesting two different levels of disorder. In Figure (a) (a low chaostat setting) the system is restrained and the patient/family likely to be risk averse. In Figure (b) (a high chaostat setting), the patient/family are less restrained and more chaotic.

and 5.2(b) Maria. The art of Jackson Pollock can be compared with that of Piet Mondrian to provide an additional illustrative contrast. Anna has a *chaostat* set at a low level of disturbance. She is averse to risk, always very restrained and careful. Maria, in contrast, has a high setting. She constantly takes risks and probably gets quite out of control at parties, having taken drugs and alcohol. Their behaviour, though, is related to set boundaries. If Anna finds her life getting too interesting (a man at work takes a very strong liking to her) she might well pull back her eating, become even more obsessional, and bring her life back to its accustomed level. On the other hand, she might, if her life becomes so humdrum as to be to her unbearable, add a little spice by having something new, but low calorie, to eat. At the other end of the scale, Maria often finds life boring, and has a wide repertoire of behaviours designed to increase the excitement level, such as bingeing and vomiting when she should be reading a document for work, turning up late for an interview, or harming herself and turning up to accident and emergency. If Maria's life gets too interesting, she is probably in danger. She might have taken a near-fatal overdose, had unsafe sex or been imprisoned for causing death by dangerous driving. Under those circumstances she may wish to turn down the level of excitement and, perhaps, go into therapy, attend Alcoholics Anonymous or start keeping a food diary and follow a self-help book for eating disorders.

In general, people keep to their own, characteristic chaostat setting and range presumably determined by both genes and experience. They do sometimes change, as complexity theory would predict, often as a result of relationships, social, sexual and therapeutic, and seem to be following the equations of a different *strange attractor*. Thus therapy can be seen as a way of using a relationship to alter an individual's strange attractor or chaostat.

There are, of course, couples and families that have lower or higher chaostat settings. Some couples are like Jean and her partner Simon, and others are more like Natasha and Justin. Jean and Simon never argue, plan their lives in minute detail, and live in unchanging stasis. Natasha and Justin live on the wild side. If their lives are a bit boring, one of them will turn up late, have an affair or spread a rumour, and they end up having a furious argument, which might lead to a tearful and passionate reconciliation in bed. If things get too hot, they might try and cool it. Of course, if the hostility gets so great they might split for good, in which case each has a chance of establishing a new relationship with a different chaostat setting.

This approach to behaviour has clinical implications. Patients and families can be encouraged to examine their own tendencies to order and disorder to help understand how they find themselves in difficulties due to extremes in either direction. The discovery that an individual has a high chaostat setting, leading to disorder, or a low setting, leading to extreme order, can lead to a search for ways to change the setting. This is most commonly done in the context of a relationship, although biological interventions such as drug prescription, also appear to influence the setting (look at the influence of lithium salts on the cyclical attractor seen in people with bipolar affective disorder). Lastly, the appearance of similar patterns of order/disorder at different levels of a system suggests the presence of a *fractal* structure, another concept from chaos and complexity theory. Fractals are mathematically derived structures that repeat at increasing levels of magnification. A good illustration is the Mandelbrot set, the subject of many wall posters. They are abundant in nature: the shape of an entire fern can be discerned in the tiny leaflets of which it is made. In the mammalian lung, the shape of the bronchial tree is repeated at different levels of magnification down to the most microscopic. It may be that individual and family behaviour could be analysed to reveal a fractal structure that could help explain processes which seem to repeat at different levels of a system.

DISCHARGE

When a patient with a psychiatric disorder asks the doctor or therapist 'How long will I be coming to see you' some are tempted to reply 'Till one of us dies' (see reference to Sleeper, above, page 83). This is a recipe for increasing workload, long waiting lists and unnecessary patient dependence. In general psychiatric practice, some patients see a junior doctor twice yearly for a 'check-up'. The junior doctor stays six months in a post, so the patient always sees someone new! The doctor has no time to digest the problems in the case, and is rarely confident enough either to change medication or discharge the patient, so the latter stays on drugs and gets another appointment. As a matter of course I require all trainee doctors in our service to either discharge their patients before they move to another post, or ask me to follow them up. Regarding patients seen in individual therapy, they are all discussed with supervisors and the question asked 'What is therapy for, in this person, at this time?' This discussion can result in the patient being discharged, after a reasonable interval, to another service, such as in primary care, and the therapist can then take on a patient from the waiting list. We have, because of a burgeoning waiting list for therapy, discussed the proposal that we see people for a time-limited therapy. We have always rejected this proposal, but some therapists work on recurring three-monthly contracts so that therapist and patient think regularly about the purpose of the work, and the appropriateness of continued specialist therapy.

Chapter 6

DAY CARE

WHY DAY CARE?

The decision to establish a day hospital is a big one. The organisational and clinical tasks are substantial, and a beginning service should consider establishing outpatient and liaison and outreach before embarking on day care. An exception to this rule applies when, as occurred at the Royal Free, the day hospital is replacing established inpatient beds. The effort of establishing and running a day hospital is, however, less than providing 24 hour a day care in an inpatient unit, and the change will prove a relief.

The most obvious question about day care is to ask whether it works or not. We do not have a definitive answer, although we will look at some outcome data on patients who have received day hospital treatment. There is no adequate trial comparing day care with either no treatment, outpatient or inpatient controls. The St George's study (Gowers, Norton, Halek & Crisp, 1994) looked at outpatient and inpatient care and found no significant differences in outcome between the groups. There are significant dangers in day care that should be kept in mind. In Edinburgh, a day service for eating disorders at the Royal Edinburgh Hospital found that patients became attached to the day hospital and could not be discharged. The problem was solved in a dramatic way: the day hospital was closed, the patients managed using outpatient care, and admission when required (Freeman, personal communication).

Anorexia nervosa in adults can be termed an almost 'evidence-free zone' when looking for treatments which could contribute to an 'evidence-based medicine' approach. This appeared to be the conclusion of the NICE guideline development group after an extensive review of the literature (National Collaborating Centre for Mental Health, 2004). The professional treating this disorder can either move to another area of work, or like the psychiatrists dealing with schizophrenia before 1950, do what seems reasonable, and hope to avoid the worst side effects of the recommended treatments which, for schizophrenia, included ECT, leucotomy, the spinning chair, the immersion bath, cupping and the strait jacket.

In the face of such a lamentable dearth of evidence from Randomised Controlled Trials, the clinician may reasonably come up with principles that seem to embody good practice, even if they have not been shown to be better than placebos. One such dictum might be 'Apply the least restrictive treatment that, for that individual, seems to have a chance of helping to promote better health'.

The outcome of this approach is to provide a number of levels of treatment, spanning the least restrictive to the most, and to offer the treatment towards the top of the list, and graduate to treatments further down as the others fail or seem inappropriate.

A suggested sequence is as follows:

1. self-help
2. guided self-help
3. outpatient individual therapy
4. outpatient individual and family therapy
5. day care
6. voluntary inpatient care
7. involuntary inpatient care.

Day care (termed partial hospitalization in the USA) comes quite a way down the list, and is an intensive intervention. This graduated approach to care has been termed the 'stepped care' approach. Some patients, when first seen, are clearly not suitable for the earlier 'steps'. A patient who is at death's door due to malnutrition and refuses treatment may well end up with step 7 as soon as she is referred.

A second question can be 'Are we, in this area, suitable for a day programme?' The ideal geographical area for an eating disorder is fully or partly urban, so that a substantial proportion of the population can travel to the centre within an hour. However, even if the population density is very low, a day programme can be run in association with an eating disorders hostel, in which patients reside during the week while the day hospital is running. The establishment of such a hostel is discussed in Chapter 9.

This chapter is arranged to provide a guide to establishing and running an effective day programme within a comprehensive community oriented eating disorders service. The essentials are to manage the staff, provide good nutritional guidance and develop a therapeutic programme of care, backed up by emergency provision, including weekend care, should things go wrong.

MANAGING DAY CARE

The optimum size for an eating disorders day hospital is 8–12 places. Fewer than six and groups have too little input to be therapeutic and interesting, and over 12, groups and particularly meals become unwieldy. If the demand is so great that numbers need to be exceeded, it might be necessary to have two sets of groups running contemporaneously, or even two programmes. This is most unlikely to be required, however. Too few is more common and if numbers are consistently four or below, the need for a day hospital should be reviewed. It is possible, if numbers are low for a while, to redeploy team members to outreach, liaison and outpatient roles while a list of patients for the day hospital is built up. In our experience, a population of around a million, mostly urban, generates enough referrals to warrant a day hospital with 8 to 12 places.

Most of the staff in the day hospital will be splitting their duties with the other main domain, outpatients, and also be available to provide the occasional outreach visit. Team members working in the day service will therefore have a management relationship with both the day hospital manager and the outpatient service manager, and care needs to be taken to make sure that conflicts do not cause difficulty. The outpatient load must be managed so that time remains for the individual worker to spend time working in the day hospital. The occasional staff member providing specialist input, for example of dance movement therapy, may work exclusively in the day programme, and usually works part time. The day hospital manager (DHM) can be any profession, and is a member of the senior management group which meets monthly (see Chapter 2). In our service, the role has been filled by a nurse, an occupational therapist, an art therapist and a dietician, each of whom has brought a unique and different combination of skills and priorities to the post. The DHM holds the waiting list for the day programme, and decides whether a patient can be accepted into the programme, by an assessment, followed by a report back to the multidisciplinary team meeting. The DHM is also accountable for the functioning of the day programme to the service manager and the consultant psychiatrist, and issues such as waiting time, time spent in the day programme, attendance rate, the group programme, and weight gained in a specified time are all quality measures that form part of a regular (almost always friendly!) discussion between the DHM and other senior management in the team.

The main functions in the day hospital, and the staff who usually fulfil them are as outlined in Table 6.1. There is a good deal of flexibility, although some roles seem to fall naturally to certain professions. Meal supervision, for example, is more commonly provided by nurses than by doctors. Over time merging of roles of different professions has occurred, and meal supervision, now, is commonly provided by psychologists, although doctors

Table 6.1 Day hospital activities and the staff involved in supporting them

Activity	Staff	Usual Professions
Overall management	Day Hospital Manager	Nurse, OT, dietitian, art therapist
Key working/therapy	Key worker	Nurse, psychologist, OT
Meal support	Meal support staff	Nurse, any (+students)
Psychodynamic group	Open group facilitators	Psychologist, trainee psychiatrist
Open art group	Facilitator	Nurse, any
Creative therapies (art, dance movement)	Facilitators	Specialist therapists + any team member
Carer's support group	Facilitators	Any two team members
Weekend planning and review	Facilitator	Nurse, any

still remain down the league. The specialist treatments, such as psychodynamic groups, art therapy and dance movement therapy, are run by a specialist therapist with someone who is a non-specialist in the field (e.g. nurse, psychology trainee) as co-therapist.

The key worker role, also known in other contexts as the care coordinator, has a number of different important roles. The key worker meets weekly with the patient for an hour, providing individual therapy, reports on the patient's progress at the team meeting, supports the patient during interviews with other team members, if necessary, may attend family therapy on request, completes statutory documentation relating to health and assists the patient in applying for state benefits, housing and activities related to further rehabilitation such as referral to sheltered workshops and to community psychiatric resources and drug rehabilitation. The key worker–patient relationship can, as will be apparent, be a very close and dependent one for the patient and appears to be a major element of importance in a successful experience of day care. The key worker gets to know more about the patient than anyone else in the team, and is in an excellent position to assist the team develop strategies for helping a patient who has reached an impasse. Occasionally, the relationship can be so close, particularly if there is strong mutual identification, that a split can appear with the patient and key worker on one side and the rest of the team, often making unreasonable demands on the patient like insisting on weight gain, on the other. When such a split happens it must be recognised as quickly as possible and dealt with in supervision, sometimes in a three-way, with a supervisor, the key worker and another team member with whom there seems to be a conflict over the patient. Such meetings are unpleasant, but not nearly as bad as the chronic dysfunction that can ensue when splits are not managed adequately.

PATIENT CRITERIA

The team needs to decide on the scope of the day programme. Is it primarily for anorexia nervosa, and so having a clear focus on weight gain, and, if possible, weight recovery, or will patients of normal weight with bulimia nervosa be admitted, and those overweight, mostly with binge eating disorder? At the Russell Unit, we have chosen the first option, and patients on the day programme are judged to some extent according to their weight gain or lack of it. Other types of patients with eating disorders may, however, benefit from day care, including those with bulimia nervosa and binge eating disorder unresponsive to outpatient treatment, and those satisfying criteria for borderline personality disorder, for whom there is Randomised Controlled Trial evidence in favour of a psychoanalytically oriented day hospital (Bateman & Fonagy, 2001).

The assessment for suitability for day care is usually made by the day hospital manager and one other professional, who may be any experienced member of the team. Key to the assessment are the linked issues of motivation and commitment. The motivational stages of DiClemente and Prochaska (1998) are borne in mind, namely precontemplation, contemplation, determination, action, maintenance and relapse management when assessing motivation, and patients accepted for the day programme should be in the action stage. The patient should also be ready to give up their whole week to tackle the eating disorder and this means no work or education in the initial stages of the day programme. Physical state is also assessed. The patient should not be too ill. In general, we have found that patients with a BMI over 14 are better able to cope physically and mentally with the day programme, and we have tried to find other ways of helping patients under that BMI until they reach it and can join the day programme, including intensive outpatient care and brief inpatient stays.

FOOD GLORIOUS FOOD

It is in the dining room that the day hospital approach can be seen to be superficially most similar to the inpatient approach, but in reality it is at its most different. If the inpatient dining room could speak it would say 'You are not leaving this table until you have eaten enough to make you put on weight'. What would the day hospital dining room say? Perhaps 'You have met with day hospital staff, probably a nurse or a dietician, and chosen what food to have today. It may not be enough to make you gain, but it is a lot more than you have had hitherto. We will support you so that you can eat it and choose to eat more in the future so that, eventually, you will put on weight'.

It will be seen that the day hospital dining room is a good deal more chatty than its terse inpatient cousin. Weight gain is usually slower as a day patient than as an inpatient. Although it is unproven, our impression is that patients who gain weight as day patients appear to hold onto it for longer than those who have been admitted and fed on inpatient units. Weight gained as an inpatient sometimes seems to belong to the staff, and is got rid of as soon as possible. In the day patient the weight often seems to be the patient's, and so the history of day patients is that they either put on weight and keep it, at least for a while, or they don't put it on at all. We await with impatience the controlled study that will consign our impressions to the recycle bin.

Patients begin attending the day programme having developed, over years, sometimes, a diet which, as they often assert, is very 'healthy' being full of salads, proteins, vegetables and water, but in fact very unhealthy, as it lacks the very fuels of life, namely carbohydrates and fats. Decisions about diet to be taken begin with an assessment of what the patient is already eating, as a basis, acceptable to the patient, on which to build. The patient is weighed and height taken, unless already known. A session is arranged with the dietician, the aim of which is to agree a meal plan which the patient accepts she will consume on the day programme. At the beginning it may not be adequate to gain weight, although it will usually maintain. Within a few weeks the patient is eating a weight-gaining diet. Her weight is measured every week, and discussed at the day programme team meeting on Wednesday morning (see below).

Meals are supervised by an experienced member of staff and usually a less experienced one (occasionally the consultant) who is there to chat, observe and learn. There should be no argument about the food provided, because the meal plan has been pre-agreed. However, hospital meals being what they are, mistakes can happen, and the wrong food may be sent up. In such a case, the staff will negotiate with the patient for her to have a nutritionally equivalent meal that is available. This can be very difficult, especially for a patient who is rigid about her diet, and it cannot safely happen frequently.

The patients are called into the kitchen, where the food is served, one by one, and the staff member dishes up the meal. When all have been served, the meal starts. It is in a pleasantly furnished dining room, with two dining tables. At one, the staff members sit with the patients who are deemed to require extra support. At the other table sit patients who are more 'senior' and can cope with less supervision. Conversation is encouraged, and tends to be about subjects that interest young girls, such as pop concerts and personalities. Patients who are having problems eating are supported although challenges are often reserved for after the meal.

Clinical description 6.1

A patient attending the day programme had ordered fish with mashed potato. At the table she covered the meal with tomato ketchup, then squeezed on a layer of brown sauce, then a layer of black pepper, finishing the dish with a layer of mayonnaise. She then pushed the plate away as she regarded it, probably correctly, as uneatable. She was challenged by other patients in the post-meal group, but refused to comment.

Clinical description 6.2

A patient who was very underweight with a BMI of 13.5 attended the day programme. She had ordered a full meal but was only able to take a couple of spoons of soup. A staff member commented that she appeared to be having great difficulty eating. She immediately burst into tears and was unable to have any more to eat.

After the meal there is a post-meal group. The patients sit with staff and comment on how the meal has gone for them, and how the behaviour of other patients has affected them. It lasts 15 to 30 minutes, depending on the number of patients.

Patients beginning the day programme are required to attend five days a week, for two main meals. Breakfast is not usually taken at the day hospital, although it can be provided if the team view is that it would be helpful. Equally, meals are not provided at weekends, unless patients are having particular difficulty at weekends, in which case extra hours are offered to staff members so that at least one meal per day at the weekend can be provided.

Some patients, particularly at the beginning of day care, are unable to eat at all, having survived on liquids, sometimes with little or no nutritional content. These patients are at some risk for refeeding syndrome and acute gastric dilatation (see Chapter 8). However, the risk is probably less than with inpatient refeeding because the patients, not being under constant supervision, increase their nutrient intake at a lower rate. Patients at most risk from these complications would also be most likely to be admitted for the initial stages of refeeding. Those who continue to find solid food repugnant may be permitted to begin refeeding using meal replacement drinks such as Clinutren© or Ensure©. Calorie intake can begin at 500 per day and increase over the first few days to 1000–1500, whatever level results in weight gain. The occasional patient never gets onto solid food.

Clinical description 6.3

A 20-year-old woman was a refugee from persecution in her country of origin. Members of her family had been imprisoned and she had been subject to sexual abuse. She had lost weight to a BMI of 14 and become significantly depressed. She was thought to have an atypical eating disorder with depression. During day care she took liquid food replacement drinks which restored her weight and, to a large extent, her mood and self-esteem improved. She was never able to eat a full diet, although was able to take some soup after a year.

CREATIVE THERAPIES

Anorexia nervosa is a complex set of behaviours. It is also an art form. The patient behaves in such a way that her body adopts certain forms. These forms, like other works of art, convey different messages, depending on the artist, the observer, and, unusually in art, also on the medium (the patient). The message might be very difficult to render in language, but some themes can be discerned, often emerging in psychotherapy. One such theme is a hunger for closeness, and an inability to achieve it. Both elements are well conveyed by a skeletal body. The message is made more poignant when, as sometimes occurs, the patient collects soft toys which can reach hundreds, and whose chubby fluffiness contrast starkly with the patient's own emaciation. Another is a sense of worthlessness and another a denial of sexuality, increasing as the body first becomes boyishly masculine, then losing all sexuality in a skeletal body looking more like a corpse than a woman.

It is no surprise, therefore, that patients often find it difficult to express the way they feel in words. They are, after all, going to a lot of trouble to express their feelings through their bodies. Words often seem pale by comparison. Alternatives to the *sit down and tell me about it* type of therapy are the *show me* therapies. These include art therapy, dance and movement therapy, massage therapy and some techniques used in family work, namely sculpting already described in Chapter 5.

The action therapies have their dangers. Many of the patients are obsessive and perfectionistic and may already have had experience of art and dance. Their tendency is to try and be the best in the group, without allowing themselves to learn. Art therapy can take a number of forms. At the Russell Unit we have two types of art group. One is facilitated by an art therapist, patients are invited to produce some work and then talk about it either privately to the therapist or, preferably, to the group. The other is less 'psychotherapeutic' and is termed 'projective art'. Patients are provided with media for producing work and they may or may not wish to talk about what they have produced. Themes in both forms of art group are repetitive. Perfection is often there, as is an idyllic family scene, often contrasted with a dark area, occupied by the patient, with an uncrossable river or barrier dividing the patient from the idyll. The illness is often depicted as a prison or cage with the patient trapped inside, sometimes being tortured. Perhaps the most striking aspect of the art of patients with anorexia nervosa is the aloneness that emerges from the work, a combination of desperate loneliness and aloof superiority.

In dance and movement therapy, patients are asked to use their bodies publicly. They are encouraged to pull silk scarves, bounce and throw balls and to convey how they feel using physical movement, as well as experimenting with different sorts of movement, which demonstrate ways of being such as confidence or assertiveness that are quite alien. Patients who are quite unable to express aspects of themselves, such as anger, verbally, are able to do so using movement therapy. They also begin to find their bodies again and even to enjoy them.

In massage therapy, patients are seen individually. The problem being addressed is the alienation many patients have from their bodies. They often do not look after their skin, which, as a result of nutritional deficiency as well as lack of care, becomes dry and scaly. The patient often asserts that she actively hates her body and punishes it by failing to care for it. The aim of massage therapy is to reconnect the patient with her, or his, body via massage. The massage therapist sees the patient alone in a quiet room with a couch, and provision for playing music. The initial session will be concentrated on description of the process, an explanation of what is going to occur, and a discussion about body care. The actual massage begins with the least challenging part of the body, usually the hands, and subsequent sessions are planned to coincide with the patient's wishes. Some patients who find the whole process of recognising that they have a body and who are averse to any form of physical contact difficult, find the process of gradually extending massage very liberating, and they may begin to look after their bodies, using creams suggested by the massage therapist, and beginning to have a completely different relationship with their bodies. The massage therapist generally asks patients to complete a visual analogue scale, rating their level of tension at the beginning and end of each session, and almost always finds an improvement. There is some weak evidence in favour of the use of massage therapy in eating disorders and this does appear to be confirmed in our patients, although we have not studied it systematically. Doubts are sometimes raised about the wisdom of using a therapy involving touch in conditions in which a history of sexual abuse is commonly reported, and in which sexual exploitation by therapists is not unknown. This is, of course, a very important consideration. Our approach to it is rooted in our confidence in our massage therapist, in her training, and supervision, and in the belief that were anything untoward to occur, even without the therapist being aware of it, it would be very likely to come to light in the therapy itself, and in other conversations that the patient has with other team members. In our service, massage therapy is rated as one of the most popular treatments, and our view is that it is safe, as long as it is appropriately supervised.

GROUPS AND GROUP PROCESS

Group therapy is an essential part of any day programme. The weekly programme of groups is given in Table 6.2. They vary from groups in which the weekend, unsupported by the day programme, is planned, and then reviewed, to a CBT group for anorexia nervosa, to a psychodynamic open group, as well as the specialised creative therapy groups for art and dance movement. The result is a full programme with a very wide variety of therapeutic approaches. There is ample opportunity for patients to challenge each other and they are encouraged to do so. The balance of the patients in those attending the day hospital is very influential. Usually there are a few patients who are forging ahead with recovery, and this strongly influences the others, who will do their best to join in, even though they may not be able to make as much progress. Some patients in the 'forging ahead' category may be acting out a script they have assumed within their families that they cope with adversity and help the rest of the family through. The anorexia nervosa may have represented a way to escape from the 'super-coper' role. When they appear to be leading the group in recovering, they may need to be reminded that there are, perhaps, some unresolved issues that need to be addressed.

Clinical description 6.4

A patient of 19 was attending the day programme following a brief hospital admission during which she gained weight at a very high rate (2–3 kg per week). In her subsequent day hospital treatment, she continued to gain, although not as quickly. In the groups she took on a therapist role, and did not seem to be dealing with the difficulties that had led to her illness. In her family she had taken the lead at the age of 13 when her father became psychotically depressed and her mother had barely coped. When it was pointed out that, once again, she was sacrificing her own needs for the group she became more introspective, her weight gain ceased for a while, but then resumed as she began to benefit from the group therapy.

Table 6.2 Day Hospital Weekly programme

	Monday	Tuesday	Wednesday	Thursday	Friday
11.15–12.15	Weekend review	Goal planning	Team meeting	Nutrition group (incl Lunch) –1.00	Weekend planning
12.15–1.00			Lunch		
1.00–1.15			After lunch group		
1.45–3.00	Creative art	Art therapy		Expressive group	Open group
			Snack		
3.00–3.30	Relaxation	CBT	Creative group	Social group	
			Supper		
			After supper group		
17.00					
17.30	Carers' support				
19.30	(first Monday of the month)				

Other patients adopt solitary roles, which reflect their own histories and difficulties. Some try to be the best patient (as above) or the worst patient, breaking all the rules, keeping weight down, and passing judgement on other patients for betraying their anorexia by gaining weight, and sometimes on staff for being fat. The latter can be particularly difficult for a staff member who has sensitive issues about weight and shape. Others remain aloof in groups, giving the impression that nothing that is said could ever be of help. One such patient, for example, insisted on flossing her teeth during the post-meal group, without saying anything to contribute to the group. The danger such behaviour courts is of being ostracised by the other patients, often re-enacting the patient's previous role in her family or in her social relationships, and consolidating it in the present. When other patients challenge the behaviour the patient's view of herself as hateful is confirmed. It is up to staff to interpret the process and demonstrate how the behaviour and the group's response reinforce each other in a pattern which is destructive to the patient and can have negative consequences for the group (such as guilt and self-blame) if, for example, they successfully force such a patient out of the day programme.

TEAM MEETINGS

The weekly team meeting (sometimes archaically called the 'ward round' – where is the ward, and who goes round?) has a number of functions. The meeting is split into three. The first hour, 9–10 am, is the Current Concerns meeting (see Chapter 2) during which any patient giving rise to concern is discussed, including newly referred patients not yet seen. From 10 to 10.15 refreshments are brought in, with tea, coffee, biscuits, cheese and whatever other goodies team members have elected to provide. This break certainly involves more high-quality food than is usual at clinical meetings, and may represent the team acting out their wishes for the patients to be eating more. From 10.15 to 12 is the day hospital team meeting, with the first 45 minutes (10.15 to 11.00) devoted to reviewing reports of all the day patients and during the hour from 11 to 12 a proportion (about half) of the day patients are interviewed by the consultant in the presence of necessary team members and their progress is discussed and further plans made. The first part of the day hospital team meeting is attended by all staff who work in the day hospital, as long as they are present at the time. In its entirety, the team meeting is such an important place to exchange information, make referrals within the team, and obtain support and advice, that any worker coming to the team is encouraged to make Wednesday morning one of their sessions.

The reports section is chaired by the day hospital manager and the consultant, and each patient is presented in turn by the key worker, starting with her current weight and changes in weight. A graph of weight over the time the patient has been attending the day hospital is available and is a useful aid in judging progress. Naturally weight is not the only criterion, and psychological and social changes are also reported. If the patient is not gaining weight, however, it is taken as a sign that something needs to change. After the key worker has given her report, other team members report on different aspects of care including behaviour at meal times, issues arising in specific groups including art, dance movement and the psychodynamic open group and other domains including family therapy and massage therapy. The time is quite brief and chairing has to be effective if all patients are to be given approximately equal time in the discussion.

The patient is seen for 10–20 minutes, in the presence of the key worker and all team members relevant to her care. She is asked to agree to students being present and if she does not they are excluded for her interview. If the patient is a local student, other students in the same course are excluded as a matter of course. Relatives are sometimes invited with the consent of the patient to help keep them informed and to talk about issues that affect them such as weekend management. The aim of the interview is to pick up areas that are going well, and to recognise that, and to talk about things that are not going so well, and to develop and agree a plan for dealing with them. Tissues are always available, as sensitive topics are, not unusually, touched upon. Other staff members usually feel free to join in, ask questions or make comments. After the patient has left there will usually be some comments from staff on the helpfulness or otherwise of the interview. Patients are aware that they are expected to be seen in the team meeting every fortnight, and there is a certain amount of trepidation requiring substantial key worker support prior to the meeting. At the meeting the key worker sits beside the patient and acts as a support during the meeting. Patients usually value the meeting, even though they may find it stressful, and regard it as an important opportunity to review their progress. There is often a feeling among staff and patients that the key worker–patient–consultant meeting evokes a mother–daughter–father family group and it may be that at a symbolic level, the process acts as a recapitulation of childhood experience. If so, it is vital that we avoid making the experience controlling or abusive, and emphasise support, encouragement and sympathetic listening, while setting boundaries that help patients/children grow towards health/maturity.

AIN'T MISBEHAVIN': PATIENTS WHO BREAK THE RULES

At the initial assessment it is vital to make it clear what the expectations of the day programme are. Generally a full programme will be arranged, and the patient is expected to attend it all. If there is an unavoidable clash which requires the patient to miss a session, this would need to be discussed with the key worker and agreed with the team. After a two-week assessment period during which motivation is assessed, a decision is made on both sides whether day care is the appropriate treatment at this stage.

The most common problems observed in day hospital care are failure to gain weight and failure to attend the full programme. A number of different patterns of the weight chart are seen:

- Failure to gain above a certain level: weight goes up initially, and then levels out. It may go up one week, but if it breaks through the patient's self-imposed barrier, it goes down the following week. The barrier is usually a numerical one, and is to some extent culture bound. For those still on avoirdupois, it might be 7 stone (44.5 kg), for Europeans it is commonly 40 kg and for Americans it is often 100 lb. For those *cognoscenti* who have consulted the ICD (Internation Classification of Diseases, 10th Edition) it can be a BMI of 17.5. All the levels, apart from the BMI of 14, are in the upper part of the anorexic range, and patients are sometimes fixated on lower barriers such as 6 stone, 35 kg etc.
- Weight goes up to a level, as above, then plateaus, but the patient is looking increasing ill, pale and thin and her SUSS test scores (Chapter 4) are getting lower. In this case, the patient is probably falsifying her weight (see Chapter 4) and should be examined before weighing, and 'spot weighed'. Spot weighing means weighing the patient without warning, and takes considerable assertiveness on the part of staff.
- Weight goes up and down substantially (saw tooth pattern). This is usually an indication that the patient is gaining weight by bingeing and losing it by purging. Keep an eye on her electrolytes and discuss her meal pattern. She may require specific therapy aimed at curbing bulimia nervosa.
- Weight goes up gradually then takes off, rising by several kilograms every week. This suggests that weight gain and improved nutrition have triggered the development of binge eating. It is frightening for the patient and quite difficult to control. It tends to level off as a healthy weight has been reached. Patients with a history of being overweight may find that weight tends to stabilise at the previous level.

A plan for managing failure to gain weight depends on the circumstances. If a patient has a chronic disorder (over 10 years) and has joined the day programme in an attempt to gain weight which has proved impossible, it may be best to accept that she is at a low but stable weight and that outpatient support may be the most useful approach. If weight is very low

(BMI 14 or below) it may be worth considering more intensive measures such as weekend support, family therapy directed at weight gain, and if these measures are impractical or unsuccessful, to consider hospitalisation (Chapter 8) until BMI is, say 15, and try again. If the patient's motivation is evenly balanced between change and staying the same, it may be worth giving her a period of 'time out' of the programme, say for a week, and for her then to return and indicate whether she wishes to terminate day care or come back with a commitment to gain a minimum amount of weight, say 0.5 kg per week. If after four weeks this has not happened, she would be discharged to outpatient care. It is important to avoid labelling the patient as a failure for not achieving weight goals. She will already have labelled herself as a failure, as well as regarding herself as a success for avoiding weight gain. To what extent can someone be held responsible for symptoms of an eating disorder? This is an important question because it determines to some extent how the patient is treated. If a patient fails to gain weight because she undereats and exercises at the weekends, is she responsible or is it anorexia? The answer is that sometimes it makes sense to give the first answer and sometimes the second, and sometimes to combine the two. The argument has something in common with the political left–right dialectic between those regarding our actions as determined by genetics and environment, and those who posit free will. One approach to the weight gain problem might be for the team to convey to the patient a statement such as the following:

Anorexia leads you to engage in behaviours which prevent weight gain. We want to encourage and strengthen that side of you which wants to gain weight and so lead a more normal life. At present anorexia has the upper hand. We believe that if we demand of you that you gain weight as a condition of attending the day programme, this will strengthen the non-anorexic side and help you move forward.

This partly externalises anorexia, that is, it defines it as an alien force. However, it must also be acknowledged that anorexia often feels to the patient anything but alien. The more the patient believes that her ultra thin self is 'me' the lower the motivation to change, even if the patient acknowledges that her physical health could be better if she gained weight.

Patients who fail to attend the full programme as agreed have a meeting with the key worker, and, perhaps, the day hospital manager to see if a modified programme, acceptable to both sides can be agreed. If not the matter goes to the day hospital team meeting and a decision on whether the patient should continue in day care is made after consultation with the patient. Naturally, further treatment to replace day care depends on the physical and mental state of the patient but might include regular physical monitoring and individual therapy.

INVOLVING RELATIVES AND CARERS

Adults over 18 have the right to exclude members of their family from any or all aspects of their care, even if they are residing with the family, who therefore are in daily contact with the patient and the evidence of her illness including weight loss, bingeing, vomiting and self-harm. This naturally causes much disquiet for families, especially parents, and as a group, parents of patients with eating disorders have quite reasonably demanded more information about their children's treatment so that they can be more adept at dealing with the disorders as they manifest at home. Professionals dealing with eating disorders must tread a narrow path between breaking confidentiality and excluding relatives. Most patients are not averse to their relatives being part of treatment, and in such a case, the family, including parents, siblings and partners can attend family therapy, the family support group, multifamily groups and parental or partner counselling sessions. It is important to observe the rule that no information given by the patient in other contexts must be revealed in a family session unless the patient has given prior consent. If the patient does not give consent for family therapy, she may still allow her parents to be seen for support and counselling, as long as information about her history and physical state, especially her weight, is not disclosed. In the extreme situation in which the patient is adamantly against all contact, parents can attend information sessions provided by organisations such as the Eating Disorders Association, unrelated to the clinic treating their daughter, in which questions about eating disorders can be raised without specific reference to the patient in question.

The team meeting, in which the patient is seen, is a context in which families can be included, informed and advised, with the patient's consent, and usually in her presence. In England, a system called the Care Programme Approach (CPA) has been developed (Chapter 7) in which the patient, carers (usually family or partner, occasionally friends) and professionals meet to establish the care programme and to identify who will be responsible for each element of it. As part of the CPA, there is provision for a carer's assessment, in which carers can state their own needs in caring for the individual with the disorder, and services have to meet those needs if possible and reasonable.

DISCHARGE

When weight is increasing steadily, and the patient has reached a BMI of 17 or so, she may wish to consider life beyond the day programme. In a patient whose social and occupational life is intact, she may start by arranging a morning or afternoon back at her job. If she agrees, a letter to the employer approved by the patient can be helpful. It is important to emphasise to the patient that she is still unwell, and that continued weight gain is expected. A patient whose occupational links have been broken by chronic anorexia nervosa will need a rehabilitation approach (Chapter 9) and voluntary work, attendance at a sheltered workshop and, perhaps, referral to a hostel, may all be relevant. If weight has increased to a BMI of 19 and menstruation has not resumed, it is useful to request a pelvic ultrasound scan (Chapter 4) to monitor ovulation and help determine healthy weight.

Discharge from the day programme is usefully staged over a number of months, with groups and meals gradually dropped and a final discharge date set well in advance. During this process a CPA meeting, which should occur whenever there is a major change in treatment, is arranged and outpatient treatment planned.

EFFECTIVENESS

The effectiveness of a service for anorexia nervosa can look at body weight, BMI, menstrual function, social and occupational functioning, depression and eating disorder symptoms. These should be measured before and after treatment, and compared with a control group receiving non-day care treatment, such as inpatient care or outpatient treatment. Unfortunately such a controlled study does not exist as yet. However, we can look at apparent functioning by examining a single service, looking at the above outcomes, and including patient and carer satisfaction rating. At the Russell Unit we collect some of this data and will present it here.

Audit of all patients referred to the service in a year

In an audit of patients referred in 2002 the numbers of patients being treated in different locations were as follows:

- Total number assessed: 176
- Outpatient treatment only: 156
- Outpatient and day patient treatment: 15
- Outpatient, day patient and inpatient: 6

Amongst the 15 day patients, the Eating Disorders Inventory, (EDI) (Garner, Olmstead & Polivy (1983)), and the Bulimia Investigatory Test Edinburgh (BITE) (Henderson & Freeman (1987)) symptom and severity scores but not the Beck Depression Inventory (BDI) (Beck, Ward, Mendelson, Mock & Erbaugh (1961)) depression rating, reduced significantly.

Day hospital outcome audit

A further audit of all 24 patients with anorexia nervosa (22 females, 2 males) discharged from the day hospital between January 2001 and December 2005 and followed up a variable time after discharge demonstrated the following:

History of previous specialist treatment: 18/24, i.e. this was a severely ill group.

Duration of day treatment: 58.5 weeks + 9.96 (standard error)
Follow up period (from discharge): 34.6 weeks + 7.77
BMI on admission: 14.5 + 0.46
BMI on discharge: 16.5 + 0.54
BMI at follow up: 16.9 + 0.55
Analysis of variance of BMI on admission with repeated measures at discharge and at follow up:
$F(2,71) = 20.6$, $p<0.0001$
Post-hoc analyses:
Admission BMI vs Discharge BMI: $p<0.01$ (Tukey's test).
Admission BMI vs Follow up BMI: $p<0.01$.
Discharge BMI vs Follow up BMI: Non-significant.

Admissions during day care:
10 to Specialist Inpatient Eating Disorders Unit (SIEDU)
1 to Medical Ward and SIEDU
1 to General Psychiatric ward
Analysis of variance of BMI on admission with repeated measures at discharge and at follow up comparing patients admitted with those not admitted:
Admitted vs not admitted: $F(1,71) = 1.66$, $p>.2$
Time $F(2,71) = 21.9$, $p<0.0001$
Interaction, Admitted by Time: $F(2,71) = 2.44$ $p = 0.1$

Menstrual outcome:
Menstruation in 7/22 female patients
BMI >17 at follow up: in 13/24
Conclusions

The vast majority (89%) of patients with anorexia nervosa were treated as outpatients. Those attending the day hospital showed improvements in weight and in eating disorder symptoms. About half the patients attending the day hospital were admitted at some time during their day hospital care. As a group the day hospital patients had already had specialist treatment, spent about a year in day care and significantly improved their BMIs, and those admitted did slightly, but not significantly, worse than those not admitted. About a third of patients were menstruating at a mean of 8 months follow up and about half had a BMI over 17. Lastly, although there was some improvement in BMI between discharge from the Day Hospital and follow up the change in BMI was not significant.

Chapter 7

LIAISON AND OUTREACH

INTRODUCTION

Sometimes the complexity of a patient's problems demands a degree of flexibility and creativity from the eating disorders service so that her needs can be fully met. Some conditions seem to be in an unholy alliance with each other, intensifying and perpetuating each other's symptoms. Diabetes mellitus, combined with an eating disorder, provides a good example. Diabetes causes weight loss, depression and poor self-esteem and its treatment leads to weight gain and dietary restriction all of which may have adverse consequences in a patient with an eating disorder. Anorexia and bulimia nervosa, by dietary restriction or loss of control, can profoundly affect diabetic control and lead to repeated diabetic coma and early appearance of complications such as blindness, kidney problems and neuropathy. These, in turn, by increasing chaos and decreasing self-esteem, can exacerbate the eating disorder. Similar alliances can be discerned between eating disorders and other physical conditions such as inflammatory bowel disease, conditions of uncertain diagnostic home such as irritable bowel syndrome and chronic fatigue syndrome, substance misuse disorders, personality disorders, especially with deliberate self-harm and psychiatric disorders such as depression, obsessive compulsive disorder and psychosis. Management of patients with these combinations of problems can be very challenging. It can be helpful to appoint a team member whose main responsibility is to liaise with other teams (liaison role) and to arrange visits to patients who are at high risk but are unable to make it to the clinic. The two roles not infrequently overlap, for example in the case of a patient with chronic fatigue syndrome and anorexia nervosa who may require home treatment from both chronic fatigue syndrome and eating disorder services, so that it makes clinical sense to integrate treatment and visit the patient together.

LIAISON EATING DISORDERS PSYCHIATRY

This section is organised according to the team charged with handling the non-eating disorder condition. The variety of settings for liaison work is wide. Within the psychiatric field are community mental health teams (CMHTs), psychiatric inpatient units, child and adolescent and drug and alcohol services. Liaison with units in the rest of medicine can bring the worker in contact with general practitioners, medical inpatient and outpatient and obstetric and gynaecology services. The work is stimulating because of this variety, but it is also a challenge to learn so many languages! The sources of referrals representing the majority of cases are depicted in Figure 7.1. The following discussion covers the professional sources. Work with patients and carers is discussed under outreach (p. 138).

Community mental health teams

The most significant factor determining whether a community mental health team (CMHT) is involved in treatment is the referral pathway (see Chapter 1). If all referrals have to come via the local CMHT then it is fairly

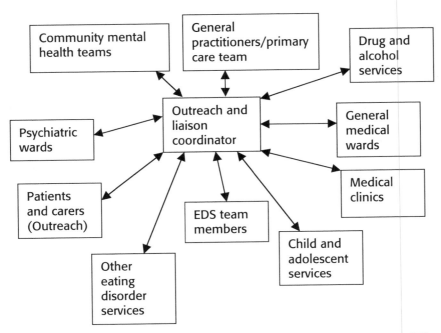

Figure 7.1   Map of an Eating Disorders Liaison and Outreach Service (EDLOS)

likely that the team will accept some responsibility for the patient's care. If they refuse there can be a number of processes at play. They may consider that the problems presented by the patient do not meet their threshold for working with a patient. In order to limit the constituency of people who have a call on their limited resources CMHTs need to set a fairly high threshold of severity so that the 'worried well' do not exhaust their resources, and this is right. Sometimes patients with eating disorders who should meet these criteria are deemed not to because of an ignoble mixture of ignorance, fear and prejudice. When this occurs, it is a good idea to talk with the team manager who usually acts as the gatekeeper, and try to get invited to a referrals meeting where you can put the case for the patient receiving CMHT services.

The eating disorder service should develop its own ideas of the sort of patient who should be co-managed. The list of criteria may include:

1. Patients with multiple problems including eating disorder, deliberate self-harm, suicide attempts, substance misuse.
2. Patients with social problems such as homelessness, or a need to move accommodation and difficulties with financial benefits.
3. Patients with chronic illness requiring rehabilitation (see Chapter 9) beyond the resources available to the eating disorder service.
4. Patients with very severe eating disorder requiring frequent medical and psychiatric hospitalisations, or those recently discharged after long-term hospitalisation.

Once the patient has been accepted by the team there are several pitfalls to avoid in co-working. The most common is splitting, 'But Dr X says I don't need to put on any weight!' The next is disagreements between the teams, 'I'm a qualified social worker and should have been invited to any discussion about the patient!' Perhaps the most dangerous is each team thinking the other will be doing something, 'We look after her depression and the eating disorders team look after her weight'. All these problems have occurred in our experience and could have been avoided by better communication.

The initial meeting about the patient is the most important and, if it is missed out or mishandled, subsequent meetings will be patching up a poorly done job. First, the correct individuals must be invited. Sometimes a patient is discharged from hospital to a mental health team without the eating disorder service even being involved. The shortlist for the meeting should be:

- the patient
- a relative

- a key worker from the currently responsible team
- a prospective key worker from the receiving CMHT
- a liaison worker from the eating disorders team
- the general practitioner
- consultant psychiatrists from all three teams.

The agenda must include:

- main areas of risk.
- proposed management of each area, including the name of each responsible worker.
- warning signs of relapse, proposed management if such signs are detected and names of individuals responsible for detection and action.

A fictitious but illustrative case example follows:

Clinical description 7.1

Mary is an 18-year-old woman who is being discharged after eight months in a private eating disorders unit for treatment of anorexia nervosa. A meeting, one month before discharge, was arranged according to the above-mentioned guidelines. A professionals meeting was held just before the formal discharge meeting. It was clear that, although Mary was near a healthy weight, she had been extremely resistant to treatment as an inpatient and was at high risk of relapse.

A care coordinator was allocated from the CMHT. Mary was to see a therapist from the eating disorders team on a weekly basis. If she failed to attend a session, and did not attend when contacted, a nurse from the general practice would visit her armed with a weighing machine. Her GP agreed to monitor medication and blood tests. A follow-up meeting was planned for three months hence. Signs of relapse were agreed to be falling weight and action agreed in such a case was an urgent review by the eating disorders team doctor and discussion with the consultant.

In English psychiatric practice, the document resulting from the first meeting is known as the Care Programme Approach (CPA) form and this document follows the structure outlined as follows:

- demographic details
- problem areas

- action proposed
- staff member responsible for monitoring and implementing plan
- responsible psychiatrist
- any unmet needs
- detection of relapse
- action in the event of relapse
- names and contact information on all those present and relevant individuals not present.

Troubleshooting guide:

- Problem: the patient refuses to see the eating disorder service key worker, but will see the CMHT key worker or the GP.
- Risk: the danger here is that the patient is being followed by a non-specialist who may not be as knowledgeable about risk factors.
- Action: the frontline worker must be intensively educated and supervised by the eating disorder service worker, preferably a senior nurse who may have the role of managing the liaison service. Concentrate on essential information that will give a clear idea of how at risk the patient is. Use the guidance given in Chapter 4 on risk management. Lastly, treat non-attendance at monitoring sessions as a reason to consult urgently and to find a way of seeing the patient for monitoring.

Perhaps the most important aspect of the care of a patient considered at risk who seems to be evading attempts at monitoring is to generate a high and rising level of anxiety about her welfare and for one senior individual, generally the consultant psychiatrist in eating disorders, to demand information (accepting the fact that people may see him as difficult) until he is satisfied that the risks are being adequately managed.

- Problem: the patient is being monitored regularly, has lost some weight but is now maintaining. It is decided to try and avoid another admission so close to her discharge from a long stay in hospital. However, her parents are extremely anxious and constantly press for admission.
- Risk: well, they may be right! Parents are well placed to assess the needs of their child, and we must never arrogantly dismiss their views. There are occasions, however, when rising anxiety in the parents is related to unresolved family issues rather than the realistic risk to the patient. A parent whose child has had repeated admissions since childhood may have learnt to deal with anxiety by seeking admission, and it may be extremely difficult to break that mould.

Clinical description 7.2

A patient aged 18 who had been in psychiatric units since the age of 12 had been discharged from an eating disorders facility six months before she was referred to the Russell Unit. She was not grossly underweight although she suffered from bulimia nervosa. She found the outpatient and day programme difficult to cope with and made veiled threats of self-harm. Her mother found the anxiety unbearable and persuaded a local consultant psychiatrist to admit her to another inpatient eating disorders facility who were unable to discharge her after two years.

In this case, the mother was determined for her daughter to be readmitted and recruited another system to achieve that end. It demonstrates the importance of working with the family and with colleagues and the unpalatable truth that such liaison sometimes does not work.

- Problem: the patient with a very long history peppered with hospital admissions is discharged to a flat. She has major needs in a number of areas including general support at home, and psychiatric rehabilitation as well as help with diet, food purchasing and preparation and weight maintenance. The eating disorders team contact the CMHT and ask for help. The CMHT turns down the referral on two grounds. First anorexia nervosa is not severe enough for their service. Secondly they know nothing about eating disorders and would not know how to manage the patient.
- Risk: the patient could be managed by the eating disorder service, but would then miss out on some very important aspects of rehabilitation and probably end up in hospital again.
- Action: this is mainly an issue of training and attitudes. Many health workers, including those in psychiatry, hold the view that eating disorders are rather trivial problems presented by silly rich girls who diet too much. This form of stigma is best approached by visiting the team, explaining the problems that the patient presents and arranging to see the patient together with a member of the CMHT. Staff who have actually met and got to know the history of a patient with a severe chronic eating disorder will often modify such prejudicial views.

Psychiatric inpatient units

Patients with psychiatric illness in medical or surgical wards, especially if they have harmed themselves, are often treated with hostility and may not receive proper care, being discharged as quickly as possible so that a more deserving patient with a 'proper' illness can be admitted. At a different level of the health system (see fractals, p. 102) patients with certain diagnoses in psychiatric wards receive less sympathy than others from psychiatric staff ('We've got a ward full of acutely psychotic patients and this manipulative anorexic is giving staff the run around'. Comment by a consultant psychiatrist about a patient with bulimic anorexia nervosa on the ward). These diagnoses include eating disorders, personality disorders and drug and alcohol dependence. Why do patients with eating disorders attract opprobrium from staff whose role is to care for the sick? The public believe that people with eating disorders, along with drug and alcohol addicts, are responsible for their disorder, and should pull themselves together. People with eating disorders are very challenging to treat, often trying to maintain a low body weight, by hiding food, falsifying weight by drinking large amounts of liquid, or by interfering with weighing machines (see Tricks of the trade, Chapter 4, p. 69). As a result, staff can find themselves with a very sick patient who has deteriorated under their eyes, and who might die as a result. This is very serious stuff. The death of a psychiatric patient is usually treated as unnatural, and is accompanied by exhaustive and distressing enquiries, often critical of staff. Not too surprising, then, that mental health workers in general units feel ill-equipped to deal with such patients, and if they have to without adequate training and support, they feel resentful and angry, feelings which sometimes translate into negative attitudes towards the patient herself.

Patients with eating disorders can only be managed in general psychiatric units if a specialised team of doctors and nurses is available to provide specific eating disorders input. The main business of inpatient psychiatric wards is increasingly to deal with patients with acute psychosis who, because of the risk to themselves or others, cannot be managed in the community. The skills of such an inpatient psychiatric team are, therefore, greatest in the treatment of this group and range from close observation of those at risk of suicide, control and restraint of patients with violence as a result of paranoid or manic illnesses, support for patients receiving psychiatric treatments such as medication and ECT and involuntary hospitalisation and treatment. Patients with severe eating disorders requiring hospitalisation might be treated by a general service if the nutritional problems, specifically low weight and hypokalaemia, are stable and do not require specific eating disorders input such as supervised meals and close observation to prevent purging. Admissions to such a service are likely to be triggered by clinical problems other than the nutritional such as suicidal behaviour or intent or severe deliberate self-harm.

In a number of services, specialist eating disorder beds have been established in general psychiatric wards. The patients are nursed by general mental health nurses, and there is always a specialist eating disorders trained senior nurse on duty to supervise the work of the more junior staff. Consultant responsibility is taken by an individual consultant with a special interest in eating disorders psychiatry, rather than a series of general psychiatrists, and junior medical staff are supervised and trained by that consultant. Weekly team meetings are held for the eating disordered inpatients.

In other services in which beds have been established on general psychiatric wards, there has been substantial pressure to move to a separate, dedicated unit. These pressures come from a variety of sources. Patients with eating disorders are perceived, and perceive themselves, as different from the general psychiatric population, and it is the case that our waif-like patients do seem out of place in general wards which contain a minority of patients, more often male, who may be threatening, especially to a young female patient. The problem of harassment of female patients in general by males has resulted in the establishment of separate inpatient facilities for women in many hospitals, and these may be more suitable for, at least, the female patients with anorexia nervosa who require inpatient care. The other pressure, more subtle, has been that because many areas lack their own inpatient facilities, a dedicated inpatient unit can attract outside funding by offering inpatient services to those areas, which is very attractive to management, and which can lead to a miraculous improvement in attitude to eating disorders when the balance sheets appear in management meetings.

In the Russell Unit, we have done our best to avoid admissions and to resist establishing our own beds so that we can be free of the financial inducements of a specialist inpatient service. As will be discussed at length in Chapter 8, we have established that between three and four inpatient beds are required per million. Where those beds should be is a matter for discussion. If eating disorders care is rationalised, it is likely that community services will be established for smaller populations, say 1 million, and inpatient units for larger areas of 5–10 million population. Some patients will still require general psychiatric admission and liaison with the general psychiatric staff will continue to be required.

General medical inpatient units

Admission to a general medical ward (see Chapter 8) for treatment of severe malnutrition or electrolyte disturbance can be life-saving. In order for it to be successful, eating disorder and medical services need to be speaking a language each understands. It is probably fair to say that many eating disorder psychiatrists could know more about nutrition, and physicians could know more about eating disorders. Mutual distrust still unfortunately exists between medicine and psychiatry, and reflects society's misconceptions. In the UK, psychiatric services have moved away from medicine and towards social services, with movement from hospitals into community locations and this has disrupted the 'corridor culture' which facilitated communication between physicians and psychiatrists in management meetings and canteens as well as corridors. Liaison between eating disorder services and the medical team has, therefore, become even more essential. In the following case, the opinion of the eating disorder service was not effectively transmitted to the medical team, with disastrous results for the patient.

Clinical description 7.3

A 20-year-old patient with an eight-year history of anorexia nervosa was transferred from an inpatient eating disorders unit to a medical unit because of persistent low BMI (<12) resistant to treatment. The medical unit was requested to tube feed the patient against her will. The patient seemed in excellent health apart from the catastrophically low BMI, and wandered around the medical ward greeting other patients, who were often confined to bed, with a smile. The physician did not think that forced feeding was ethical, even under the Mental Health Act. Arrangements were therefore made for the patient to be transferred to a specialist inpatient eating disorders unit (SIEDU). On the weekend prior to transfer the patient, who was receiving 'special' nursing from two nurses who did not have experience in treating eating disorders, starved and micro-exercised (see Chapter 4) continuously and on Monday morning fell into a hypoglycaemic coma which she did not survive.

This tragic case teaches us a number of lessons, as do all deaths. For the psychiatrist, be as assertive as you need to be to persuade your colleague, not specialist in your field, to follow your advice. For the medical consultant, do not be misled by the apparent health of patients with anorexia nervosa. They may be driven to overexercising to the point of death. They may appear mentally sound, and they may be so in every area but this one compulsion to be thin which will kill them. Avoid compulsory treatment when you can, and use it when you have to. For the SIEDU, extend medical care of your patients as far as you can. I would suggest that most patients who do not require an intravenous infusion or a cardiac monitor should be manageable on a SIEDU. This means that expertise and equipment for passage of a nasogastric tube must be available, the expertise kept up to date with training and the equipment regularly inspected and updated.

A particular problem in a patient admitted to a medical unit is refeeding syndrome (RFS). This occurs when a profoundly malnourished patient is provided oral, nasogastric or parenteral nutrition. It is described in Chapter 8. It is caused by electrolytes travelling into cells as soon as food, specifically glucose, is available and the most dangerous changes are hypokalaemia and hypophosphataemia. Phosphate is probably also depleted by rapid synthesis of adenosine triphosphate, the substance the body uses to convey energy to cells, as soon as glucose levels increase. These changes can vary rapidly and patients at risk should have daily monitoring of electrolytes, including phosphate and magnesium, on a daily basis until the clinical team decides to monitor less frequently. From the point of view of liaison in eating disorders psychiatry the question is, 'Who constitutes the clinical team?' and it is very important that discussions take place at an early stage, preferably prior to any admission, to agree the following.

Consultant responsibility is shared by the general physician and the eating disorders psychiatrist. This means that instructions from *either* consultant (e.g. frequency of monitoring in RFS) must be followed. Any inconsistency must be resolved the same day.

On admission, clear goals for the admission should be set (e.g. BMI >14, potassium stable on oral treatment for >3 days, normal ECG for 2 days) and recorded clearly in the medical notes. Reviews of the patient should include a representative of the eating disorders service (be aware that this may require attendance at 8 am, unusual in a psychiatric setting!). Consultant notes on the management plan should be updated at least twice weekly. A discharge date should not be set without the approval of the eating disorders psychiatrist.

Liaison with other medical services

Our patients may turn up at a number of other clinics, sometimes without telling us.

Clinical description 7.4

A 32-year-old patient with moderate anorexia nervosa (BMI 17) withdrew from outpatient follow up while she pursued fertility treatment on a private basis. She became pregnant with twins after clomiphene (hormone stimulating) treatment. Her nutrition during pregnancy was poor, and the twins grew at a sub-optimal rate. Both died soon after birth in a special care baby unit.

Clinical description 7.5

A 25-year-old patient was attending monthly outpatient follow up and had gained weight from a BMI of 15 to 17. She was feeling increasingly uncomfortable with her weight and withdrew from outpatient treatment. She attended a gastroenterology clinic for treatment of irritable bowel syndrome (abdominal pain, bloating, diarrhoea) and was prescribed dietary treatment, namely wheat exclusion. Unfortunately this resulted in rapid weight loss and the gastroenterologist contacted the psychiatrist requesting urgent resumption of psychiatric care. The patient subsequently required urgent medical inpatient care for extreme weight loss with hypothermia and ECG changes at a BMI of 12.5.

These two cases have a number of lessons for both eating disorder specialist and non-eating disorder specialist. In the first case the patient was determined both to achieve a pregnancy and avoid too much weight gain. The fertility specialist was probably aware of the dangers to the foetus of pregnancy in a woman of poor nutrition, but may have been influenced by the desperation of the patient. It may also have been a factor that the fertility treatment was provided in private rather than national health care and this may have shifted the odds in favour of providing a treatment that was of arguable advisability. In countries in which private care is the norm, such as France or the USA, such occurrences might be more common. When it is known that the patient is consulting another physician, discussion of the case with that physician can be helpful. In the second case the patient was being given treatment for one condition (IBS) which adversely influenced the outcome of the eating disorder. The psychiatrist was unaware of the medical consultations, and the medical consultant would have been advised to keep the psychiatrist aware of treatment changes and, particularly, changes in the physical state of the patient.

This problem is not uncommon, and consultation is frequently impossible, usually because the patient prevents it from happening, dividing her carers in order to rule them. Action at a higher level in the system may well be required. In the UK a system of Royal Colleges has (for the time being) a certain influence on the training of doctors in different specialities. Consultation between the Royal College of Psychiatrists and those of Obstetricians and Gynaecologists, and Physicians could be helpful in laying down some rules for their members to consider, perhaps publishing leading articles in relevant national journals. That this has not yet occurred is, perhaps, an indication that impediments to collaboration continue to exist.

Two areas of medicine that our patients access commonly are diabetes and pregnancy care. Diabetes and eating disorders are dread companions, as has already been mentioned. Patients with bulimia nervosa omit insulin as a way of purging calories. The lack of insulin allows the blood glucose to rise above the level at which glucose 'spills' into the urine and is lost to the body just as surely as if the food had been vomited. However, the rise in blood glucose triggers a number of other chemical changes that can result in the condition DKA (diabetic ketoacidosis), which often requires hospital admission and which carries a high mortality. Thus, whenever patients omit insulin to purge calories, they are running a high risk of DKA and possible death. If it happens regularly then over a few years the chance of a fatal outcome is high. Diabetes can present diagnostic problems for the eating disorders specialist. Missing out insulin happens commonly in adolescents and young adults with diabetes, and when that practice leads regularly to high blood glucose a substantial amount of glucose can be lost in urine, and weight loss ensues, as it does in untreated diabetes. The weight loss may be enough to stop menstruation, so that two criteria for anorexia nervosa (self-imposed weight loss and amenorrhoea) are satisfied. The question of whether an eating disorder is present therefore rests on the third criterion, body image disturbance. This is, however, sometimes denied in patients with undoubted anorexia nervosa and is inferred from behaviour intended to keep weight low. Hence the difficulty in diabetes, if the patient denies any problem with her body image and denies that the reason for her omission of insulin is to do with keeping her weight down. The importance of the distinction is that if the condition does not fall within the diagnostic area of an eating disorder, then it could be argued that the general psychiatric or psychological service should be providing the mental health input. In our experience eating disorder services are usually involved, even though the patients may not fulfil strict eating disorder criteria.

Patients with eating disorders may, of course, get pregnant. If they are normal weight, and suffering from bulimia nervosa, the eating disorder often remits or improves during pregnancy and returns after the baby is born, when the patient is faced with trying to recapture her previous body shape. The role of the eating disorders key worker is to support the patient through pregnancy and treat the likely but not inevitable postpartum relapse. In anorexia nervosa there is evidence that low maternal weight and nutrition leads to poor foetal growth, low birth weight and increased perinatal mortality (Treasure & Russell, 1988). The risk appears to be greatest in the last trimester although whether this is due to increased restriction by the patient in the face of a burgeoning abdomen is unknown. In practice the obstetricians are well advised to monitor foetal growth more frequently than in the case of normal pregnancies, especially in the last trimester. A letter to the consultant obstetrician (from the consultant psychiatrist) referring to the literature can be helpful.

After the birth the issues are to do with the patient's anxiety about her size, and difficulties in feeding the baby. Little is known about the impact of lactation on a woman with an eating disorder, although it could be predicted that a proportion will wish to avoid breast feeding in order to limit the size of their breasts, while others might encourage lactation as a way of using up calories. It is known that at one year, women with eating disorders of various types (anorexia, bulimia and atypical forms) have difficulty in feeding their infants (Stein et al., 2001), find mealtimes very stressful and are intolerant of mess at mealtimes (a particular disability when a toddler with a bent plastic spoon is using the bowl of pureed food as a percussion instrument). Most worryingly, they sometimes perceive their (normal weight) babies as fat and may attempt to slim them by giving them diluted feeds. In the worst cases infant malnutrition and growth retardation can occur and this effect seems to be most marked in female children (Treasure & Russell, 1988; Hodes, Timimi, & Robinson, 1997).

In any patient with an eating disorder who becomes pregnant, the eating disorders team needs to set up liaison with the obstetric team before the birth, attending at least some ante-natal appointments with the patient, and partner if he and she wish, and to be in touch with the GP and health visitor (in the UK) and, elsewhere, with the family physician and the person responsible for monitoring the health of the new baby. The key signs to look for are as follows:

- Foetal growth problems. Using ultrasound, the head size and femur length of the foetus can be measured and plotted in a graph. The measurements, relative to the normal population, can be expressed as a *percentile* that is, the percentage of the population with that level. The average being the 50th percentile and abnormally low and high levels being under the 5th and over the 95th percentiles. The percentile follows a curve and the norm is to stay on that curve. If foetal growth fails to follow a percentile curve and crosses to a lower curve, this is an indication that growth may be slowing. The nutrition of the mother will need to be looked into as a matter of urgency, and admission to a specialist eating disorders setting considered in order to improve nutrition for the remainder of pregnancy.
- Feeding and growth problems in the baby and child. Most women with eating disorders are aware of their difficulties with the nutrition of their baby and welcome the opportunity to discuss it and to have some practice feeding sessions with a therapist in order to identify and address some of the difficulties. Involving the partner can also be helpful. If the patient is not cooperative and the child is growing poorly (crossing growth percentiles post-natally) contact child psychiatry or paediatrics and arrange for an assessment of the child. The end result might be involvement of social services and care procedures in order to protect the child.
- General psychological disturbance in the child. In addition to problems with feeding, growth and weight there seems to be an increased

likelihood of conduct and emotional disorder in the children of women (there are no studies of men) with eating disorders. The eating disorders team needs to maintain an awareness of such problems so that advice can be conveyed to the GP to arrange child psychiatric referral if required.

Lastly, patients who are severely obese (BMI >40) may be referred to a surgeon with an interest in bariatric (i.e. weight reducing) surgery, usually laparascopic gastric banding or an intestinal bypass procedure for patients with very high BMIs. It is extremely useful to have a good relationship with a skilled surgeon in this speciality. Fortunately, health purchasers in the UK are realising that investment in this form of surgery can save substantial health care costs (as well as suffering for the patient) by reducing the risk of diabetes mellitus, arthritis and heart and respiratory disease and more such surgical treatments are being funded. The surgeons require psychiatric support both preoperatively, to ensure that any eating disorder has been adequately treated and to establish that the patient is in a reasonable psychological state prior to surgery, and postoperatively to help with some of the difficulties a proportion of the patients have, including eating disorders modified by the operation. Our policy has been to accept for assessment and treatment patients who have, or who are suspected to have, eating disorders (we hand out the DSH IV criteria for binge eating disorder quite liberally). Screening for psychiatric disorder, including eating disorders, could be done by general psychiatric services, but is probably better arranged via a session with an eating disorders psychiatrist (funded by the surgical budget) to provide both eating disorder and general screening, assessment and treatment.

Liaison with general practitioners

Many of the issues in relation to GP liaison have already been covered. One of the strengths of the National Health Service is the network of general practitioners that serve the whole population and act as gatekeepers to specialist care. As a result, once a patient is referred to specialist care they have already been assessed by the GP and the latter is usually in a good position to share responsibility for care. This is seen, in other systems (e.g. in the USA) as an infraction of the patient's freedom to choose their own doctor. However, in a system in which the whole population has free access to all medical care, specialist care, being limited, has to be reserved only for people who require it. Some eating disorders can be treated in primary care. Treasure et al. (1996) have shown that a significant proportion of patients with bulimia nervosa can be helped using guided self-help. In this model the patient is given a treatment manual and is seen briefly by a therapist in order to support the self-help programme and monitor progress. Counsellors in primary care may well be suited to provide this sort of guidance, although they need training in the process in order to do so.

GPs often see patients who undoubtedly have eating disorders but who are unwilling to attend specialist services. The eating disorder service can support the GP by offering to discuss such patients, and suggesting that the assessment can take place in the surgery, together with the GP.

Clinical description 7.6

A young woman with severe anorexia nervosa (BMI 14) refused to be seen at the hospital-based specialist service. She was seen by the consultant, with the GP, in the surgery over several months and eventually admitted to hospital for treatment.

GPs can have a very important role in monitoring patients with eating disorders and alerting specialist services when required.

Clinical description 7.7

A 47-year-old patient had been suffering from severe anorexia nervosa since the age of 19. She worked as an administrator and usually managed to maintain a BMI of 13. She was seen fortnightly by her GP for weighing, SUSS (see Chapter 4) and bloods. The eating disorders consultant saw her every three months. Her mother developed a terminal illness and the patient lost weight. The GP contacted the consultant who saw her earlier and advised the GP on criteria for hospital admission.

The GP has to cover a vast range of conditions, and will generally find it useful to have available a clear guide to use in a number of situations:

- Physical monitoring of anorexia nervosa (see Chapter 4).
- A list of self-help manuals for bulimia nervosa.
- A reading list including self-help leaflets for patients with eating disorders and their families.
- Diagnosis of binge eating disorder to use when considering whether to refer patients with obesity.

Lastly, given the high rate of eating disorders in the population (about 10 000 in a population of 1 million served by an eating disorders service) and the low level of specialist treatment (about 1000 treated over five years in a specialist service) many patients with eating disorders are, if they accept treatment at all, being seen in primary care. Specialist services should provide adequate support to primary care, even if it is just telephone availability to discuss a difficult case.

Drug and alcohol teams

When a patient with an eating disorder combined with a serious drug problem is referred the eating disorder service is faced with a dilemma. To the patient, her eating and drug problems are just two of the sets of behaviours she uses in order to feel good, or, at least, not so awful. To the agencies, the expertise to look after her is split between eating disorder and drug and alcohol services. To be sure, treating a patient with CBT for bulimia nervosa when she arrives at sessions stoned or drunk is very difficult. She has to get 'clean' before the CBT–BN can start. She could be referred to substance misuse services while she is placed on the waiting list for individual or group therapy, in the hope that she will be off substances when she is allocated for therapy. The problems with this approach are first that substance misuse services are not always interested in patients who are not either on heroin or cocaine, or addicted to alcohol. Those with problem drinking or heavy cannabis abuse may not receive very much help. Secondly substance misuse services, like Alcoholics Anonymous, may not suit everyone, and, as they often work with self-referral rather than agency referral, motivation on the part of the patient is extremely important, as it is in eating disorders treatment, so the patient may not get to treatment for her drug problem, but still turn up with major eating difficulties.

This is a difficult problem to solve, but one approach that may help is to have a member of the team trained by the substance misuse service to provide basic counselling to patients misusing cannabis and abusing but not addicted to alcohol. The remaining patients, with more serious drug abuse, can be referred to or refer themselves to the appropriate service.

Child and adolescent teams

While it is a very challenging field, it must be so glorious to work in child and adolescent psychiatry. No matter how unwell patients are, you always know that on their 18th birthday you can refer them on to adult services. (Interestingly this is not the way it works at the other end of life. Older age services will not always accept a 65-year-old patient with schizophrenia from a general adult team to the frequent irritation of the latter.)

The group presenting the most difficulties are those who have been in hospital for a prolonged period of time. The transfer of this group to adult psychiatric and adult eating disorders services is a complex procedure fraught with danger. Consider Mary, a patient described above (page 125). She had been under the care of the adolescent service who placed her in a private adolescent eating disorders unit and she turned 18 while in hospital. In this case adolescent outpatient services were not involved in the transfer of care. Consider the following, however:

Clinical description 7.8

Gemma is a 17 year old with anorexia and bulimia nervosa who has been seen in the child and adolescent outpatient eating disorders service for two years during which time she has received thrice weekly psychoanalytic psychotherapy. Her weight has been maintained at a BMI of 17, but continued vomiting has caused a hypokalaemia varying between 2.7 and 3.2 mmol/l. Because her 18th birthday is three months away, the adolescent department suggest a meeting with your service to arrange transfer of care.

The danger here is that because such intensive psychotherapy is not usually available in the adult department, its withdrawal could result in a further relapse of her condition. It was decided in this case to extend her therapy for six months, during which time the therapy would be concluded and weekly monitoring instituted in the adult department together with parental support. Moving from one service with such an intensive level of treatment, to one with somewhat less, is a little like a diver's transition from the deep to the surface. The patient may suffer a psychotherapeutic equivalent of 'the bends'.

OUTREACH

Outreach is an important extension to a service but can only be provided if there is enough therapist time to accommodate the occasional outreach case. The time taken to reach a patient may add two or three hours to the session, so that, unless several such patients are in the same area, one therapy session will require the whole afternoon or morning.

Outreach is required whenever a patient is, for any reason, unable to attend a clinic for treatment. This may be due to the apparent or actual severity of the eating disorder, a complicating illness, or to non-compliance with treatment.

Severity of the eating disorder

In the case of the patient in Clinical description 1.1 (p. 13) whose mother thought he was too frail to attend the day hospital, her anxiety, which led to treatment refusal which fitted with the patient's ambivalence, was allayed by a reassuring discussion with the team at her home, in the presence of the patient and, crucially, his father.

Complicating illness

The illness is one that makes attendance at a clinic difficult for the patient. Examples include agoraphobia and chronic fatigue syndrome.

Clinical description 7.9

A woman of 33 had suffered with chronic fatigue for five years, she was resistant to treatment and had not left her home, where she lived with her elderly parents, during that time. Her GP referred her because, over the previous 12 months, she had been undereating and losing weight. A doctor and a psychologist visited her at home and a diagnosis of anorexia nervosa complicating chronic fatigue syndrome was made. She received visits from a dietician and an occupational therapist monthly for the following year during which time she recovered much of her lost weight. Her chronic fatigue syndrome continued as before.

Non-compliance with treatment

Considering that the vast majority of people with eating disorders do not seek treatment, those who do appear at the eating disorders service may have a level of motivation to change that does not allow them to engage fully in treatment, even after using motivational enhancement techniques. Our practice is to refer such patients back to their GPs in the majority of cases, after discussion at the Current Concerns meeting (Chapter 2). In a few cases the patient is actively and assertively followed up. This occurs when the patient is of low weight, particularly when weight is known to be falling, or when she has been considered in the category of high risk (Chapter 4, p. 73). Another category would be a patient with multiple problems, who is under the care of the CMHT, and who has significant and dangerous eating disorder symptoms, such as low weight or purging behaviours associated with hypokalaemia. In such cases, every effort will be made to see the patient, at the clinic, at home, at the GP surgery or at the

CMHT base. If all fails, a meeting is scheduled with whoever the patient is willing to see, or failing that with a family member, usually a parent, and the 'frontline' worker is given guidance on how to manage the risk in a way that is as safe as possible.

ORGANISATION OF THE LIAISON AND OUTREACH SERVICE

Anyone in the team can work with patients or staff outside the clinic. It makes sense, however, for one or two team members to take responsibility for the service and to persuade others to take on individual pieces of work.

Clinical description 7.10

A nurse with two years of general and two years of eating disorders experience took on the task of coordinating the EDLOS (eating disorders liaison and outreach service). The consultant, who screened all referrals, passed suitable cases to her. She brought them to the Current Concerns meeting (Chapter 2) and a number of team members took on pieces of work. A doctor with a liaison and outreach brief as part of the job description was appointed, and it became apparent that one of the psychologists and one other nurse were particularly interested in this type of work. This group, together, at times with the dietician, then took on most of the liaison and outreach work, although other team members knew that they were at liberty to 'bid' for a case if they wished.

This demonstrated how aspects of the team's work can develop in an organic fashion, responding to external demands by both shifting roles and recruiting new staff with different job descriptions to those they replace.

INPATIENT CARE

INTRODUCTION: A SERVICE WITHOUT BEDS

When the Russell Unit was redesigned in 1997, there was broad agreement that the new service should be community oriented with minimal reliance on inpatient care. There were already eight beds in a separate eating disorders ward, of which six were used. The new service was to concentrate on delivering high-quality outpatient, day patient and outreach services and to use beds as necessary, but as little as possible. The funding body (the Camden and Islington Health Authority) at the time was positive about the new proposals, contacted the management of the Royal Free Hospital (we were then part of an Acute Trust, together with medical and surgical colleagues) and indicated that as it had spent a considerable sum the previous year on inpatient services outside the Royal Free (in spite of having eating disorder dedicated beds at the Royal Free!) it would be willing to offer us the amount it had spent (about £200 000) as long as we didn't come to them for more money for inpatient care. This was a very tempting offer, and coincided with discussions within our service that we could probably do without major inpatient provision, as long as we had good community services, and had access to the odd bed when we needed it. This, at the time, went against the way most other specialist services for eating disorders were managed and I became known as the one who was trying to do it without beds (which, as we will see, is a distortion). I was invited to speak in debates with titles such as, 'Dedicated beds are unnecessary in specialist eating disorders units'. I always lost the debates, mainly because I was trying to propose less emphasis on large inpatient units often far from people's homes, and more reliance on up-to-date community services similar to those adopted by general psychiatric services after they had emerged from the days of the 2000-bed hospitals in the middle of nowhere, with psychiatrists called alienists and allowed to retire early because it was all so awful. The audiences in these debates tended to split between a few radical anti-psychiatrists who, embarrassingly, voted for me, as did the chairman out of pity, and the majority who seemed to think I was against admission

in all circumstances. The elements of modern psychiatric practice (even in
1997) that I was interested in applying to eating disorders were local care
based on community mental health teams with access to crisis resolution
and response teams and assertive outreach teams, as well as traditional
day hospitals and supported hostel accommodation. More recently early
intervention has appeared, and may make its mark on eating disorder services. The prospect of young person early intervention services, focused
on 14 to 25 year olds, is particularly interesting because of the onset, in
adolescence, of the majority of patients with anorexia nervosa, and of a
substantial number of patients with other eating disorders. The separation
of adult and child psychiatry, both at the levels of services and training
in many countries, means that a giant creative leap by both clinicians and
managers (not unknown, but not frequently observed) will be required.

Among the staff of the Russell Unit, the idea of reorienting the service
towards a community model was very popular. Some of the nurses working on the inpatient unit were not happy with the work, and when I suggested closing the beds, one of them went looking for a spanner to disman-
tle them! The team then was very small, with two doctors, some dietician
time, a senior nurse and a few inpatient nurses. The nurses had, because
of the lack of outpatient services, already begun evaluating patients themselves, and this practice formed the basis for our outpatient assessment
described in Chapter 3. With the money provided by the health authority
we started recruiting new staff, and closing the beds released more staff
from inpatient duties. Because nurses who worked less unsocial hours in
the new service earned less, their previous pay was protected for a year
after the change. What we needed in order to close the beds safely was
a therapeutic team that could address the problems of the patients who
would, otherwise, be admitted. Our agreed priorities were more nurses, a
psychologist, a family therapist (as a family therapist, I was biased) and
more dietician time. We started discharging the inpatients, which turned
out to be less difficult than we had expected. They had mostly been in the
unit for several months, and were therefore not acutely ill, and by October
1997 all had gone except one stalwart from the east who finally packed
her bags in November by which time we had begun taking people into
the day programme and had made the transition we had planned. The
task then was to provide as much care as possible in outpatients, the day
hospital and, later, in liaison and outreach, but to admit patients when absolutely necessary. We had not used up all the funds allocated at the start,
as we had been asked to bear the costs of specialist inpatient care if we
admitted patients, and we had £100 000 to use for this purpose. The service therefore minimised the use of beds and we can state with reasonable
confidence that the majority of patients we have admitted could not have
been treated without admission. Therefore, our estimates of the number
of beds required can be taken as a minimum for an urban population. The
latter has been a developing story. In the first few years we required very

few beds of any sort. However, each year we saw one or two new patients who had very severe disorders and who required either medical or eating disorder unit admissions for long periods. After five years of providing a service to a population which varied between 840 000 and 1.2 million, the number of beds required reached a plateau, and we now (after eight years) have a reasonable estimate of the needs of such a population which could be used by other services. Be aware, however, that when a service for an area is set up, there is a lag of several years before the true and enduring requirements of the population are apparent. These figures are provided in the last part of this chapter.

WHEN DOES A PATIENT REQUIRE A BED?

The short answer is, 'When they need treatment that cannot be provided in the community'. When all the resources available to the community eating disorders service are exhausted, namely outpatient individual therapy, day care, weekend support, family support and therapy, home care and liaison to other agencies, inpatient care should be considered, and arranged if it is thought that such care is likely to be helpful. There are some situations that demand immediate inpatient care, and these are a substantial, imminent threat to life from malnutrition (deteriorating BMI, muscle tests, liver function tests, creatine kinase, ECG), electrolyte disturbance due to restriction or purging behaviours, high suicidal risk. Other admissions are less urgent, and the decision may be reached during a period of outpatient or day patient treatment. The patient may seem unable to benefit from psychological treatment due to nutritional disturbance, and a period of inpatient care may be useful to improve nutrition and render the patient more amenable to psychological interventions. This may be due to organic effects of malnutrition upon the brain, or to psychological barriers to eating certain foods, or gaining weight beyond a certain threshold (see Chapter 6), which, it is hoped, might be helpfully overcome during a period of inpatient care.

The patient's history is of substantial influence in determining the threshold for admission. If a patient has a history of repeated relapse and disengagement from treatment, then admission might be better arranged, under compulsion if necessary, earlier in her progress down the weight chart, rather than waiting until she has reached a weight at which a long period of inpatient care will be required.

Clinical description 8.1

A 22-year-old woman had suffered from anorexia nervosa since the age of 15. She had been sexually abused by a family friend and also was thought to be in an ongoing incestuous relationship with her father. She presented extremely unwell and was admitted to a medical ward where she developed severe muscle weakness and a refeeding psychosis. On discharge she was partially weight recovered but quickly relapsed and was readmitted, very unwell to a medical bed. She was then placed on a compulsory order (Section 3 of the Mental Health Act 1983) and transferred to a specialist inpatient eating disorder unit where she gained to a normal weight and was moved to a hospital hostel. The compulsory order was lifted as a result of an appeal to the Mental Health Review Tribunal, and she went home and relapsed over the next five months, her father barring all contact with services. She was subsequently readmitted to the eating disorders unit under a further compulsory order, when the social worker insisted on seeing the patient, using powers of forced entry.

There has been substantial debate about the use of compulsory hospitalisation and treatment in eating disorders. Whereas involuntary admission to hospital is found in the psychiatric services of all countries, there are substantial differences between them in the criteria required for such treatment. In some only patients with psychotic illness, such as schizophrenia or mania, can be subject to compulsory treatment, while in others, including England, a patient with any mental illness can be treated compulsorily as long as the condition is threatening to health or safety and requires treatment in hospital. Whether the different laws are associated with different mortality rates for anorexia nervosa is unknown. To many it seems strange that patients with the eating disorder that makes you thin can be treated against their will and, perhaps, 'saved' while eating enough to make you fat cannot be treated compulsorily. The argument goes that the former have a mental illness but the latter do not. However, even when a patient with severe life-threatening obesity does have an eating disorder (binge eating) which is leading to the obesity, the Mental Health Act is not used. A libertarian view might be that both should be able to choose whether or not to have treatment, while those emphasising the mentally ill person's right to treatment even when it is refused, would say that both should be considered for compulsory treatment.

The existence of the Mental Health Act has profound influence on patient behaviour. It is not unusual for there to develop a highly dependent relationship between patients and hospital staff, and patients with anorexia nervosa not infrequently state that they feel safer when detained on a compulsory order. This process is usually better avoided, because patients on an inpatient unit can sometimes compete with each other for more intensive treatment, whether it is one-to-one nursing or a Mental Health Act 'Section'. This is one of the traps into which staff and patients can be lured during inpatient care, with patients becoming increasingly dependent and staff increasingly controlling and coercive, and is a good reason to avoid compulsory treatment as far as possible.

WHAT SORT OF BED CAN BE ARRANGED?

An eating disorders service needs to decide whether it is going to provide all services to its patients or to restrict its interventions to those directly related to the patient's eating disorder. Patients with anorexia nervosa and bulimia nervosa can have many difficulties, and because everything is linked to everything else in the universe, one could make a case for dealing with all the patient's problems. One reason to do otherwise is that funds are limited, demand is not, and if we provide every possible service to our patients, our waiting lists will grow or our service will become more expensive as we require more staff. Of the variety of problems requiring inpatient care that the patients present, the majority can be classified as those to do with:

1. Weight loss and malnutrition.
2. Purging behaviour and electrolyte imbalance.
3. Depression and suicide.
4. Personality disorder and self-harm.
5. Substance misuse and withdrawal.

Table 8.1 gives a guide to how these five types of problem are dealt with, in particular, which service is deputed to deal with the problem. In a number of cases, care is shared between two services. In such cases, clear agreement is required by a meeting of at least one representative from each service, so that each knows what their agency and the other agencies have agreed to do.

A degree of flexibility can be very useful in dealing with difficult clinical situations in which a patient is at high risk. It is advisable to become aware of all potential residential placements in the area and how to access them.

Table 8.1 Problems demanding intensive community and inpatient care and the services involved in providing the care

Problem	Community care	Inpatient care
Weight loss and malnutrition	EDS/Primary care	EDS/Medical unit
Purging behaviour and electrolyte imbalance	EDS/Primary care	EDS/Medical unit
Depression and suicide	EDS/Gen Psych Service/Primary care	Gen Psych Service
Personality disorder and self-harm	EDS/Gen Psych Service/Primary care	Gen Psych Service
Substance misuse and withdrawal	EDS/Substance Misuse Service/Primary care	Substance Misuse Service

They may vary in different boroughs. In our area, the following residential services are available to at least a proportion of patients:

- Return to parental home (immediate hospital admission not required).
- Stay in hotel while attending the day programme (immediate hospital admission not required).
- Stay in local hostel (immediate hospital admission not required).
- Admit to women's section of general psychiatric ward.
- Admit to medical ward under joint medical and psychiatric care.
- Admit to specialist eating disorders unit.

Which facility to use depends on the clinical situation and the patient's wishes, but a combination can be useful.

Clinical description 8.2

A 24-year-old patient with frequent deliberate self-harm lost a lot of weight rapidly and fulfilled criteria for anorexia nervosa. Although her BMI was 15 she was physically compromised, and was admitted to a medical ward where she received nasogastric feeding until her physical state stabilised. She was assessed by inpatient psychiatric services, but they felt that with her deliberate self-harm she would be unlikely to benefit from a general psychiatric admission. She was therefore referred to a highly supported hostel used as an alternative to admission where she was accepted.

General psychiatric beds

Admission to general psychiatric wards carries a series of problems, which have been described in Chapter 7. In a service providing care for a million or so population around two beds would be required. The eating disorders service needs to come to a decision about where those beds should be. One solution is to establish two beds in an adult general psychiatry ward, and to provide clinical leadership and training to equip the ward to manage the occasional patient. An alternative and preferable model is to establish a larger unit serving five million with 15 beds or so, to which the smaller community units had access. If general psychiatry beds are used, they are better placed in a women-only section of the ward, or even better, a women's unit, where they exist. Naturally, any male patients requiring admission will be accommodated in a male bed. Because admissions will be uncommon, and rather few, a formal 'ward round' will be difficult to arrange. However, it is usually possible to identify an hour in the week for a discussion, with relevant staff, of the eating disorder patients on the ward. There should be at least one nurse trained in eating disorders on duty during meal times, and an eating disorders nurse should attend both the inpatient discussion and the Current Concerns discussion (Chapter 2, p. 22). Ideally, the inpatient unit should be on the same site as the eating disorders day hospital, so that patients admitted can attend the day hospital programme if it is deemed appropriate.

What can be expected of such inpatient care? First, it is useful to indicate what is unlikely to be achieved. There will not be a group of patients with anorexia nervosa who can be treated as a group in which process may exert a therapeutic influence, particularly in the area of food intake. It will, therefore, be more difficult to achieve weight gain in this context. Secondly, also because of the few patients, there will not be a substantial group of nurses skilled in the management of patients with anorexia nervosa, although with time, knowledge and skills will increase. In other words, one cannot create a miniature version of an inpatient eating disorders unit with only one or two beds. There is also a limit on the severity of medical illness in patients admitted to a psychiatric bed. As a rule patients who are not mobile, or those who require an intravenous infusion or a cardiac monitor are not suitable for a psychiatric bed. The boundary is often set around nasogastric tube feeding. Some ward managers are happy for their suitably trained staff to pass a nasogastric tube with support from their medical staff, and to administer nasogastric feeds daily, others are not. The impetus to change may come from above. The management may become aware that if one or more of their psychiatric wards would allow nasogastric feeding, referral to expensive facilities could be avoided. The argument is that if a patient is so malnourished that she is unable to benefit from day hospital therapy, a relatively brief admission for, say three to four weeks of nasogastric feeding could improve her BMI and general nutritional state to a point at which day care could be tried again, and a prolonged inpatient stay avoided. This process, of persuading nursing staff to change policy, can take some time and needs to be conducted with the support of the senior nurses in the organisation. The other professionals that need to be persuaded of the appropriateness of admission of patients with anorexia nervosa to general psychiatric wards are psychiatrist colleagues, especially if they are being asked to give up general psychiatry beds to eating disorders, even occasionally. The appearance of a new service for eating disorders is an opportunity to relieve colleagues of a group of patients who are difficult to manage, especially by non-specialists, and occasional use of beds can be acceptable under those circumstances. If there is already a community service that is requesting access to psychiatric beds, the welcome can be less enthusiastic and the financial argument may need to be made, together with senior medical management. These caveats taken into account, patients on a general psychiatric ward can do remarkably well. The treatment of one very complicated patient is described:

Clinical description 8.3

A 42-year-old lady had chronic anorexia nervosa since the age of 18 with food restriction, laxative abuse and near total social isolation. She was referred by her GP who had found her at home, emaciated in a squalid flat. She made a practice of consulting numerous specialists for various ailments, and she had been prescribed a large number of different medications. GPs had found her very difficult to manage and she had moved from one to another either because of her own dissatisfaction or theirs. She had never seen a psychiatrist and asserted that all of her problems were due to physical conditions. She was admitted against her will to a general psychiatric ward and was allocated a key nurse on the ward. The latter was not a specialist in eating disorders but received regular support from the nurses on the adjacent Russell Unit. The patient refused most solid food, but did take a specific brand of meal replacement drink that had to be obtained from outside the hospital. Her weight rose steadily. Her medical problems were fully assessed and appropriately treated. She was withdrawn successfully from laxatives. Discussions with staff and patient occurred weekly and all aspects of these very complex problems were managed. She was discharged home after six months in hospital, and was followed up by her GP, psychiatrist, physician and surgeon.

In this case the patient's underweight responded well to general nursing care and discussion of nutritional intake by her nurse and members of the Russell Unit, including the dietician. However, many patients in general psychiatric beds are unable to eat enough to gain weight, because of the strength of their drive for thinness. The first change to make is to increase the intensity of nursing care to close observation (one-to-one nursing care) during meal times. If the patient begins to eat, but still fails to gain or loses weight, she may be vomiting, exercising or finding other ways to avoid weight gain, and a 24-hour one-to-one nurse may be needed.

If such intensive nursing fails to result in weight gain, the clinical team needs to consider more intrusive methods of nutrition. In some units, 'assisted feeding' is practised, in which the patient is held and food pushed into her mouth with a spoon. It is felt that this practice is preferable to nasogastric feeding, because it does not involve an abnormal passage into the body, and because patients often agree to eat voluntarily rather than go through 'assisted feeding' again. This is a difficult argument to resolve, mainly because the practice is so difficult for nursing staff to perform. It is a question for each team to resolve, and is more relevant to specialist units, where it will be further discussed.

If it is decided that nasogastric tube feeding needs to take place, most general psychiatric ward managers will wish the passage of the tube to take place in a medical ward and this is not unreasonable when the patient is of very low BMI, because of the risks of refeeding syndrome and gastric dilatation initially. However, once it is established and the patient is stable, it should be possible to continue tube feeding on a general psychiatric ward. The ward management will need to discuss this alongside arrangements for patients with severe depression or catatonic stupor, who also may require nasogastric feeding to support nutrition. Let us suppose, however, that our patient has resisted all attempts to persuade her to eat, and nasogastric tube feeding is recommended to be initiated on a medical ward.

General medical beds

Admission or transfer to a medical bed is necessary in rather uncommon but very important circumstances, and it must be clear to the eating disorder service what those circumstances are and how to proceed. The key is to identify the correct doctors at the different levels of the system. It is advisable to seek out a senior medical consultant in the hospital who has an interest in patients with nutritional or psychological problems, and to have a general discussion mainly to show that you have an idea about medical issues and do not conform to the weirdo image of psychiatrists that very rarely fits. Psychiatrists in the eating disorder service should arrange to undergo a refresher in their medical knowledge and if possible should have gone through a course in clinical nutrition. (It is also useful to include attendance at the medical grand rounds to keep up with changes in the language of medicine as well as to remind physicians that psychiatry is a medical speciality by making the occasional useful comment in these meetings.)

Beds are almost always required very soon. We are not going to wait around if we have seen a patient with a potassium of 1.5 mmol/l. In general, there is a reasonably experienced physician on call (under various names – duty medical registrar, duty physician etc.) who will have completed four or five years of postgraduate medicine. They are likely to know relatively little about eating disorders and be cautious about admitting a psychiatric patient to a medical ward. Some are found to be reluctant to take information from a psychiatric nurse, however experienced, very seriously, and the same can be true of a trainee psychiatrist, so the consultant should be prepared to call the physician and engage in a robust discussion about the patient's need for admission. In general the more contact you have with the physicians in your setting, the more you will understand the sort of pressures they face (such as bed shortages) and the better the outcome for your patient.

Before admission to a medical bed is arranged, the following should be determined, at least provisionally:

- What are the reasons for admission?
- What treatment will the medical staff be asked to administer?
- Who are the senior clinicians in charge? (Generally a named psychiatrist and a named physician.)
- How will the patient's psychiatric needs be covered?
- Who is the eating disorders liaison worker who will provide regular support to the medical ward?
- What are the aims of admission, and under what circumstances could the patient be discharged or transferred?

Treatment in the medical ward depends of course on the problem being treated. The most common reasons for admission listed and principles of treatment are outlined below.

Hypokalaemia or other electrolyte imbalance: if potassium is very low and ECG changes have been observed, the patient should usually receive ECG monitoring while potassium is corrected. In general, cessation of vomiting and resumption of regular meals and adequate fluid intake will correct the electrolyte imbalance, and it is helpful to prescribe oral potassium chloride tablets, although the latter can cause gastrointestinal irritation. Many patients will be dehydrated by vomiting and laxative abuse, will have raised serum urea levels, and are likely to receive an intravenous infusion of dextrose saline with potassium chloride. There is a real risk of overprovision of potassium, with resultant and potentially fatal hyperkalaemia, when potassium is given intravenously and this is an argument against parenteral potassium correction. Daily electrolyte measurement and ECG monitoring can detect such an occurrence, but it is probably better avoided by more judicious and less enthusiastic potassium treatment. A patient who is known to have chronic hypokalaemia should not be given large amounts of potassium quickly. They will have adapted to the condition and oral rehydration and potassium supplements are safe and adequate, unless ECG changes demand more aggressive measures. If the patient is being given a drip with dextrose (i.e. glucose) in it be aware that she may well interfere with the drip to reduce her calorie intake.

Clinical description 8.4

A patient of 18 was admitted to a medical ward in an emaciated state with acute renal failure. An attempt was made to save her renal function by rehydrating her with a 5% dextrose infusion. She repeatedly switched off the infusion because of her fear of calories. She died in the early hours of the following morning.

Many patients with eating disorders are unable to stop vomiting or abuse of laxatives. This may continue in hospital, especially in a medical ward where supervision from the ward nurses has to compete with many other priorities, and even one-to-one nursing can be inadequate to prevent purging, especially if the nurses are not experienced in eating disorders. If potassium continues to be low, even with oral replacement and close observation, it is worth trying a proton pump inhibitor (PPI). These curiously named drugs (they are not part of the nation's nuclear defence strategy) prevent the stomach from secreting hydrogen ions or H^+ (protons). This stops the body's acidity from falling and it is this acid loss (alkalosis) caused by vomiting which causes potassium to be secreted by the kidney with consequent hypokalaemia. Preventing H^+ loss with a PPI such as Lansoprazole can reduce hypokalaemia. Sometimes this works so well that potassium shoots up, and needs to be monitored regularly whereas sometimes it doesn't work at all.

Very low weight: admission to a medical ward for treatment of straightforward emaciation usually needs to be discussed in principle, in advance with a medical consultant who is willing to share responsibility. If this is not done, the patient is likely to be discharged as soon as they do not need a 'tether'. The latter can be an intravenous drip, or a cardiac monitor, but it represents a clear signal that the patient needs to be in hospital, in a medical bed, while queues of trolleys bearing patients with heart attacks and strokes build up in accident and emergency. Once the tether is removed, the patient gets up and presents a picture of (thin) health, racing round the ward and greeting fellow patients loudly. (One emaciated patient who was on an elderly care ward terrified her fellow patients who thought the Angel of Death had arrived for them when she visited them by night.) Referring to the criteria mentioned above (p. 150), the following provisional decisions may have been made:

Patient *Amanda V*

- What are the reasons for admission? *Emaciation (BMI 12), muscle weakness, raised liver enzymes.*
- What treatment will the medical staff be asked to administer? *Bed rest, nasogastric feeding, monitoring for refeeding syndrome.*
- Who are the senior clinicians in charge? (Generally a named psychiatrist and a named physician.) *Dr Freud and Dr Fleming.*
- How will the patient's psychiatric needs be covered? *Daily visits by EDS liaison team, special psychiatric nursing.*
- Who is the EDS liaison worker? *Nurse Florence.*
- What are the aims of admission, and under what circumstances could the patient be discharged or transferred? *BMI over 14, SUSS test 3/3, liver enzymes falling.*

Unless there has been prior agreement and the required training to support nasogastric feeding, the latter is usually performed on a medical ward, although it can be continued on a psychiatric unit once the patient is medically stable. It is best done using a fine bore indwelling tube, inserted by a nurse or doctor with substantial experience of the procedure. Afterwards, fluid from the tube is aspirated using a large syringe, to check that it is acid (i.e. gastric), air is syringed into the tube while the stomach is listened to for bubbling, and an x-ray may be taken if there is any doubt to ensure that the end of the tube is in the stomach.

If the patient's diet has been very low in nutrition for some time (> one week) then she may be at risk of refeeding syndrome and daily electrolytes, including phosphate and magnesium, should be measured. The initial feed (assuming a feed of 1 kcal/ml) can be 500 ml per 24 hours, and this can be increased over five days to 1000 ml per 24 hours, watching for signs of refeeding syndrome (low potassium, phosphate or magnesium), water retention (development of oedema, rapid weight rises, signs of cardiac failure) and gastric dilatation (swollen, tightly stretched stomach, involuntary vomiting). Fluid intake, in a patient who is drinking, can be monitored, along with urine output. If she is refusing drink, total fluid intake can start at 500 ml and be increased over a few days to 1000–1500 ml, depending on body weight and physical state. If fluid overload is a problem, a higher concentration of feed (1.5 kcal/ml) can be used.

In patients who adamantly refuse all nutrition and who will die if not fed, nasogastric feeding may be necessary against the patient's will, under legal compulsion using a Section of the Mental Health Act, or its equivalent in countries other than England. Forced feeding against the patient's will is very occasionally required, and it must be done as safely as possible by a team of doctors and nurses who are experienced in the procedure. Several staff, up to five nurses, experienced in control and restraint techniques, may be required, and the patient may need sedation using oral or intramuscular Lorazepam with or without Haloperidol. The procedure is hazardous because of the unpredictability of a low weight malnourished patient's response to medication. Dosage should start low (e.g. 0.5 mg oral Lorazepam) and built up slowly, giving time between doses to avoid toxicity due to accumulation. In practice, benzodiazepines can be disappointing in their sedative effect, possibly because the patient is extremely aroused, and perhaps because of a different response to these drugs in the malnourished state. Commonly, a small dose of Haloperidol (2.5–5 mg) is required orally or intramuscularly in order to sedate a patient enough to pass a tube. Because of the unpredictability of response, it is recommended that a senior clinician, experienced in clinical pharmacology, be consulted before attempting to sedate a patient with severe anorexia nervosa. The most serious adverse consequence of sedation is probably hypotension, in a patient who may have a starting blood pressure of 80/50, and this needs to be monitored closely during and after drug administration. Low weight is associated with ECG changes (Chapter 4, p. 68) and neuroleptic drugs such as Haloperidol can exacerbate these, and an ECG is mandatory. In general, the sedation of a patient with anorexia nervosa is similar to rapid tranquillisation of a patient with an acute psychosis with the additional complication of malnutrition.

After a tube is inserted in such circumstances, the patient may well not allow it to stay, and the team may need to insert the tube daily, in order to provide nutrition. When the patient is out of the BMI danger zone, and still refuses nutrition, a decision needs to be made whether to continue to feed or to discontinue forced feeding in view of the fact that the patient's life is no longer at risk. This can be difficult in practice, because a patient who is refusing all oral intake, including water, can become very unwell from dehydration within a few days of stopping feeding. It may be worth stopping feeding once the patient gains weight, but if feeding has to be reintroduced within a short time because of dehydration, consideration will need to be given to the possibility of regular (usually daily) forced refeeding over a long period. Such an eventuality is very rare, but in every large service one is likely to turn up every few years, and it is important to have discussed a policy for its treatment in advance.

Clinical description 8.5

A 34-year-old refugee who had been in the UK for 10 years was admitted to a medical ward emaciated and dehydrated after refusing food and drink over the previous three weeks, claiming that eating caused her to have abdominal pain, organic causes for which had been excluded. She was rehydrated intravenously, and began to eat a little. She was discharged but readmitted several times for the same reason. She was not thought to have an eating disorder, but abnormal illness behaviour, with a possible somatoform disorder. However, she became unmanageable on both medical and psychiatric wards and was transferred to an eating disorders inpatient unit where she refused all oral intake and was tube fed under sedation (BMI 13, Lorazepam 4 mg IM, Haloperidol 2.5 mg IM). She continued to refuse to eat or drink and, following a second opinion, tube feeding was discontinued. Over four days she became extremely unwell, and developed renal impairment and electrolyte disturbance, even though her weight was not too low (BMI 17). It was decided to resume daily forced nasogastric feeding. It was surmised that she had become terrified of discharge due to assaults she had suffered while working as a prostitute and that her starvation provided a way of remaining safe in hospital, although she strongly denied any suggestion of this.

Should nasogastric feeding fail, either because the staff do not have the necessary expertise, or because the patient sabotages it by, for example, secretly leaking the feed into her pillow, the patient will need transfer to a specialist inpatient eating disorders unit.

Less common reasons for medical admission

There are many physical problems the patient may present which require inpatient medical intervention. The principles remain the same, however, as illustrated by the following case:

Clinical description 8.6

A 25-year-old woman was admitted to a coronary care unit with a BMI of 12, a temperature of 33.5 °C and widespread inverted T waves on her ECG. She was wrapped in a hypothermia blanket, her heart was monitored, and a dextrose saline infusion was started. She was offered meals, but refused them. A visit by the consultant in eating disorders, an EDS liaison nurse and the EDS dietician at the time of the daily review by the medical team resulted in a meal plan together with nursing supervision to try and ensure that the patient complied with it. She gained weight, to a BMI of 14, her temperature and ECG normalised and she was discharged to the EDS day hospital.

This demonstrates the importance of being in the right place at the right time. The best contact is often the most junior doctor, who should be contacted to find out when your patient is likely to be reviewed by the team. At this point you can suggest that they could visit her at 9 or 10 am, rather than the unsocial hours many medical teams keep. (I once attended a 7.30 am handover meeting to be greeted by the slightly bizarre sight of 20 or so trainee physicians having jam doughnuts provided by the makers of an anti-ulcer drug.) Make sure that a member of the EDS team is present at least three days a week on rounds, and be particularly vigilant when discharge might be discussed. It can occur without warning on the day before the ward is due to be on emergency intake, to clear beds.

Clinical description 8.7

An 18-year-old woman with anorexia nervosa was admitted to a medical ward because of severe weight loss (BMI 12.8) and weakness. No blood abnormalities were discovered and three days after admission, she was reviewed by the registrar (senior resident) the day before the ward was 'on take' and discharged.

She was unable to raise her feet, due to leg weakness, but she made it as far as the pavement outside the hospital. However, she was unable to raise her foot onto the kerb, and was carried to her parents' car. Her parents issued a formal complaint against the hospital, and the patient was readmitted for nutritional treatment.

In this case, the EDS team had been a little slow in catching up with the patient in hospital and she was inappropriately discharged with potentially disastrous consequences. Lastly, a patient can be admitted to a medical ward for treatment of deliberate self-harm, generally a serious overdose, a physical complication of the eating disorder, such as a rectal prolapse, or a complicating condition, such as diabetic ketoacidosis. A member of the team should make contact with the admitting unit, determining whether there are any eating disorder issues that demand immediate attention, such as very low weight, and make arrangements to see the patient and report back to the EDS team if the view of the team looking after the patient is that this would be helpful.

Specialist inpatient eating disorder beds

In your community-oriented service there are many options to try before you opt for an inpatient specialist eating disorders unit, namely outpatient, day patient, outreach, liaison, brief medical admission, and psychiatric admission with day care. You have reached the point where you have tried, or at least considered everything else, and are convinced that the only way for the patient to have a chance of recovery is to admit her to a specialist inpatient eating disorders unit (SIEDU) bed. You have seen patients who have been sent to inpatient units and discharged after three years of treatment costing, perhaps half a million euros.

The question is affected to some extent by who is paying the bills. If you have a certain amount of money set aside for inpatient care, and you have to spend it wisely, so that one patient does not use it all up, or if your employing authority is responsible for funding inpatient care, then you will be very interested in the subject, will try to provide care in the community as much as possible, and, when they have been admitted, think carefully about alternatives that have a good chance of helping the patient. If you are working for a hospital with a patient whose care is being paid for by a distant, anonymous trust with which you do not have much contact, your motivation to do all these things is just a shade less. My advice to funding bodies is to get an experienced clinician involved in monitoring the inpatient stay so that someone not being paid by the inpatient unit is giving views on the most appropriate management.

Clearly the most important question in all care is, 'What is the most helpful care for the patient at this time?' Different agencies do not always agree in attempting to answer this question. A patient who has reached a BMI of 17 in a unit may be deemed by the community team ready to start day care, but the inpatient team may well have a policy that states that patients should reach a menstrual weight prior to discharge. The fact that the patient has had four previous admissions and failed to maintain a menstrual weight in the community does bear on the matter, but it could be argued, as the patient, and parents, may well do, that 'this time it is different' and it may be!

A community service should have developed some criteria and policies around SIEDU referrals:

- criteria for admission (all required)
- failed in outpatient and day patient care
- failed in joint EDS and medical or psychiatric inpatient care
- at high medical risk from symptoms of anorexia nervosa
- selection of unit
- cost, competitive – look out for hidden extras (e.g. high price for one-to-one nursing)
- clinical service (must be on the EDS 'preferred provider' list)
- location: as near to patient's home as possible
- liaison
- willing for a senior member of the EDS to attend team meetings
- a senior member of the EDS willing to commit to attending team meetings
- written reports provided by SIEDU every one to two weeks
- patient is discussed at EDS Current Concerns meeting.

In selecting units for the EDS 'preferred provider' list, the unit should be visited by a senior clinician and the service manager from the EDS. The accommodation should be inspected and the senior clinical (especially nursing and medical) and management staff interviewed. It should be established that the staff on the SIEDU view the treatment of eating disorders in a way that is compatible with the work of the community EDS. Policies regarding age group, one-to-one nursing, the Mental Health Act and nasogastric feeding should be sought, views about admitting medically ill patients, including the quality of medical cover and the experience of senior and junior nursing and medical staff in management of eating disorders. A description of the therapeutic programme should be obtained and enquiries made about individual and family therapy and family support and the eating disorders experience of the therapists.

The following information about inpatient care derives from joint work between the Russell Unit and the Capio Nightingale Hospital in London, which has a private eating disorders unit where some Russell Unit patients have been admitted. As inpatients, patients normally gain weight at 0.5 to 1 kg per week. They are generally eating with other patients although in the first few days, a new patient might be eating in her room with a nurse, especially if she has great difficulty eating. For very starved patients, refeeding syndrome (Solomon & Kirby, 1990) should be sought over the first five days. A patient should see a primary nurse weekly and an associate nurse should also be allocated. Group therapy should start as soon as the patient is fit enough as should individual and family therapy.

If the patient does not gain weight, she should be challenged and consideration can be given to more intensive observation such as 24-hour one-to-one nursing, to detect exercising, vomiting or other eating disorder behaviours. Laxatives can be detected using urine testing. If the staff suspect that the patient might be water loading (see Figure 4.2, p. 64) she can be spot weighed without notice. If, after leave from the unit, the patient has unexplained diarrhoea, she and her room can be searched for evidence of laxatives and a patient subject to deliberate self-harm can be searched for blades on return from a trip out. The SIEDU should have clear policies dealing with the above procedures for voluntary patients and those detained compulsorily. If after attention to these matters weight still does not rise, consideration may be given to nasogastric tube feeding if weight is low, or discharge to outpatient or day care if BMI is over 14 and physical state is stable.

The patient's progress should be monitored in a weekly multidisciplinary meeting with medical and nursing staff and staff from the group programme, a unit individual therapist, the dietician and the family therapist. Other therapists should attend while their patients are being discussed. The meeting should be properly and legibly documented in case notes.

Discharge can be planned when the patient reaches a preset target which might be menstruation or a 'safe' weight at which outpatient or day care can reasonably be resumed (such as a BMI of 14 or 15). In some cases, the aim of discharge is to transfer the patient to a hospital hostel, as described below. If transfer is to be back to the community EDS there should be a formal Care Programme Approach meeting as described in Chapter 7, and enough time given for the patient to say goodbye to the staff that have been looking after her in the inpatient setting.

Specialist eating disorder hostel beds

A few SIEDUs have, attached to the inpatient unit, a hostel in which patients can reside while attending the eating disorders clinic at the same hospital. This is an interesting model of care, especially for patients with long-term anorexia nervosa who usually require rehabilitation (see Chapter 9), over a prolonged period of time, sometimes several years. The patient stays at the hostel, and attends the day hospital or outpatients department every day. The day programme may have a strong rehabilitative element with occupational therapy sessions geared to coping with everyday life, and a major effort is made to discharge such patients to appropriately supported residential placements. Transfer to the hostel can be flexible, as patients who are used to long inpatient stays have great difficulty in managing step-down care. They have excellent experience of refeeding and relapse, but have trouble with recovery. If the inpatient unit and the day unit each have their own distinct programme of care with separate dining rooms and therapy programmes the patient can be encouraged to develop her own programme of transfer into hostel and day care treatment. It is important not to impose this, because one thing patients with a lot of inpatient experience can do really well is resist changes in treatment with which they disagree. One patient may decide to continue the inpatient nutritional and therapy programme, while spending at first one night at the hostel, building up slowly. Another will prefer to stay in an inpatient bed, but gradually increase the number of meals and groups they attend per week in the day programme. The aim is full attendance at the day programme with seven nights a week at the hostel, and this may take several months to achieve. Be prepared for the patient to have dips in mood as she negotiates the new terrain, which has a chance of landing her in the real world with all its demands. Sensitive individual and group therapy, key working and family support (mothers especially can get extremely anxious during this process) are all essential to help the patient finally make it back into the world. The staff also have to let go of someone they have been closely observing for a long time and the patient allowed to have some symptoms in private while they negotiate the bridge to their own version of recovery. Orpheus lost Euridyce because, as he was leading her out of the underworld, he just had to check that she was following him as planned. Well she was, but as a result of his look (Lot's wife had a similar problem) she was drawn back across the Styx and lost forever.

AN AUDIT OF HOSPITAL ADMISSIONS

A case-notes audit of patients who had been admitted over a seven-year period was conducted. Case notes for all patients admitted by the Russell Unit between 1 January 1997 and 31 December 2003 were reviewed by the author. Admissions were included only if they occurred from the community. Transfers between inpatient units were excluded. In each case records of physical assessment performed in the period preceding the admission were inspected, and recorded in a structured manner. Both Russell Unit and inpatient unit notes were inspected. The aim of the survey was to

Table 8.2   Reasons for admission in 20 patients admitted a total of 36 times over 7 years

Test	Medical bed (15 admissions)	Psych bed (7 admissions)	EDU Bed (14 admissions)	Total (36 admissions)
Falling BMI	6	5	11	22 (61 %)
Falling SUSS	5	3	5	13 (36 %)
Failure to improve BMI	2	1	2	5 (14 %)
Raised creatine kinase	0	1	4	5 (14 %)
Hypokalaemia	3	1	0	4 (11 %)
Leukopaenia	2	0	2	4 (11 %)
Raised transaminases	1	0	3	4 (11 %)
Family concern	0	0	4	4 (11 %)
Professional concern	0	2	2	4 (11 %)
Uraemia	1	1	1	3 (8 %)
Hypoglycaemia	2	0	0	2 (6 %)
Hyponatraemia	1		1	2 (6 %)
Hypomagnesaemia	1			1 (3 %)
ECG changes	1			1 (3 %)
Hypothermia	1			1 (3 %)

identify the processes that had resulted in admission. In addition to physical measures, psychiatric state, and the influence of family, other social contacts and professionals were considered. A few patients were admitted to general psychiatric services for non-eating disorder problems, such as depression or suicidality, and these admissions do not appear in these figures. Results of the audit are summarised in Table 8.2 which provides the number of patients admitted to each of three types of inpatient unit (medical, general psychiatric and eating disorders) and the most important reasons for the admission.

Figures for occupied bed days were taken from management data and include patients transferred between inpatient units.

Results

During the study period there were 36 inpatient admissions from the community, among 20 patients. Fifteen admissions were to medical beds, seven to psychiatric beds and 14 to specialist inpatient eating disorder units. There was a substantial increase in these admissions between the first four years and the last two years of the survey, with three admissions in each of the first three years, four in the fourth and 11 in each of the last two years (regression of beds with years: $r = 0.86$, $p < 0.03$, slope $= 1.86$ bed increases per year).

Reasons for admission

For each of the three types of unit falling BMI was the most frequent reason for admission, with falling scores on the SUSS test next and various medical tests including blood tests, ECG and body temperature making up the remaining reasons. The number of reasons for which patients were admitted ranged from 1 to 4, with a mean of 1.914.

- BMI: 22 of 23 patients admitted because of a falling BMI had a BMI under 13 (mean 12.02 ± 0.84 sd, range 10.7–14.8). Dividing all admissions into those under and over a BMI of 12, those with an admission BMI under 12 were significantly more likely to have multiple reasons for admission than those with a BMI over 12 (chi squared comparing one reason with >1 reason $= 6.22$, $p = 0.013$). Admissions to medical beds were less likely to be for falling BMI, although this was not significant (chi squared $= 4.92$, $p = 0.085$). In five admissions, the patient was brought into hospital in part because of failure to gain weight, rather than because of physical problems due to a falling BMI.
- SUSS: this test was introduced as a simple, semi-quantitative measure of muscle power in anorexia nervosa (Chapter 4). In the present series it was a reason for admission in 36 % of episodes, although in only three cases (8 %) was a falling SUSS test not accompanied by a falling BMI level. In one case, a patient's BMI appeared to be stable at 11.3. However, scores on the sit-up test fell from 2 to 0 and the patient was admitted against her will under the Mental Health Act (1983). The day following admission her weight fell to a BMI of 9.9 and she revealed that she had been water loading prior to weighing, consuming up to 3.2 litres of water each time.
- Hypokalaemia: this was a common reason for medical admission, and sometimes occurred in the absence of other risk markers. Admission was considered when the potassium level fell below 3 mmol/l, the lowest level on admission being 2.0 mmol/l. One patient had a history of a cardiac arrest when her potassium was 2.3 mmol/l and this influenced the threshold for medical admissions in her case. All patients with hypokalaemia had anorexia nervosa, bulimic subtype, or purging bulimia nervosa.
- Failure to improve BMI: in these five cases, patients had presented in a stable physical condition with a BMI between 11 and 12.5, but in spite of intensive community treatment no progress had been made in raising BMI. In three cases there were additional causes for concern, with falling SUSS test and white cell count in two cases, and concern from an outside professional in a third.

The following concerns were relevant in four admissions: raised creatine kinase, leukopaenia, raised transaminase levels, family concern and professional concern.

- Creatine kinase (CK): rises in CK were sometimes marked, with a maximum of 1169 u/l. CK-MB (the cardiac fraction of CK) was measured in 13 samples with a CK > 220, and varied from <5 % (normal) to 21 %. It was abnormal (>5 %) in 8 out of the 13 samples. One patient was a compulsive exerciser. She was admitted to hospital at a BMI of 11.6, at which time her CK was 1037 u/l (CK-MB 4.8 %). She was placed on close observations and her CK fell to 86 u/l. The close observations were removed, and a CK a week later was 914 u/l.
- Leukopaenia: this was mild, with a minimum observed total white blood count of 3.08 (cells/microlitre)/1000), neutrophils of 0.7 and lymphocytes 0.91.
- Raised transaminase levels: aspartate transaminase (AST) rose to a maximum of 168 u/l (NR (Normal Range) 5–40) and alanine transaminase (ALT) to 244 u/l (NR 5–40). Of the other liver function tests, alkaline phosphatase was generally normal, but on one occasion rose to 133 u/l (NR 42–128) and bilirubin was never raised.
- Family concern: this was recorded when family expressed extreme concern including frequent, sometimes abusive calls and bringing a lawyer to appointments. In two cases this appeared to lead to admission at a BMI higher than usual (14.8, 15).
- Professional concern: this was recorded when professional intervention from outside the team altered the management decision of the eating disorders team. On two occasions a consultant psychiatrist from another team (one general psychiatry, one GP-liaison) independently arranged a bed for a patient, in accordance with family wishes for admission. In one case the patient's BMI was 15, in another it had been chronically at around 12.
- Uraemia: in three patients, a urea level above the normal range was present in patients just prior to admission. In fact, a low urea level was frequently observed in our patients, with levels in the range 1.5–2.8 mmol/l. This low level of urea is likely to reflect a low protein intake, with a consequent reduction in the hepatic amino acid substrates for urea production. The levels observed in the three admitted patients were 8.4, 10.2 and 12.5 mmol/l (NR 3–6.5).
- Hypoglycaemia: this was responsible for two admissions in one patient whose glucose level fell to 1.8 and 2.1 mmol/l (NR 2.9–5.3). The hypoglycaemia was detected on routine testing and was not symptomatic.
- Hyponatraemia: this appeared to contribute to admission in two cases, one patient with restricting and one with bulimic anorexia nervosa. The

levels were 121 mmol/l and 126 mmol/l respectively, and there were no reported symptoms of hyponatraemia.
- Hypomagnesaemia: one patient with anorexia nervosa bulimic sub-type and laxative abuse had persistently low magnesium levels of 0.53 mmol/l (NR 0.7–1). She was admitted for a few days into a medical bed when outpatient treatment failed to elevate magnesium levels.
- ECG changes, hypothermia: one patient developed ECG changes (T wave inversion in anterior leads) while very underweight and hypothermic (t < 33 °C) (see Figure 4.4, p. 68).

Lessons from this audit

In the audit, the following questions have been addressed:

- What are the best measures to use when assessing physical risk in a patient with a severe eating disorder?
- At what level of risk should inpatient care be introduced?

The best measure in adults remains body mass index. However, some patients falsify their BMI and others become ill because of electrolyte imbalance which may be unrelated to BMI. Additional measures are, therefore, required. The SUSS test can identify patients who are falsifying by, for example, water loading, and is recommended. Other physical measures such as the presence of postural hypotensive symptoms and hypothermia can sometimes add useful information as can an electrocardiogram. Among blood tests, urea, electrolytes, glucose, creatinine, creatine kinase, white blood count and transaminase levels all have their place. Abnormalities not found in this series such as a raised amylase and prolonged QTc interval on the ECG should also be sought.

In approaching the regular monitoring of a patient with anorexia nervosa who has a BMI in the critical range (below 15), it may be helpful to suggest a basic set of data that should be obtained at routine visits. From the experience reflected in this study, the set would include BMI, SUSS, temperature (low reading thermometer), ECG, urea, electrolytes, liver function tests, white blood count and creatine kinase. Other tests would be ordered depending on signs, symptoms and basic test results.

Deciding when to admit a patient with anorexia nervosa to hospital is difficult. Our experience suggests that under a BMI of 13 complications become increasingly numerous, and the recommended minimum safe BMI at which it is possible to work with a patient in the community appears to fall between 13 and 14. This assumes that no other measure, such as potassium concentration, has reached dangerous levels and that a specialist team is available, able to offer intensive monitoring and treatment. We suggest adopting a BMI of 14, below which admission for reasons of physical safety should be seriously considered. Some patients, usually with chronic anorexia nervosa, who maintain lower BMIs out of hospital for prolonged periods, and who have, presumably, adapted to low BMI, might be considered to be exceptions to the admission BMI threshold of 14.

Among patients admitted, there were few differences between the three different types of bed utilised. Most psychiatric wards have difficulty maintaining an intravenous infusion, and the need for a 'drip' probably indicates that a medical bed is required. Similarly, cardiac monitoring would be difficult to provide outside a medical unit. Lastly, some treatments are more appropriately provided in a medical ward, for example management of severe hypothermia, and extreme cachexia, because they each require intensive monitoring of, respectively, cardiac function and refeeding syndrome, which require medical facilities.

In a few cases, family concern, sometimes expressed very strongly, and the concern of professionals outside the team, resulted in the admission of patients at a BMI at which community treatment would usually be advised. Such cases require sensitive handling of communication between the eating disorders service, the family and other clinicians. Anxieties cannot, however, always be allayed.

HOW MANY BEDS ARE REQUIRED?

The crucial issue for a service is the number of beds that will be required for a defined population. The present discussion applies to an urban population in north London. Rural populations might need more beds simply because patients are unable to readily attend therapy as a result of poor transport and long distances. It will be seen from the graphs (Figure 8.1, Table 8.3) that overall bed usage has increased significantly since 2001. The

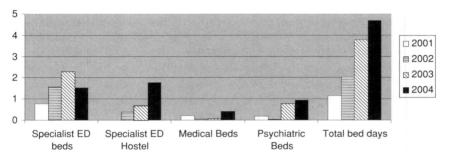

Figure 8.1   Beds per million population required by the Russell Unit service each year from 2001–2 to 2004–5.

Table 8.3   Beds required over 4 years showing an increase in total beds and an increasing proportion of hostel beds (beds per million population)*

Year	SIEDU	Specialist Hostel	Medical	Gen Psych	Total
2001–2	335 (0.76)	0	92 (0.21)	79 (0.18)	506 (1.16)
2002–3	684 (1.56)	171 (0.39)	31 (0.07)	16 (0.04)	895 (2.04)
2003–4	1001 (2.29)	287 (0.66)	36 (0.08)	328 (0.75)	1652 (3.78)
2004–5**	470 (1.53)	545 (1.77)	134 (0.43)	293 (0.95)	1442 (4.68)

Note:
* SIEDU: Specialist Inpatient Eating Disorders Service.
Specialist Hostel: Unsupervised hostel located near to and linked with a specialist eating disorders day hospital.
Medical: General medical bed.
Gen Psych: General psychiatric bed.
** Base population up to 2004 1.2 m, after 2004 0.844 m.

increase appears to be levelling off, and we are using the 2004–5 figures to indicate the likely continuing need for inpatient beds.

First, note that there is a rather small but consistent requirement for medical beds, running at 0.43 beds per million (BPM). That is, we are likely to have a patient in a medical bed just under half the time. Secondly, we are using general psychiatric beds up to a level of 0.95 BPM. Thirdly, we have steadily increased our use of SIEDU beds over the years, with a decrease in the past year to 1.53 BPM. This reduction has been offset by an increase in our use of specialist hostel beds to 1.77 BPM. Interestingly, probably as a result of random influences, bed usage in 2005–6 has markedly declined to a total of around 2 BPM (including 1.3 BPM SIEDU). I suggest however using the more realistic 2004–5 figures which more probably reflect average requirements.

What have we learnt from our experience? First, in the first few years after a community service is set up, relatively few beds will be needed. However, subsequently, each year one or two new patients will be referred who do not respond to any of the community approaches outlined in this book, and require inpatient care which may be life saving. They may have to stay in hospital a long time, and, partly because of this, they require prolonged rehabilitation for which a hostel is a very useful facility. In conclusion, referring to the latest complete year (2004–5) we can say that for an urban population of one million people, a combination of two SIEDU beds, two hostel beds, one general psychiatry bed and 0.5 medical beds, totalling 5.5 beds per million population, represents a reasonable provision of inpatient care, as long as an active community eating disorders service, of the type and extent described in this book, is available.

Chapter 9

REHABILITATION: DEALING WITH SEED

SEVERE AND ENDURING?

Clinical description 9.1

A 37-year-old male patient with anorexia nervosa since the age of 18 had been in hospital for most of his adult life, and was referred to a community mental health team after spending 18 months in a SIEDU for treatment of yet another relapse. He suffered from long-term moderate depression, and had no close relationship with anyone apart from a very dependent female patient with an eating disorder who he found impossible to cope with, as he had never had a relationship before. He had multiple long-term disabilities in a number of domains, including social and occupational functioning, psychiatric and physical symptoms and difficulties with his accommodation. He was rejected for CMHT care on the grounds that he did not have a 'severe and enduring' mental illness.

There has been substantial discussion about what is meant by the terms severe and enduring mental illness, or just severe mental illness. In some definitions the patient has to have a psychosis, in others not. I suggest that a mental disorder that has a mortality several times higher than that of schizophrenia should not be excluded from disorders carrying the severe and enduring label. The latter is important, because, in England, it brings eligibility for funding, as the case above shows. In this chapter, I present a particular approach to eating disorders rehabilitation from the point of view of a psychiatrist. The subject is hardly dealt with in most publications on treatment of eating disorders, most of which focus on recovery and cure. It was not mentioned, for example, in the report on eating disorders by the National Institute for Clinical Excellence (National Collaborating Centre for Mental Health, 2004 (NICE)). The field is one shared among all professions dealing with eating disorders and approaches from other professional standpoints, especially occupational therapy and mental health nursing, would be most welcome.

IDENTIFICATION OF PROBLEM AREAS

Patients with severe and enduring eating disorder (SEED) have disabilities in every area of life, namely physical, psychological, family, social, occupational and regarding accommodation. However, the pattern of problems is different for many other people with SEMI (severe and enduring mental illness), for example due to schizophrenia. Let us step through the areas mentioned above, and with the help of an individual with SEED, identify what could be done to help in each area of disability. In the UK a useful system of documentation of management plans called the Care Programme Approach (see Table 9.1) has been developed. This, among other things, lists the problem areas (e.g. medical, psychological, occupational, family, social), indicates the interventions that are being made to address the problems (e.g. dietician appointments, individual therapy, exploration of opportunities for voluntary work, family support) and crucially, who is responsible (in addition to the patient) for implementing each. A care coordinator or key worker responsible for the whole programme is also named. This general structure will be used in the following discussion.

PHYSICAL PROBLEMS

Our patient is the 37-year-old man mentioned at the beginning of this chapter. He has a number of physical problems. He has a BMI of only 16, and finds it very difficult to maintain this outside hospital. He has some weakness of his legs, but that does not stop him walking everywhere, even though he has been advised to take buses. He has been told that he has osteoporosis, but that did not affect him until he suffered pain in his mid-thoracic area and found that he had lost 2 cm in height. The reduction in height increased his BMI, and he argued with his doctor (who was not convinced) that he was recovering. He vomits every day, and has had some faints, probably due to dehydration, although his potassium has been below normal at times, so a cardiac cause is possible.

Addressing physical needs includes dietary advice to maximise his level of nutrition. If he will not eat more or vomit less, he might be persuaded to take a combination of vitamins (e.g. Forceval® 2 daily) and calcium and vitamin D (e.g. Calcichew D3 Forte) to avoid micronutrient deficiency. If his potassium is low, potassium supplements may be necessary, and if persistent, a proton pump inhibitor (see p. 151). His walking might be

Table 9.1   Summary care plan for a patient with long-term anorexia nervosa

Care plan for patient P

Present: Patient P, Key worker K, Consultant C, Dietitian D, General Practitioner G, Occupational Therapist O, Family Therapist F

Problem area		Intervention	Responsible individuals
Physical Problems	Muscle weakness	Optimise nutrition Increase weight	P, K, D
	Osteoporosis	Increase weight Refer to rheumatologist	P, K, D C
	Electrolyte imbalance	Minimise vomiting Provide potassium chloride	P, K G
	Dehydration	Minimise vomiting Provide electrolyte solution	P, K G
Psychological/ Psychiatric Problems	Depression	Optimise nutrition Consider SSRI.	P, K, D C
	Obsessive-compulsive symptoms	Optimise nutrition Gain weight Consider SSRI	P, K, D C
	Social anxiety	CBT, outings to café	P, K, O
	Insomnia	Optimise nutrition Yoga Consider tricyclic	P, K, D O C
Social and Occupational Problems	Social isolation	Café group, Day centre	P, O
	Difficulty eating out	CBT, Café group	P, K, O
	No close relationship	Day centre, voluntary work	P, K, O
	Extreme dependence on mother	Family therapy	P, F
	Lack of daily occupation	Day centre, voluntary work. Course in computer skills	P, O
Financial Problems	Not receiving benefits	Help with application	P, K
Accommodation Problems	Requires independent flat	Apply for housing	P, K
Carer assessment	Parents require support	Parental and family therapy	F
Relapse identification	Weight loss		P, K
Relapse plan	Discuss with medical team member		K
Next meeting Signed: Patient Signed: Key worker	20th October 2007	Eating Disorders Unit Date Date	K

reduced by advice, perhaps combined with an arrangement for him to hand in bus tickets or keeping an exercise and transport diary. If his faints are found to be related to dehydration and low blood pressure with a marked postural fall in blood pressure associated with dizziness, an oral electrolyte replacement such as Dioralyte® may be considered. His osteoporosis is severe, as it has led to a spinal crush fracture. He should receive a bone mineral density scan and be referred be for treatment at an osteoporosis clinic where biphosphonates may well be considered. He clearly needs to gain weight and stop vomiting and overwalking. However, as these are extremely entrenched aspects of his eating disorder progress might be slow and limited. He should, however, see a key worker regularly to discuss his progress in these areas and to try and persuade him to make changes.

PSYCHIATRIC/PSYCHOLOGICAL NEEDS

His depression is likely to have origins in undernutrition, social isolation, chronic illness and genetic predisposition (his father was a pastor with bipolar affective disorder). As above, his nutritional needs should be met as far as he and his anorexia will allow, his individual therapy may include a cognitive-behavioural approach to his depression, and an antidepressant may be considered. Social isolation is dealt with below (Social and occupational difficulties).

He is found on evaluation to have obsessive compulsive symptoms. These are also likely to be multifactorial in origin. He was a nervous child with extensive rituals prior to the onset of the eating disorder. His father was also obsessional, and consulted a psychiatrist because of blasphemous obsessional thoughts. The patient's obsessional thinking and behaviour became significantly worse after the onset of the eating disorder and have made the eating disorder more entrenched by, for example, extending the length of meal times, and reducing the amount of time available for meals.

Treatment of these symptoms can be very difficult, but also essential if we are to keep our patient out of hospital. Again nutrition must be optimised. CBT can be used for obsessive symptoms, and it may be helpful for the patient to spend some time in a day hospital where encouragement to eat and not ritualise can act as a form of response prevention. Attention to body image in therapy can, in the unlikely event of it being effective, reduce the tendency to ritualise because eating is not feared as much. Lastly, some antidepressants, notably SSRIs, in large doses. Fluoxetine, starting at the usual dose of 20 mg but increasing if necessary up to 80 mg per day, can have an effect on obsessional thinking and may be worth trying. Involvement of carers can be helpful as they sometimes get drawn into joining in with the patient's obsessional behaviour, as can be seen most clearly in Clinical description 5.1 (p. 89).

His next problem is social anxiety. He has a terrific fear that if he says anything in a group, he will make a mistake and appear foolish. This appears to have its origin in the social isolation which stemmed from his anorexia nervosa. He became fearful of going out with friends, in case he was required to eat or drink something that was not on his permitted list. This symptom can be approached indirectly by day hospital treatment, including group meals and group therapy, and more directly using CBT to reduce the fear of social interactions and encourage social experiments.

Lastly he complained of insomnia. This can be related to both depression and malnutrition, lack of a daytime occupation and pain from his back. Treatment with hypnotic drugs is risky because of the probability of dependence. Secondly they may not work. In the face of underweight (which reduces the need for sleep) and hunger (which makes falling asleep difficult) drug treatment is unlikely to help much. Psychological approaches including relaxation techniques are to be preferred. If drugs are used, tricyclics are not addictive, and may help. One of the newer neuroleptics, olanzapine, has been thought to be helpful in anorexia nervosa because of its tendency to increase weight, and it sometimes helps insomnia. Neuroleptic drugs carry the potential risk of tardive dyskinesia, a movement disorder caused by damage to the brain which may be irreversible, and the patient should be fully informed of this.

SOCIAL AND OCCUPATIONAL DIFFICULTIES

Our society has so much invested in food and its consumption, that it is not at all surprising that someone with an eating disorder has serious social problems. Almost every social activity involves some sort of consumption. Every family celebration and religious festival, including fasts, involves a celebratory meal, and sometimes a particular type of food. People with eating disorders, especially anorexia nervosa, are often terrified of restaurants, because they imagine that they will not be able to choose anything on the menu except Perrier. Difficulties eating in company can make social arrangements so onerous that social life becomes impoverished and attenuated as the patient refuses more and more invitations and friends lose interest and fall away. The patient may then prioritise eating disorder symptoms, such as bingeing, over social arrangements, and may avoid agreeing to go out because 'I might want to binge'. Social isolation is a highly significant disability, and one shared by many people with psychiatric disorders. Its management is similar to the approach to social isolation in schizophrenia or severe obsessive compulsive disorder, but also distinct because of the specific problems that difficulty eating in public presents.

First, an assessment of the patient's social network needs to take place by asking the following types of questions:

- How many people do you know?
- For how many of them do you have a phone number?
- How many of your contacts know each other?
- How many people could you call at 3 am in an emergency?
- In a week, in how many social activities would you engage?
- How many of these activities involve eating?
- Do you have a close relationship with a person to whom you could tell intimate personal information?
- In a week, how many of your contacts would call you?
- Do you have a sexual relationship?
- Do you regard yourself as socially isolated?

A conversation in which these issues are covered will give you an idea of the size (number of contacts), density (contacts who know each other) and quality (intimacy) of the person's social network.

Helping build a social network: general measures.

- Regular contact with a team member: this can take the form of therapy, key working, medical monitoring or other reasons for seeing the same person regularly. Sometimes such contact can be the only time the patient talks to anyone.
- Attendance at a psychiatric day centre: some patients reject the idea of such a centre, and do not wish to be identified with a chronically ill psychiatric population. However, they may be surprised to find that they have a lot in common with people with severe chronic obsessive compulsive disorder, anxiety and depression. At a day centre the patient may make friends and at least will have the opportunity to discuss problems with others.
- Attendance at a psychiatric day hospital: this experience can provide some general help with socialization and communication, and some specific therapy in relation to disabling symptoms such as depression, obsessive compulsive symptoms and social phobia.

Specific measures

Fear of eating out: this can be addressed by using an educational approach and an exposure programme. The factors that lead to the fear are explored. They are usually one or more of the following (or any of a host of other anxieties): (i) I won't find anything acceptable on the menu. (ii) If I have a salad, they'll say I'm being anorexic. (iii) If I have a cake, they'll think I'm greedy or bingeing. (iv) They won't be able to cope with my food rituals. (v) I'm so fat they'll think I shouldn't be eating at all.

Once the nature of the fear is established, the next step can be to embark on 'thought experiments'. For example, 'Imagine what would happen if you went into a café and had a latte?' followed by detailed planning of an actual outing. It is useful if this occurs in a group, and patients attending an eating disorders day hospital or an outpatient group can be very supportive when trying this sort of challenge. Naturally, the item chosen will be different for each person, depending on the precise fears and how much they have already been addressed.

Difficulties with close relationships: many people with SEED are without a sexual partner. There are numerous reasons for this. The most obvious is that when weight is low, so, usually, is libido. However, the panoply of eating disorder symptoms including restricted eating, obsessionality around eating, depression, sleep disturbance and bulimic symptoms can conspire with lack of libido and when changes in physical appearance due to low weight as well as infertility are added, it is, perhaps, not surprising that it is an unusual person who will accept as a partner someone with severe and enduring anorexia nervosa. Helping this problem covers all areas of treatment. Some patients engage in a non-sexual intimate relationship, sometimes with another person with a severe eating disorder. This can be helpful, because of the sympathy that a fellow sufferer can bring, and also has potential dangers, as there can be competitiveness in areas such as weight, which can make matters worse. 'Couple' sessions can help to address such dynamics and might direct the partner towards appropriate therapy for her condition.

There are other ways in which a patient might make moves towards a relationship. It may be possible to provide a 'buddy' through social, psychiatric or volunteer services or religious organisations while there are many organisations (the Eating Disorder Association, Overeaters, Alcoholics and Narcotics Anonymous in the UK) that have provided support, friendship and guidance to patients with eating disorders.

Family members may be the only social contact remaining to a patient with SEED and meeting the patient with a member of the family with whom they are close can help to preserve and improve the relationship. When the close relative is a spouse, couple therapy or multi-couple groups may help the partner support the patient.

Over-dependence on a family member: the person in question is usually but not always the mother. If the anorexia has begun in childhood, the parent may have endured several episodes during which the child's life was at risk. Over the years the mother's relationship with her husband may have suffered, perhaps due to the strain of the illness, and the bond between mother and child becomes even closer. By the time the patient is in her 20s or 30s the relationship can be extremely interdependent and the other parent can become quite estranged.

As a general rule, the expectation of therapists when the patient is 12 is that the family should, if they can, pull together and feed her. When the patient is 25 the opposite may well be more appropriate. Treatment of the eating disorder is now the responsibility of the patient together with the doctors, nurses and therapists and other professionals. The family therapist may therefore encourage the family to withdraw and allow the services to deal with nutritional problems that arise. This may be very difficult in a family all of whom have been affected by the eating disorder and parents, especially mothers, may experience considerable guilt at giving up the role of food provider to her daughter. She must be encouraged to view the change as a positive one, and, interestingly, allowing parents to disconnect from the feeding of their child can sometimes have a beneficial effect on the patient, just as releasing in the water a child learning to swim can expedite the learning process. In Clinical description 5.4 (p. 93) the illness had fostered a dependent relationship between daughter and parents which ceased to be appropriate or helpful when the daughter reached adulthood. In the following case history, the dependence was even more extreme.

Clinical description 9.2

A young girl developed anorexia nervosa at the age of 11. She was admitted to a child psychiatric facility and gained weight but refused to get to a healthy level. She was discharged to her family and her mother gave up her job and supervised every meal. Her weight stayed constant. After three years she expressed the wish to go on a school trip for a weekend. She went on the trip and lost 5 kg. Maternal supervision resumed and at the age of 20 she moved to a placement in a residential supportive community abroad. There she lost some weight but stabilised at a BMI of 15. Her mother had fed her for nine years almost without respite.

We have moved on from Gull's view about the family (p. 93) to regard the family as an important resource that can contribute in a major way to the patient's recovery, often with help from eating disorder services. As can be seen, however, parental feeding of the patient, when the illness has become severe and enduring, can impose an intolerable burden and the aim of family therapy may be to help the family withdraw from a relationship in which the patient's health and even life depends on a parent being present at every mealtime. The transition of care between family and eating disorder service needs to be negotiated with caution. When it is accomplished successfully, the parents can sometimes establish a different and more independent life and the relationship between the parents and patient can improve.

5.30–6am	Wake and wash
6–6.30am	Morning exercises (Yoga)
6.30–7am	Prepare breakfast
7–8am	Eat breakfast
8–10am	Walk off breakfast
10am–12.30pm	Tidy flat, do chores
12.30–1.30pm	Prepare lunch
1.30–3.30pm	Eat lunch
3.30–5.30pm	Walk off lunch
5.30–7.30pm	Prepare supper
7.30–9.30pm	Eat supper
9.30–10.30pm	Exercises
10.30pm	Night time crisp bread
11.00pm	To bed

Figure 9.1   Daily routine for a patient with Severe and Enduring Eating Disorder.

Lack of daily structure and occupation when symptoms have reduced

Some patients complain that our constant exhortations to give up their symptoms is equivalent to asking someone to give up their way of life with nothing in return. The day of someone with SEED, living alone, may well be as depicted in Figure 9.1.

This daily programme allows no time for social activities and shopping, and is the schedule of someone with restricting anorexia nervosa. For a patient with a regular bingeing and vomiting pattern, exercise, housework, preparing and eating meals as well as sleeping usually give way to buying and consuming binge foods and purging.

How can we help the patient break out of this veritable citadel of activity? As the comment at the beginning of this section implies, we must help the patient put something reasonably interesting in its place. Our patient is spending 24/7 in the world of anorexia, how can we tempt him into ours?

The problems are complex and require a number of different interventions. Specific therapies aimed at reducing eating disorder behaviours (including food-related obsessional behaviour) are central. If that can be achieved, and some time can be released to spend on other activities, a start can be made on filling that time in ways that can make recurrence of the eating disorder less likely, because the patient is getting so much out of the new occupations. Because many people with anorexia nervosa have a perfectionistic character, they (and sometimes their parents) may be content with nothing less than a university degree. The patient and family may need to accept lower initial expectations and to recognise that a long and serious illness is not going to disappear in a few weeks. In someone attending an eating disorders day programme, it may be a good idea to start with a couple of hours in a voluntary position, or engaging in a class of interest to the patient. At this stage it is important that expectations are not even slightly too high. Any course must be without formal assessment, and voluntary work must be closely supervised and not involve managing others. When that has been accomplished, the number of hours can be extended but always bearing in mind that the patient will feel guilty for not keeping up with people who do not have eating disorders and try to push himself too hard. Sometimes a combination of psychiatric day centre or day hospital and voluntary work or education can work, with one foot in the treatment camp and one in 'the world'. Patients vary, of course, and some will be able to move more quickly. In general, however, if a person has dwelt in the anorexic cave for a number of years, without an occupation other than symptoms and treatment, it will take several years to establish occupational and social life beyond the illness.

Once eating and obsessional behaviour have come under better control, and the patient has established a foothold in the world of work (including voluntary) or study, he will start to meet people and may be able to embark on some social life. This may well start with other people with eating disorders, as a visit to a cafe with someone who understands the problems is much less awkward, and social life may be restricted to family members and other patients for some time. Only when the patient is able to handle social situations involving food better, and this may include giving information to other people about difficulties with food, may it be possible to make social contacts with people without eating disorders.

As a further important step towards social recovery, a referral to a sheltered workshop may be made. The ideal place accepts people with a history of treatment for mental illness and provides a full range of activities from the more mundane, such as packaging and posting, to the more elaborate, like design, accounts and public relations, so that patients can find a niche which reflects their experience but also their current capacities, and move through the organisation as the latter improve.

FINANCIAL DIFFICULTIES

Patients with anorexia nervosa are often seen as middle class and well off. A few are, but several years of SEED with no gainful employment will exhaust most resources and many people in this position are poor. Some people, particularly with restricting anorexia nervosa have great difficulty spending money. This appears to be a form of hoarding, in the way that some patients hoard food, and may be an example of patients attempting to live in the most frugal way possible, eating and spending as little as possible in order to get by, in a way reminiscent of the lives of religious hermits. The patient may have spent very little income, and public benefits may have accumulated to a sizable sum in the bank, large enough for some public organisations, such as social services, to refuse to provide services such as home support without payment. Management of 'pathological frugality' is similar to management of undereating, with discussion of the costs and benefits of underspending, diary keeping and plans to increase spending to an appropriate level. Another common problem is failure to apply for benefits to which the patient is entitled, and work to encourage applying, in the face of the patient's guilt and sense of unworthiness, can be helpful. Lastly, the authorities frequently fail to acknowledge the disabilities imposed by SEED, and they may need to be described in detail in official application forms, with medical support, before the appropriate level of benefits is paid.

ACCOMMODATION PROBLEMS

For someone who has been in and out of the hospital system for a number of years, the prospect of living independently without relapsing may be a novel and frightening one. The pattern hitherto has been: several months in hospital gaining weight, then gradual discharge home to outpatients or day patient care, followed by slow relapse and readmission. If the admission is far from home, follow up may be inadequate and relapse usually comes more quickly. If this familiar cycle is to be avoided, discharge must be gradually effected to a highly supported environment. Initially this may be to a hostel attached to an eating disorders unit (see Chapter 8, p. 157) and this placement may be required for up to a year. During the latter part of this time, applications are made either for supported accommodation (a room in a house with mental health trained staff) or an independent flat with support from the eating disorders service, the community mental health team and any other organisation that is willing to help. Before moving into independent accommodation, the patient should have sessions to practise food and clothes shopping, food preparation and consumption in the flat, and any other identified areas (such as use of transport) in which experience is lacking.

CARER ASSESSMENT

The role of the family has been alluded to several times in this discussion. In a patient with SEED the family may still be closely involved or may have become completely separate. If a family member, or a close friend or partner, can be identified, the full range of interventions for carers can be offered, including information and advice sessions, single and group family therapy, home visits and support groups. Illness in the carer is not uncommon, and can include depression, eating disorders, alcohol misuse and physical illness developing in an elderly parent. Such illness may emerge if the carer is seen individually for a carer's assessment, which is increasingly performed. When the relationship with the patient has been close, death of a parent can be followed by a relapse of the eating disorder as a manifestation of grief, although weight loss and bulimic symptoms may actually serve to help the bereaved avoid the process of grieving and so store up problems for the future. In one case the father's death was followed by a complete remission of a severe and long lasting anorexic illness.

Clinical description 9.2

A female patient developed restricting anorexia nervosa at the age of 19. She remained ill and amenorrhoeic throughout her twenties and thirties, in spite of intensive individual and family therapy, and at 35 was admitted after the suicide of her partner which was followed by major life-threatening weight loss. She remained in hospital, on an involuntary order, being fed nasogastrically, for 18 months. After discharge, having gained little weight, she developed paralysis of both hands which defied neurological diagnosis. After the death of her father when she was 41 she began to eat more, and her BMI rose from 14 to 22, and she resumed menstruation after a 22 year gap. She obtained a job as a teacher and slowly began improving her social life. She continued to be plagued by depression and self-blame, although her weight stayed normal over the following 4 years and her hands rapidly regained their strength. She admitted that there had been some difficulties in the relationship with her father, but did not reveal any specific problem that might be relevant to her illness and her remarkable recovery after his death.

In addition to service based provision, such as therapy, support and information, it is also useful to direct the family to the nearest self-help group, the Eating Disorders Association in the UK, for further help.

Chapter 10

TECHNICAL AND ACADEMIC ASPECTS

AN EDS DATABASE

Establishing a database

Most healthcare organisations will use a database to record limited aspects of their work. The identity of these data is usually dependent on the requirements of the funding agency so that referral rate, attendance and 'did not attend (DNA)' rate, and delays between referral, assessment and treatment are examples of information that may be collected, along with name, address, age and general practitioner. The staff within the service itself may be interested in this information, because if, for example, the 'DNA' rate is high, the funding body may criticise the healthcare organisation and this criticism, in the form of pressure to change, filters down to the clinical team. The problem is that the data collected is often inaccurate, mainly because the people collecting it are either temporary staff or have no particular investment in it being accurate. If data is going to be used to judge the efficiency or efficacy of your service it is highly advisable to collect at least a sample of it yourself, so you can challenge central figures before they are used to close you down.

There may be other information that you wish to collect, and each service will have a different set. It is useful to have a team day devoted to deciding what you want to be included on the database. The following is a list of questions that you may wish to ask of the system:

- Who is referring, and how often? Who is *not* referring?
- Where do the patients live? i.e., how far from the clinic?
- How many referrals are received per unit time from each area covered?
- What eating disorder diagnoses are represented in the patients?
- What treatments are being provided?
- How do the patients change with treatment?
- What is the dropout rate, and who is dropping out?

- Who is currently causing concern?
- Who is currently an inpatient/day patient?
- Can I have a list of everyone referred who has diabetes/is of non-white ethnicity/who has been ill for over 10 years/is male, etc.?

Once you have decided on what you want of a system, meet a database expert and give her a detailed specification for your system. Then find another one and obtain a competitive bid, scrape the required money from somewhere and commission the work. When it is complete, devote a day to spending time with the system developer going through the software, putting in dummy patients and checking that it will do all you want it to do. Make sure there is flexibility so that you can add data fields later. Involve other staff members who will be using the database and decide on who can access it and who can enter data. The latter is very important, and the number of people allowed to change data should be low, preferably one, with a backup for sickness and holiday leave. Any changes required can be fed to that person (often a secretary) on paper or via email.

At this point you will need to decide on how to get information from the patient to the database. There are a number of routes, and each requires its own system. If this is not thought about properly, you will end up with a database containing incomplete and largely useless information.

The referral letter: information here includes the date of referral, patient's name, address, date of birth and sometimes phone number, as well as the referrer's contact information. In systems such as that in the UK, where the GP is a key player in health care, the GP's details must be sought from the referrer if the latter is not the GP. Clinical information such as possible diagnosis and urgency could also be recorded here.

Information provided in the pre-assessment questionnaire (see Chapter 3): much useful clinical information can be gathered here, although because only a proportion of patients send back their questionnaires, and those being seen urgently may not have time to do so, data is usually incomplete.

Information obtained at initial assessment: here, a diagnosis can usually be made, and a lot of clinical information collected. It is a good idea to develop a form filled in by the consultant in the second part of the assessment, in which the assessor describes the patient's history to the consultant and other team members (Chapter 3, p. 44). Clearly this form will differ according to the needs and decisions of the team, but the form in use by the Russell Unit is reproduced as Appendix 3.2 (see p. 52). The form is on two sides of A4 paper, and is organised as follows:

- Demographic information.
- Referrer information.

- Diagnoses.
- Weight history.
- Family and social history.
- Eating disorder symptoms and complications.
- Complications of obesity.
- General psychiatric symptoms.
- Substance misuse.
- General medical problems.

Follow up: finding out how patients have done in the service can be a surprisingly difficult and frustrating task. The patient may have a poor view of attempts to collect outcome data. She has gone through the rigours of referral, waiting, assessment, more waiting and therapy and after all that we have the nerve to ask her to fill in more forms. From the therapists' point of view, they have done their best with the patient, struggled through 12 months of weekly toil, and now they've got to chase the patient for some form which might show that they didn't do that well! This area also needs a team meeting, so that all team members are signed up to the idea that assessment is part of therapy, gives individuals reasonably accurate feedback on how their patient did, and gives the managers information on how different approaches work. It is wise not to use information from individual therapists, because that can leave team members feeling somewhat persecuted, or at least nervous. Gather together all the results for individual supportive, CBT, group therapy, day programme, separately so that the approach can be evaluated. The results can be presented in a regular audit meeting and if an approach seems to result in little change, the reasons for that can be discussed, and alterations in model can be mooted. Data collected at follow up should be limited in number. A suggested list follows:

- Weight and BMI.
- Eating disorder questionnaire (e.g. EDI) (Garner, Olmstead & Polivy, 1983).
- Depression questionnaire (e.g. BDI) (Beck, Ward, Mendelson, Mock & Erbaugh, 1961).
- Bulimia questionnaire (e.g. BITE) (Henderson & Freeman, 1987).

This will give an indication of the effects of treatment for the main eating disorders. If there is no change in these measures, or a negative change, therapy has probably not been successful. A possible exception is in the chronically ill patient for whom survival and avoiding hospital admission should be deemed a success.

Ways of using the database

As a rapidly available source of information. Case notes are sometimes time consuming to obtain, and regularly grow legs and walk about hospitals, coming to rest in the offices of people who deny ever seeing them. An Australian doctor once told me that the way he dealt with the enormous pile of discharge summaries he was supposed to dictate was every few months to throw all the files into Sydney Harbour. However, with adequate investment in administration, the majority of files can be located. In addition, a properly completed database can provide information about a patient, for example during a phone call, and a consultant who, with increasing age accumulates more patients and a less effective memory, can access at least basic data on a patient seen in the service.

As a list-maker. One of the most useful lists in our service is the Current Concerns (or 'worry') list. This is a list of patients causing concern to anyone in the team. The patient may not have been seen in the service, but a phone call from a medical ward in a distant part of your area may have imparted the information, 'We've admitted this patient who is rather thin at 32 kg, but she won't eat, she keeps jogging round the hospital and we don't know what to do with her'. A phone call to the writer of the letter will have been made, basic information entered on the database, the patient placed on 'Current Concerns' and a visit to the hospital arranged during the Current Concerns meeting (Chapter 2, p. 22). Classes of patients that make their way onto the Current Concerns list are as follows:

1. Patients seen in the past week.
2. Patients causing concern, e.g. about their physical or mental state.
3. Patients in hospital beds (especially if the admission is being paid for by the service).
4. Patients seen recently for assessment. In the case of recent assessments, the tasks required, such as writing and sending out the assessment letter to the referrer, booking a bone scan, following up bloods, etc., may not have been done. This is particularly relevant for patients seen by itinerants such as trainees and medical students who always seem to go to a mountaintop clinic in Mongolia immediately after leaving our service.
5. Current day patients.
6. Patients of other services. This especially applies to patients currently being treated in child psychiatry and SIEDUs who are known to be *en route* for the service, and whose care requires detailed planning (see CPA, Chapter 9) before they are taken on.
7. Liaison and outreach cases. This group (see Chapter 7) comprises patients currently under the care of other services not as yet intended for transfer to the EDS. This includes the patient jogging round the hospital described above.

USE OF THE INTERNET IN EATING DISORDERS

Websites of interest

The internet is a huge resource for people with any problem at all. The difficulty is that a Google© search returns much that is unreliable. Websites that appear when 'eating disorders' or 'anorexia' or 'bulimia' are used as search items fall into the following categories:

- *Academic sites*. These sites often give reliable information, but are often written in technical jargon. They can be accessed via Google Scholar©, via an Athens account (http://www.athens.ac.uk/) or via the many academic websites belonging to the publishers of the principle eating disorder journals, i.e. the *International Journal of Eating Disorders* and the *European Eating Disorders Review* (both accessible via the Wiley Interscience website (www3.interscience.wiley.com under psychology). Quite reasonably, most journals charge for access to papers although the cost per paper (usually over US$25) makes the internet library only for the rich and those with multiple institutional subscriptions.
- *Non-academic sites*. These are websites geared to provide information to the patient, the family and the non-specialist professional and can be extremely useful. The Eating Disorders Association (www.edauk.com) and its sisters in the USA and other countries are user friendly and provide information on eating disorders, self-help links and access to lists of services and therapists. The 'something fishy' website (www.somethingfishy.com), established by the family of a woman who died from an eating disorder, is also a major source of information and service for patients and families, with a chat room and a somewhat chilling but touching page of candles in memory of people who have died from eating disorders.
- *Online therapy*. This has increased in recent years, and you can visit attractively designed websites offering online therapy from a person described on the site. Costs are usually less than for face-to-face therapy, often US$25–30 per email, but efficacy is unknown (although see below 'Email bulimia therapy'). Also online are many descriptions of clinics, often in fantastic locations, offering to help with your disorder, as well as teaching Tai Chi and horse riding. It is very difficult to assess the quality of care from these sites, and it is not advisable to book in without consulting someone who knows the field and could contact a clinic. Some are run by people who have, themselves, had an eating disorder or an addiction, and although such a history is not a bar to therapy, and may help understanding of the problems, it is fairly sure that someone with an active problem would not be in the best position to be a therapist to a patient. Any reputable clinic would have formal registration, and its staff would be members of an appropriate

professional organisation. It would be as well to check these before signing on.

- *'Pro-Ana' sites.* These sites promote anorexia and bulimia as legitimate lifestyles. Their approach represents a point of view akin to an extreme political position. Someone with an eating disorder who is trying to recover would be well advised to avoid these sites, just as an alcoholic would be advised not to visit pubs. It would also be a cause for concern if young girls were accessing the sites, although no patient in my experience has given a history of having been influenced into an eating disorders lifestyle by the internet. It is advisable for staff to visit Pro-Ana sites at least once so they are aware of what their patients might well be accessing. Entering 'Pro-Ana' on Google© provides any number of these sites.

Email therapy

As described, it is possible to obtain counselling for an eating disorder on-line, although there is scant evidence that it is effective. Email can be used simply to keep in touch while the patient (or you if you are a pathological helper) are away on holiday or working away. Using it for therapy is possible, and may have some advantages. In our study of email therapy for bulimia nervosa and binge eating disorder we recruited subjects from a large multi-faculty college in the University of London. An email was sent out to all 20 000 students and staff inviting them to make contact if they suffered from bulimia nervosa. Each time we sent an email about 30 people responded and after sending five emails over four years, we had recruited 97 people with either bulimia nervosa, binge eating disorder or EDNOS (eating disorder not otherwise specified). We randomised them to three groups. One group received EBT (email bulimia therapy). This was based on outpatient cognitive behavioural therapy and was delivered by members of the eating disorders team and the two researchers. Participants (the term preferred to 'patients') were invited to tell their story online and then to keep a dietary diary which they sent to the e-therapist up to twice weekly. The e-therapist then sent it back after making comments aimed at helping establish a regular meal pattern, stopping bingeing and vomiting and addressing any other issues that arose. Therapy went on for 12 weeks, at the end of which time participants were reassessed. The second form of therapy was called self-directed writing (SDW). The aim was to provide a therapy that involved access to email, writing and a response from a doctor, but without any of the specific cognitive behavioural interventions present in EBT. This intervention was designed to examine the effects of therapeutic writing with minimal therapist intervention. Participants were sent an email and asked to spend some time at least twice a week, writing about their difficulties, and to send it to the author. Participants were told that they would not receive any specific advice related to their eating. They were encouraged to write a substantial amount about their difficulties. The third group was the no-treatment control group (waiting list control, WLC). They just waited 12 weeks, were reassessed, and were then offered one of the two active treatments, EBT or SDW.

The results were surprising. Therapy was effective in reducing the number of individuals with eating disorders, and reducing their scores on the BITE. However, it was not possible to discern a significant difference between the efficacy of EBT and that of SDW. The latter may have been due to inadequate numbers in the study. The percentage of participants agreeing to follow up at the end of treatment was only 63%, which reduced the potential for finding a difference between treatments. It was also found that people in the EBT group had a significantly higher desired BMI than those in the control group. Acceptance of a higher weight is usually essential for recovery in bulimia nervosa, as it is in anorexia nervosa.

An important outcome of the study was to show that email therapy was feasible and acceptable to a group of people who, in large part, had received no treatment. Bulimia nervosa is largely a secret condition, with only a small proportion of the 1–2% of the female population suffering from the condition attending their doctors for treatment. This reticence is in part due to shame and a reluctance to face a hospital or clinic and its associated professionals. Email therapy appears to be one way in which sufferers could access help without having to brave the clinic. Email is not a very secure medium, and therapy would be better delivered via a website, which could be made private. As more and more people have access to the internet, it seems likely that therapy will increasingly be made available in this way.

IN-HOUSE TRAINING

An important part of the team's work is to keep up with advances in eating disorders and in areas which impinge on the field. A certain amount of money is kept aside for staff training, and is used to send staff on conferences and training courses. In addition, there is a weekly session during which the team meets and has a training hour. This can have several forms, which rotate through the course of a term. The sequence is as follows:

- *Journal club*. One or two relevant papers are selected and circulated before the meeting. At the meeting the chair (generally, but not always the consultant) describes the papers and gives some thoughts on the conclusions and how they are significant for the work of the service. The papers can be about eating disorders themselves (e.g. effect of maternal eating disorders on child health) or peripheral but relevant (e.g. management of personality disorders using dynamic psychotherapy).

- *Invited speaker*. The invitee may be internal to the organisation, for example, a psychiatrist in substance misuse psychiatry discussing treatment of drug problems in eating disorders, or a manager describing the latest NHS rulings on the Care Programme Approach, or an external speaker. Sometimes, a speaker will be from a sister unit heading a research project with which we are due to be associated. The visitor will give a talk on the background to the study and how our unit will be involved.
- *Team member presentation*. This may be a detailed presentation and discussion of the history and management of a particular case (clinical case conference) or an account from a team member of a conference or course she has attended.
- *Business meeting*. The first meeting of every month is devoted to a team meeting (the business meeting) at which the work of the team is discussed and any upcoming management issues, including new staff, are conveyed. The remaining three meetings form the training seminar programme, and the cycle is repeated for a three-month term.
- *Staff development*. Individuals in the team who wish to receive supervision in a specific treatment modality such as CBT or family therapy can approach the relevant practitioners in the team to take on a patient or family and receive supervision for a defined time. This can contribute to the individual's CV and, if they are in an appropriate training course, form part of their specific therapy training.

TRAINING OTHERS

This book has been written in part because of the large number of emergent teams in the country and in Europe requesting help in developing high-quality eating disorders services. The initial response to a request for help is to invite members of the team (three or fewer) to attend our team meeting including the Current Concerns meeting, the day hospital discussion meeting and, as long as patients agree, to attend the interview with day patients. There follows a meeting with the manager and the consultant to answer any questions raised. Teams who send such an emissary sometimes request more intensive help. This is sometimes provided by means of regular supervision of a senior member of the developing team, by a senior member of our team. In addition, it can be helpful to arrange a half-day meeting of the whole team with our senior team member to brainstorm the local service and talk about how it might develop.

The precise programme varies with each service. Examples of a programme for such a meeting follow.

Plan 1: Development meeting for a small service under two years old

- Introduce yourself and ask each member of the group to introduce themselves and describe their role in the team.
- Discuss the format of the day, and indicate how you intend to proceed, and what you hope to achieve.
- Ask those present to group in twos (if possible, not someone with whom they normally work closely) and to discuss one aspect of their work which is going well, and one which is going less well.
- After 10–15 minutes ask for feedback from the pairs. Ask each member of the pair to feed back for the other. Write down the issues raised on a flipchart. In your own head, begin to make a list of key areas for change. Note what the people with more power (consultant, manager, senior nurse, long established therapist) indicate as their priorities for change.
- On a fresh flipchart write down the key areas for change derived from the exercise. Some key issues might be:
  - management of acutely physically ill patients who need medical admission
  - management of transition from child to adult services at age 18
  - therapy caseload management
  - information provided in primary care referrals
  - interface with community mental health services in patients with multiple problems.
- Ask the group to form slightly larger groups, say fours, and for each group to discuss possible ways forward for a different problem area. Their response should look at four categories of intervention:
  - intervention with patients and relatives
  - processes
  - resources
  - training and research.
  This latter exercise is a much more challenging one than the first. Exercise number one is really asking the team to complain about the *status quo*, which they are used to doing. You then process those complaints into a number of distinct areas and ask them to think of approaches to the problems.
- Your last task is to bundle the flipcharts together, take them home, and, given that you will not recall what the flipcharts are meant to convey, try to write an account of the issues raised in the first exercise and the approaches suggested in the second. Then schedule a follow-up meeting in six months to evaluate your intervention!

Plan 2: A mature team which wishes to look at another team's practices to see if any of them could be applied

- After introductions, get the group talking in pairs. Even in established clinics, people sometimes hardly know what anyone else does, because many staff are part time. Ask them to pair with someone they don't usually work with and to describe to each other:
  - what they do in the service
  - one way in which they would like it to be different, then ask them to feed back on their partner
  - one new thing they learnt about their partner's work
  - one thing their partner would like to see change.
- Then give a brief (20-minute) talk to introduce yourself and your team, and indicate ways of working that you think might appeal to the host team. (You have had a discussion with the team leader and have an idea about ways in which they, or at least, a proportion of them, would like to change.) Include the most innovative and exciting elements of your service. Make your last slide 'ways of working that might interest you'. At just such a seminar in Paris, my list was:
  - assessment of new patients by all members of the team
  - the Current Concerns list
  - the liaison and outreach service
  - home treatment
  - day hospital
  - SUSS test (see Chapter 4)
  - email therapy
  - multi-family and multi-couple groups.
- After the talk, ask them to choose a different partner and in 20 minutes address the following questions:
  - describe an idea you heard in the talk that you found interesting
  - describe how it could be implemented in your clinic.
  Then feed back, as usual for each other, and have 20 minutes for questions and discussion.

TRAINING NON-EATING DISORDER SERVICES

As already mentioned in Chapter 7, local psychiatric teams have a very important role to play in the care of someone with a severe eating disorder, especially a severe and enduring one. An individual team might cover 100–200 000 population, and the eating disorders service may cover a million. It is well worth visiting each of the teams, and each of the groups of consultants involved to talk about eating disorders. The form of the visit varies according to the audience. The consultants group will be more interested in criteria for referral, whom to contact and what to expect, whereas the team are more likely to want to know about assessment of risk, diagnosis, treatment and complications. The latter subjects can also be covered in a lecture to psychiatric trainees, which the consultants sometimes attend. It is always a good idea to demonstrate the SUSS test (Chapter 4) at seminars. The spectacle is unforgettable, although it might not be so memorable when the lecturer is more athletic than the author.

Students, medical and others

Students for whom your lecture on eating disorders represents a tiny fraction of their information bank, represent a real challenge. For medical students, psychiatry is often seen as a 'soft' subject with limited diagnostic and curative techniques seen in other subjects such as haematology. On the other hand, they may well see a psychiatrically ill patient in their final examinations, a great incentive to learning. Moreover, a show of hands at the beginning of your lecture in response to the question, 'Who has known a person with an eating disorder in the family or in a close friendship circle' will yield about 35 % of the audience with their hands up. Young people are hence a group with considerable experience in eating disorders.

The following structure has proved to be appreciated by a succession of medical students (a discerning group):

1. A lecture in around 40 minutes surveying the current knowledge on diagnosis, epidemiology, complications, treatment and prognosis in eating disorders. This is accompanied by a slide show with the slides distributed before the class, or posted on a student website.
2. 10 minutes of questions and answers.
3. A videotape of a patient with an eating disorder describing her symptoms, and her occupational, social and family life. The audience are asked to make notes on the biological, psychological and social aspects of her symptoms, and the putative aetiological factors and possible treatments. They are then asked to discuss with a neighbour the list each has made, and to feed back to the whole group at the end of 15 minutes discussion. An example of such notes is given in Table 10.1.
4. A final question and answer session for 10–15 minutes. During this, it is worth providing some potential examination topics and asking for comments on them.

RESEARCH

Breaking new ground is at the same time essential and difficult. We regard our whole enterprise as a research project which began with the question, 'What will happen if we close all our beds?' We now know part of the

Table 10.1 Notes taken during a video recording of a patient with an eating disorder with biological, psychological and family/social contributions to aetiology, symptoms and treatment

	Biological	Psychological	Family/Social
Aetiology	Mother and sister had anorexia, ?genetic	Was bullied at school because tubby	Attended ballet school. Parental conflict, triangulated.
Symptoms	Starves all day then binges	Feels immense satisfaction from weight loss	Social isolation, conflict with parents
Treatment	Regulate diet to avoid binges. Improve diet and weight.	CBT approach to self-image and to encourage weight gain	Reconsider ballet, contact school, family sessions.

answer to that question, and the information is provided in different parts of this book. Formal research is organised in a number of different ways:

- Funded projects. These are almost always in collaboration with a research centre such as the Institute of Psychiatry and the University of Oxford, where the academic staff are good enough to invite us to join them in a project.
- Trainee projects. Doctors and psychologists in training often wish to complete a research project and as long as they don't go off to that crowded Mongolian mountaintop clinic before analysing the results, they can get as far as publication.
- Consultant's hobbyhorse projects. These are idiosyncratic ideas that would never get funding but which can be done in spare time. The email therapy study was one of these, and depended not only on my time, but that of my colleague Marc Serfaty, and staff members of the Russell Unit who gave time to provide treatment for the participants.

Apart from getting money for projects, the other obstacle, which seems to be growing in height all the time, is the ethics committee process. Our experience is that it can take many months for a simple project (such as administering a brief standard marital satisfaction questionnaire to a group of patients and their partners before and after a multi-couple group) to be agreed. The objections are mostly technical, the fact that a whole committee must now consider all projects, rather than the chair who could, in the past, give the go-ahead between meetings, the decision being ratified at the next. It must be acknowledged, however, in these days of murderous GPs, failing heart surgeons and body-snatching pathologists that doctors are just not trusted to do the best for their patients, and this tightening of research ethics is certainly a manifestation of that sad development.

In spite of these difficulties, and the relentless pressure of clinical activities, research forms a part of the team's work, a part which should increase as more multi-centre projects are carried out in order to look at areas in the field which are, sadly, without a definitive answer. This long list includes an evidence-based treatment for anorexia nervosa, treatment for bulimia nervosa resistant to standard treatments, genetic factors in eating disorders and the relative roles of admission to hospital, day care and outpatient treatment in the treatment of severe anorexia nervosa.

REFERENCES

Bateman, A. & Fonagy, P. (2001) Treatment of borderline personality disorder with psychoanalytically oriented partial hospitalization: an 18-month follow-up. *American Journal of Psychiatry*, **158**, 36–42.

Beck, A.T., Ward, C.H., Mendelson, M., Mock, J. & Erbaugh, J. (1961) An inventory for measuring depression. *Archives of General Psychiatry*, **4**, 561–71.

Colahan, M. & Robinson, P.H. (2002) Multi-family groups in the treatment of young adults with eating disorders. *Journal of Family Therapy*, **24**, 17–30.

DiClemente, C.C. & Prochaska, J.O. (1998) Toward a comprehensive, transtheoretical model of change: stages of change and addictive behaviors. In W.R. Miller & N. Heather (eds), *Treating Addictive Behaviors* (2nd edn, pp. 3–24). New York: Plenum Press.

Garner, D.M., Olmstead, M.P. & Polivy, J. (1983) Development and validation of a multidimensional eating disorder inventory for anorexia nervosa and bulimia. *International Journal of Eating Disorders*, **2**, 15–34.

Gleick, J. (1996) *Chaos: Making a New Science*. Minerva.

Gowers, S., Norton, K., Halek, C. & Crisp, A.H. (1994) Outcome of outpatient psychotherapy in a random allocation treatment study of anorexia nervosa. *International Journal of Eating Disorders*, **15**, 165–77.

Harris, E.C. & Barraclough, B. (1998) Excess mortality of mental disorder. *British Journal of Psychiatry*, **173**, 11–53.

Henderson, M. & Freeman, C.P. (1987) A self-rating scale for bulimia: the 'BITE'. *British Journal of Psychiatry*, **150**, 18–24.

Hodes, M., Timimi, S. & Robinson, P.H. (1997) Children of mothers with eating disorders: a preliminary study. *European Eating Disorders Review*, **5**, 11–24.

Killaspy, H., Banerjee, S., King, M. & Lloyd, M. (2000) Prospective controlled study of psychiatric out-patient non-attendance. *British Journal of Psychiatry*, **176**, 160–5.

Klerman, G.L., Weissman, M.M., Rounsaville, B.J. & Chevron, E.S. (1984) *Interpersonal Psychotherapy of Depression*. Basic Books.

Laing, R.D., Esterson, A. (1964) *Sanity, Madness and the Family*. Tavistock Pubns.

Linehan, M. (1993) *Cognitive Behavioural Treatment of Borderline Personality Disorder*. Guilford Press.

Medical Research Council (1975) *Aids to the Investigation of Peripheral Nerve Injuries*. London: HMSO.

National Collaborating Centre for Mental Health (NICE) (2004) Core interventions in the treatment and management of anorexia nervosa, bulimia nervosa and related eating disorders.

Newton, T., Robinson, P.H. & Hartley, P. (1993) Services for eating disorders: 2. A consumer survey of members of the Eating Disorders Association. *Eating Disorders Review*, **1**, 10–21.

Pope, H.G. & Hudson, J.I. (1992) Is childhood sexual abuse a risk factor for bulimia nervosa? *American Journal of Psychiatry*, **149**, 455–63.

Robinson, P.H. (2000) The gastrointestinal tract in eating disorders. *European Eating Disorders Review, Special Issue – Medical complications of eating disorders: a clinical review*, **8**, 88–97.

Royal College of Psychiatrists (2001) *Council Report CR87. Eating Disorders in the UK: Policies for Service Development and Training*. Royal College of Psychiatrists.

Solomon, S.M. & Kirby, D.F. (1990) The refeeding syndrome: a review. *Journal of Parenteral and Enteral Nutrition*, **14**, 90–7.

Stein, A., Woolley, H., Murray, L., Cooper, P., Cooper, S., Noble, F., Affonso, N. & Fairburn, C.G. (2001) Influence of psychiatric disorder on the controlling behaviour of mothers with 1-year-old infants. A study of women with maternal eating disorder, postnatal depression and a healthy comparison group. *British Journal of Psychiatry*, **179**, 157–62.

Treasure, J.L. & Russell, G.F. (1988) Intrauterine growth and neonatal weight gain in babies of women with anorexia nervosa. *British Medical Journal*, **296**, 1038.

Treasure, J., Schmidt, U., Troop, N., Tiller, J., Todd, G. & Turnbull, S. (1996) Sequential treatment for bulimia nervosa incorporating a self-care manual. *British Journal of Psychiatry*, **168**, 94–8.

Treasure, J.L. & Ward, A. (1997) Cognitive analytical therapy (CAT) in eating disorders. *Clinical Psychology and Psychotherapy*, **4**, 62–71.

Treasure, J.L., Katzman, M., Schmidt, U. et al. (1999). Engagement and outcome in the treatment of bulimia nervosa: first phase of a sequential design comparing motivation enhancement therapy and cognitive behavioural therapy. *Behaviour Research Therapy*, **37**, 405–418.

World Health Organisation (2003) *International Classification of Diseases, 10th edition*. WHO.

INDEX

Notes: The following abbreviations are used: ED(s) is used for eating disorder(s), EDS is used for eating disorder service. Page numbers in *italic* refer to figures and tables.